THE KEYS
to Planning
for Learning

Effective Curriculum, Unit, and Lesson Design
SECOND EDITION, REVISED

DONNA CLEMENTI AND LAURA TERRILL

The American Council on the Teaching of Foreign Languages
1001 North Fairfax Street, Suite 200
Alexandria, VA 22314

Graphic Design by Goulah Design Group, Inc.
Edited by Paul Sandrock, ACTFL

Graphic for Curriculum Design for Learning Languages in the 21st Century (Figures 1, 6, and 14) used with permission of designers, Donna Clementi and Laura Terrill.

LinguaFolio® is a registered trademark of the National Council of State Supervisors for Languages (NCSSFL).

ISBN: 978-1-942544-59-3

Foreword

Our learners need "right now" schools with "right now" teachers. The 21st century is well into its second decade and educators are searching for guidance on how to construct dynamic curriculum and instruction to match our times. Given the remarkable pedagogical shifts occurring with access to digital tools, media production, and instantaneous connectivity, teachers seek "keys" to open the future for our students. World language learning, which supports global sensibilities and superb communication skills, provides a foundation for the contemporary learner. To assist teachers, curriculum designers, administrators, and professional developers, Donna Clementi and Laura Terrill have indeed brought us a useful guide—*The Keys to Planning for Learning: Effective Curriculum, Unit, and Lesson Design.*

Bringing years of experience in language teaching, district and organizational leadership, and teacher development to these chapters, Clementi and Terrill provide powerful strategies for rebooting teaching and learning. In many ways, curriculum design is a form of learning architecture. I believe it is here that our authors help teachers in the most direct and intimate way. Like architects, teachers make critical choices about the elements, the layout, the construction, the materials, and the style that will best serve the client and meet local standards. For today's language teacher, strategies to assist in these choices are valued. The chapters are written in a logical sequence and provide clarity as to why and how to integrate the five goal areas of the World-Readiness Standards for Learning Languages (Communication, Cultures, Connections, Comparisons, and Communities) into classroom planning. In particular, the unit design and supportive lesson plan templates are excellent blueprints for dealing with two simultaneous needs for designers. One is to support excellent interpersonal, interpretive, and presentational communication (listening, speaking, reading, and writing) in a world language and the second need is to engage our students in expanding their knowledge and appreciation of cultural perspectives.

As a futurist, I encourage the reader to note that this book is written for the "now." Clementi and Terrill not only are keenly aware of the necessary skills and knowledge that our times require of our learners, they embrace them with fresh writing on the "mindset" for curriculum writing in our times. *The Keys to Planning for Learning: Effective Curriculum, Unit, and Lesson Design* will prove to be an outstanding contribution as a launching pad into the future of world language teaching and learning.

Heidi Hayes Jacobs
President, Curriculum Designers, Inc.
Author of *Interdisciplinary Curriculum: Design and Implementation* and
Curriculum 21: Essential Education for A Changing World

Introduction

Learning a language is far more than an intellectual, cognitive challenge. It is a means to grow and mature through the experience of other cultures. It gives breadth and depth to our personalities. It allows us to approach problems differently because we have experienced different worlds; it allows us, as Proust says, to see with new eyes.

— Veronica Lacey

As we wrote *The Keys to Planning for Learning: Effective Curriculum, Unit, and Lesson Design* we strived to capture what is known about effective practices from general educational research as well as what is known from research that is specific to language learning. This book is not intended to convey how teachers might do things better, but rather is intended to focus the discussion on how we might do things differently given the need to support learners as they acquire the skills needed for a future that cannot be easily imagined. We have taken the liberty to suggest effective practices and strategies based on our combined 50+ years of experience in classrooms K–12, our work with pre-service teachers in methods courses, and countless hours engaged in conversations and workshops with other dedicated professionals about what works and what doesn't work in the classroom. The process for curriculum, unit, and lesson design shared here reflects the following beliefs:

- The learner is at the center of all that we do. The world language curriculum is dynamic and must be dynamic to accommodate the increased diversity of learners and the ways that they are learning and are able to learn languages.

- The World-Readiness Standards for Learning Languages provide broad content goals that can be tailored to the developmental needs and special interests of the learner, and to specific program model requirements. The ACTFL Proficiency Guidelines provide the pathway of progress to greater facility in communication skills.

- A dynamic world language curriculum forges connections between and among the other disciplines allowing learners to explore interesting questions and issues while acquiring linguistic and cultural proficiency. The ideas that surface as learners explore interesting topics spark the imagination and creativity of the learner, allowing learners to explore creative solutions to identified problems.

- Language is retained when it is acquired in a meaningful context; one that allows learners to use their developing language skills to learn about, interact with, and influence their world at home, in their communities, and globally.

The mindset for curriculum, unit, and lesson design presented here offers one way to structure and organize curriculum, instruction, and assessment. We know that there are other effective models. It is our hope that the ideas expressed in this book will spark conversation and continued dialogue about how to best meet the needs of today's language learners at all levels of instruction.

—Donna Clementi and Laura Terrill

What's New in the Second Edition of *The Keys to Planning for Learning*

The second edition of this book builds upon the information shared about effective curriculum, unit, and lesson design by introducing current research and thinking related to curriculum design. The information presented in this second edition also captures insights and suggestions from classroom teachers who have attended workshops given by the presenters and who are now developing and implementing thematic units in their classrooms. As in the first edition, the revision presents an in-depth explanation for design of thematic units and lessons and a process for creating a curriculum that is vertically and horizontally aligned across all levels. Recognizing that educators are busy people, we continue with the goal of making this a user-friendly publication. The information provided in the second edition has been designed for all educators working to create a curriculum that is responsive to the needs of their learners while building Intercultural Communicative Competence. Each chapter continues to focus on a key aspect of curriculum design, while incorporating the following new, revised or expanded elements:

Chapter 1: Who are Today's Learners and What Do They Need?

- Updated statistics about today's learners
- An explanation of the role of Intercultural Communicative Competence in designing curriculum, and in planning units and lessons with an explanation of elements involved in Interculturality
- A re-conceptualized Instructional Repertoire with connections made to Global Competence, 21st Century Literacies, and Curiosity
- A newly developed discussion of the NCSSFL-ACTFL Can-Do Statements showing the connections between Proficiency Benchmarks, Performance Indicators and Examples
- An explanation of effective questioning strategies

Chapter 2: Why Is a Standards-Based and Text-Rich Approach to Unit Design Recommended?

- A thematic unit overview example at the end of the chapter that captures the goals of the unit, how those goals will be assessed and what learners will need to know and be able to do to meet those goals
- An explanation of key considerations when designing essential questions
- Updated thematic unit format to include Can-Do statements and 21st Century Learning

- Guidelines for development of the Toolbox with an expanded discussion of the role of grammar in determining support structures/patterns, and additional detail on the selection of Priority Vocabulary
- Explanation of key and related language functions (Chapters 2 and 4), and a re-conceptualized Functions and Sample Progression Chart (Appendix J)

Chapter 3: What does the Educator Need to Consider to Create a Learner-centered Classroom?

- An expanded explanation of self-efficacy and growth mindset

Chapter 4: How Do We Document and Assess Learning?

- An explanation of Proficiency Benchmarks, Performance Indicators and Examples in the context of a unit
- The addition of an Interpersonal scoring guide rubric
- An explanation for quick vocabulary or grammar self-checks
- A discussion of growth in Intercultural Communicative Competence
- A description of differences in *polished* and *on demand* Presentational tasks
- An explanation of the Parameters and Qualities of Performance and the role they play in rubric design
- Modified rubrics for performance assessment tasks for the Interpersonal and Presentational Modes

Chapter 5: What Does a Curriculum for Learning Languages Look Like in the 21st Century?

- A new curriculum framework overview document, a revised sample level-by-level curriculum map and a new articulation chart showing key and related functions by level

The website has also been updated with newly revised templates, units and unit overview documents.

We hope that this edition proves to be a valuable resource for all world language educators who are working to implement a curriculum that reflects the curriculum mindset outlined in this publication; a curriculum that is communicatively purposeful, culturally focused, intrinsically interesting, cognitively engaging, and standards-based. We deeply appreciate the educators we have worked with who have challenged our thinking and hope that they see the impact of their questions and insights in this edition.

Acknowledgments

The desire to connect with and learn from others has been part of both of our careers since we started in the profession. In that spirit, we would like to acknowledge those groups and organizations that have greatly influenced our thinking. Special recognition goes to our colleagues in our local school districts and state organizations in Missouri and Wisconsin. They ensured that we were challenged from early in our careers to make language learning purposeful and meaningful. Our involvement with other organizations—ACTFL, CARLA, Concordia Language Villages, CSCTFL, NNELL, NADSFL—allowed us to continue to grow professionally.

We would like to recognize Marie Trayer who served as Project Coordinator for the development of the 1996 Nebraska K–12 Foreign Language Frameworks. This body of work and the workshops presented by Dr. Trayer were pivotal in shaping how we approached curriculum development as teachers and leaders in subsequent years.

Appreciation and thanks to all of our teaching colleagues, our student teachers in our methods courses, and to our many workshop participants. You challenged us with your thoughtful questions; many ideas that are now part of this book resulted from those rich discussions.

We are indebted to those who helped to bring this book to completion:

- Our excellent reviewers—Leslie Baldwin, Adriana Brandt, Michael Everson and Cherice Montgomery. Your comments were extremely helpful and informed the final version of this book.

- ACTFL leadership—Former Executive Director Marty Abbott and Director of Education Paul Sandrock. Your insights and suggestions throughout the writing process greatly influenced the contents of this *Keys* publication.

Finally, a very special thanks to our families who were willing to let us do what we needed and wanted to do both when writing this book and throughout our careers. It would not have been possible to do this without their love and support.

—Donna Clementi and Laura Terrill

Table of Contents

Resources for *The Keys to Planning for Learning* are available at the ACTFL website (www.actfl.org/resources/store/books/the-keys-planning-learning-resources), including:

- All material in the Appendices
- Blank templates to download for curriculum, unit, and lesson design
- Access to materials or documents referenced in the publication
- Sample units for different languages and levels

Chapter 1 | 21st Century World Languages Curriculum

Education is the kindling of a flame, not the filling of a vessel.

— Socrates

Who Are Today's Learners and What Do They Need?

██████████████████████ mes to mind when thinking of today's learners. While they share many characteristics, they are still uniquely individual with diverse needs. They come from a variety of backgrounds and bring different languages and cultures to our classrooms. They come from lives of privilege and poverty. They live in rural, urban, and suburban communities. Some have never left their community, and others have traveled the world either virtually or literally. Some have strong support at home, and others are facing the world on their own. Our first priority as world language educators must be to create a strong sense of community in our classrooms so that learners feel comfortable in their first attempts to communicate in another language, encouraged to ask questions when they don't understand, and supported in their exploration of new perspectives. Once a safe, supportive community is established, we can focus on the knowledge and skills that these learners need in order to participate successfully in the 21st century.

Let's begin with the profile of the 21st century learner. In 2015, Common Sense Media, Inc. conducted a national survey of 2,658 children in the U.S. between the ages of eight and 18 (Common Sense Media, 2015). The purpose of the survey was to document how much time young people spend engaged in both screen and non-screen media activities. The results of the survey documented differences among young people by age, gender, race/ethnicity, and socioeconomic status (SES). Among the results, we noted the following characteristics for tweens (ages 8–12) and teens (ages 13–18):

- Teens spend an average of nine hours per day using media. Tweens spend an average of six hours per day using media. These amounts of time exclude school and homework time. Media include watching TV, movies,

and online videos; playing video, computer, and mobile games; using social media; using the Internet; reading; and listening to music.
- 51% of teens often or sometimes watch TV or use social media while doing homework; 60% of teens text and 76% listen to music while doing homework. Most teens do not feel that multitasking affects the quality of their work.

The Pew Research Center collected data on the media habits of youth between the ages of 13 and 17, administering the survey in English and Spanish to a nationally representative sample of 1,060 teens from September 25 to October 9, 2014, and from February 10 to March 16, 2015 (Lenhart, 2015). The survey identified the following characteristics about these youth:

- 92% of youth go online daily, including 24% who are online "almost constantly," facilitated by smartphones.
- 12% of youth said they had no access to any sort of cell phone.
- A typical teen sends and receives 30 texts per day.
- Girls use social media more than boys; boys play video games more than girls.
- 17% of youth read or comment on discussions (examples: reddit, Digg).

The Online Learning Consortium provided the following statistic:

- More than one in four students (28%) now take at least one distance education course, a total of 5,828,826 students and a year-to-year increase of 217,275 students (Babson Survey Research Group, 2016).

What do these data suggest? First and foremost, technology permeates young people's lives. Technology allows youth to explore topics of personal interest on their own time schedule. It facilitates multitasking among those who believe that they can attend to more than one activity or resource at a time.

↳ spread throughout (something)

The ability to move to different topics at the speed of a click means that learners are likely to become impatient when put in situations where they are required to focus on a single prescribed topic, and frustrated when they are not able to be hyper-connected. These young people do not like to wait for results: immediate access to communication with others is an imperative.

These habits of 21st century learners can be advantageous when learning a world language. When given some tips on how to find helpful and interesting resources, learners can increase their time spent immersed in the target language. They can watch films, television programs, videos, and listen to music in a variety of languages. They can read news and current events online, join online games or discussions, or create an avatar to participate in a virtual community, all using the language they are learning. They can sign up for free daily language lessons. No longer does physical location on the world map dictate the potential for communication with someone from another country and/or someone who speaks a language other than English. No longer is learning confined to classroom instruction.

These digital natives are more engaged in learning in and outside of the classroom when teachers:

- Design authentic tasks built around discovery and problem solving;
- Build in time and space for learners to explore their own interests and questions within a unit of study;
- Facilitate collaboration among learners;
- Allow learners choice in how to demonstrate they have met instructional goals and objectives;
- Provide learners with ongoing feedback as they complete activities independently and in small groups.

Although these statistics seem to imply that technology is ubiquitous in young people's lives, inequities in access to technology still exist. According to a Pew Study completed in 2015 on broadband access to complete homework, 83% of higher-income teens use computers weekly for homework, compared to 61% of lower-income teens. 22% of lower-income teens use computers for homework every day, compared to 39% of higher-income teens.

Approximately 29 million households in America have children between the ages of six and 17 (Pew Research Center analysis of U.S. Census Bureau's American Community Survey). Five million of these households do not have high-speed Internet service at home. Low-income households—and especially black and Hispanic ones—make up a disproportionate share of that five million. This low-income group makes up about 40% of all families with school-age children in the United States (Horrigan, 2015).

In light of these statistics, it is imperative (vital importance) to make technology available to all learners throughout the school day, before and after school, evenings, and on weekends so that all learners have access to the Internet and its vast resources. Successful participation in our 21st century global community requires that all learners, regardless of their socio-economic situation, possess 21st century literacy skills, including the ability to successfully access and manage multiple sources of information, and to interact respectfully with global audiences. Combining language skills with technology skills is critical in preparing young people for active participation in our global community.

How Does a 21st Century Curriculum Address the Needs of Today's Learners?

The focus of a 21st century curriculum for world languages is on teaching the skills needed to build target language proficiency and cultural understandings in real-world contexts. The World-Readiness Standards for Learning Languages (The National Standards Collaborative Board, 2015) (see Appendix A) includes this statement: ███████████████████ culture gives one the powerful key to successful communication: *knowing how, when, and why, to say what to whom.* All the linguistic and social knowledge required for effective human-to-human interaction is encompassed in those ten words" (p. 12). This is the overarching, enduring understanding related to the discipline of world language study.

Given the reality that young people in the United States who study a language other than English do not all begin at the same age, continue for the same amount of time, or learn the language via the same instructional model, a guide for world language curriculum design cannot dictate specific topics to include at each level of instruction. What can be prescribed are the foundational components that lead to increased competencies in understanding and communicating in world languages. Those required components are the World-Readiness Standards for Learning Languages (2015) (Appendix A), and the American Council on the Teaching of Foreign Languages (ACTFL) Proficiency Guidelines (2012a) (Appendix B).

Figure 1 is a visual representation of the interconnected elements for world language curriculum design.

Figure 1. Curriculum Design for Learning Languages in the 21st Century

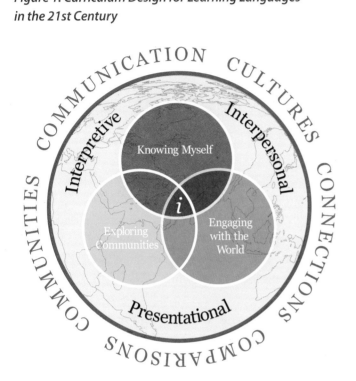

Copyright Clementi & Terrill 2013

The blue circle dominating the visual is imprinted with a watermark of the world, emphasizing communication in our global community. Surrounding the world are the 5 Cs of the World-Readiness Standards for Learning Languages: Communication, Cultures, Connections, Comparisons, Communities. The 5 Cs represent the goal areas of the World-Readiness Standards and include the 11 Standards that guide the selection of curriculum content. Printed on the world are the 3 Modes of Communication—Interpretive, Presentational, Interpersonal—which are fundamental to building proficiency in a world language. The Venn diagram in the center represents that, through communication in a world language, learners explore topics on a personal level (Knowing Myself); they explore topics related to where the learner lives locally, regionally, nationally (Exploring Communities); and they explore the learner's global connections (Engaging with the World).

In the center of the Venn diagram is an "*i*," originally intended to represent *interculturality*. Since the publication of the first edition of *Keys to Planning for Learning*, world language teachers contributed ideas that resulted in an expanded interpretation for the "*i*." Some suggest that it reflects the *individual* learner and *learner-centered* instruction. Others are reminded of the importance of using the target language continuously by both teachers and learners to create an *immersion environment* in order to build proficiency. Many teachers think of the "*i*" as a reminder to access a variety of authentic texts in the *Interpretive Mode* to serve as accurate models of the target language and culture. Still other teachers describe the "*i*" as the instructional goal of presenting new understandings of *information* to a global audience as well as sharing information, opinions, reactions, and emotions *interpersonally*. *Imagination, interpersonal, interest, interconnections,* and *identity* were also suggested. Finally, some view the "*i*" as the focus of the entire graphic: *Integration of the three Modes of Communication and Cultural Understanding* from local to global contexts in every unit of instruction with the goal of continuously developing proficiency in the target language. All of these suggestions are important considerations in the design of curriculum, unit, and lesson design, and they all are related directly or indirectly to *Interculturality*, which is discussed later in this chapter.

With these understandings in mind, and based on current discussions and readings, we believe that *Intercultural Communicative Competence (ICC)* accurately reflects the "*i*" in the center of the graphic. ICC combines the notion of Intercultural Competence with the notion of Communicative Competence. Quoting Wagner and Byram (2015):

The purpose of teaching ICC and not just communicative competence is to give students the tools in order to:

1. interpret and understand the cultural contexts of people with whom they interact—whether native speakers of the language they are learning or people using the language as a common language or *lingua franca*,
2. be able to interact with them accordingly,
3. act as mediators between two groups with mutually incomprehensible languages (and cultures), and
4. reflect critically on their own cultural context.

… we want to call for teachers to design curricula that facilitate students' ability to apply what they learn in their classrooms to an intercultural national or transnational context in and beyond their classroom and school walls.

The graphic of World Language curriculum design. (Figure 1) unites the essential elements for purposeful and meaningful instruction in world languages. At the heart of the graphic is the "*i*" reflecting *Intercultural Communicative Competence*, the overarching goal for learning world languages.

What Is Influencing Effective Practices in Curriculum, Instruction, and Assessment in Language Classrooms Today?

One of the strongest influences in how teachers teach world languages is their personal experience in learning a world language. We tend to teach the way we were taught, even if those ways were not always 100% successful for us! That said, we are fortunate to be part of a dynamic profession that continues to research and discuss how to effectively teach and learn world languages. Appendix C summarizes selected theories, methods, and approaches related to second language acquisition, and offers a brief example of language that learners might produce as the result of each method. We also benefit from the latest thinking and research on teaching and learning world languages through vehicles such as workshops, conferences, webinars, and professional publications.

Second language instruction also draws on advances in neuroscience that have expanded our understanding of how the brain learns and remembers. For example, we plan lessons according to the guideline of 20-minute learning segments that represent the attention span of the brain to focus on a single task. We use strategies such as visual representations, movement, rhythm and rhyme, and stories to move items from short-term to long-term memory. We actively apply the strategies of differentiation to meet the needs of diverse learners. These examples represent a sampling of research that has led to significant changes in how we plan for learning in the world language classroom.

Three current research-based publications related to the teaching of world languages merit special attention. *Implementing Integrated Performance Assessment* (2013), developed by Adair-Hauck, Glisan, and Troyan, "is a tool that assesses learners' progress in meeting the National Standards and attaining proficiency levels on the continuum of the *ACTFL Proficiency*

Guidelines" (p.5). Another ACTFL publication, *Enacting the Work of Language Instruction: High-Leverage Teaching Practices* by Glisan and Donato (2017), describes research on effective teaching strategies intended to "represent one answer to the question of how teacher education programs can apply results from teacher cognition research and assist teachers in creating effective learning environments for their students" (p.vii). Bill VanPatten reviews the basics of communicative/contemporary language teaching in *While We're on the Topic: BVP on Language, Acquisition, and Classroom Practice* (2017). He advocates that instructors "make curricular decisions based on ideas informed by theory and research" (p.vii).

Two other national education initiatives influence unit and lesson planning: **21st Century Learning** and **21st Century Literacies**. The Partnership for 21st Century Learning or P21 (formerly the Partnership for 21st Century Skills), founded in 2002, is a coalition of business and education leaders, and policymakers who opened a national conversation to identify and promote the importance of 21st century skills for all learners. P21 emphasizes the skills of Communication, Collaboration, Creativity, and Critical Thinking as essential for success in today's global world. The National Council of Teachers of English (NCTE) addressed the changing definition of literacy in a position statement in 2013. NCTE's statement about 21st Century Literacies acknowledges the important role that technology plays in interpreting and creating information for a global audience. Both of these initiatives will be explained in more detail later in this publication.

plans, and assessment methods continue to evolve as research identifies effective strategies and practices to facilitate learning. For many teachers, the discussion in this publication about what we teach (curriculum), how we teach (instruction), and how we know that students have learned (assessment) validates what is already common practice in their classrooms. Some teachers may find ideas in this publication that will strengthen their current instructional practices. For other teachers, the ideas in this publication may trigger a paradigm shift, a realization that the current curriculum used in their school or district or program is not sufficient to develop the Intercultural Communicative Competence that today's learners need for successful participation in our global community. In all cases, we hope that this publication sparks discussion among colleagues about effective curriculum, unit, and lesson design.

How Do the World-Readiness Standards for Learning Languages Facilitate Curriculum, Unit, and Lesson Design?

The World-Readiness Standards for Learning Languages. *Standards for Foreign Language Learning* (National Standards in Foreign Language Education Project [NSFLEP], 1996) united the profession around what learners should know and be able to do in order to understand and communicate in a language other than English. The Standards define five goal areas, the 5 Cs—Communication, Cultures, Connections, Comparisons, and Communities—and 11 Standards for those goal areas (Appendix A).

"Knowing how, when and why to say what to whom" (World-Readiness Standards for Learning Languages NSFLEP, 2015), captures the vision of what it means to communicate in a language other than English. The Communication goal area goes beyond the "what" (vocabulary) and the "how" (grammar), expanding to a more complete definition of communication indicating "why" (the purpose), "when" (the time and place), and with or to "whom" (the audience). The World-Readiness Standards give the profession a way of explaining that the instructional goal for world languages is to build learners' Intercultural Communicative Competence with other speakers of the language they are learning, and that grammar and vocabulary are tools that help learners build that competency. Because of the World-Readiness Standards, language learning is no longer limited to what learners know *about* the language, but focuses on what they can do *with* the language.

Today, the profession recognizes the visionary work done by those who developed the Standards in 1996. When they were first created, the 5 Cs offered a simple yet cohesive way to frame language learning. Over time, the complexity and richness found in the simplicity of the 5 Cs became apparent. The World-Readiness Standards align to both 21st Century Learning and the Common Core State Standards for English Language Arts and Literacy, highlighting the importance and value of language study in meeting these cross-disciplinary initiatives to prepare young people for advanced studies, work, careers, and active participation in today's global community.

Let's consider the World-Readiness Standards in the context of a unit that explores education as a topic under the theme of *Challenges*. This particular unit is designed for learners at the Novice High/Intermediate Low level of proficiency. Table 1 presents a brief introduction to the unit describing the importance of education for all young people. The complete thematic unit can be found in Appendix D. Learners explore the topic of education on three levels. First, at the personal level (*Knowing Myself*), learners share what school is like for them. Next, learners consider what school is like in their city, state, and nationally (*Exploring Communities*). Finally, learners compare their experiences with school to the experiences of young people around the world (*Engaging with the World*). Throughout the unit, learners consider possible responses to the essential question: "Why can't all young people go to school?" The unit goals reflect what learners should know and be able to do through the exploration of this essential question.

Now, let's consider how the 5 Cs—Communication, Cultures, Connections, Comparisons and Communities—are integrated within this unit.

Table 1. Introduction to Thematic Unit on Education

Language and Level/Grade	French – High School Grade 10
Performance Range	Novice High/Intermediate Low
Theme/Topic	**Challenges:** Education
Essential Question	Why can't all young people go to school?
Goals *What should learners know and be able to do by the end of the unit?*	Learners will be able to: • Describe the current status of education of young people locally, nationally, and globally. • Identify and categorize economic, political, and social reasons why young people around the world cannot go to/stay in school. • Give reasons why going to school is important to oneself and locally, nationally, globally. • Give examples of initiatives to support schooling for all young people around the world. • Connect with a school in (x) to learn more about the school; collaborate to develop a plan for continued communication.

██████ COMMUNICATION – Communicate effectively in more than one language in order to function in a variety of situations and for multiple purposes.

The Communication goal area includes three Standards representing the three Modes of Communication:

- **Interpersonal Communication: Le**arners interact and negotiate meaning in spoken, signed, or written conversations to share information, reactions, feelings, and opinions.
- **Interpretive Communication: Lea**rners understand, interpret, and analyze what is heard, read, or viewed on a variety of topics.
- **Presentational Communication: L**earners present information, concepts, and ideas to inform, explain, persuade, and narrate on a variety of topics, using appropriate media and adapting to various audiences of listeners, readers, or viewers.

In order to meet the Communication goals for this unit, learners work with a variety of authentic texts in the Interpretive Mode to learn more about why all young people cannot go to school. They participate in discussions in class and virtually with learners in other parts of the world to share information and opinions about schools locally, nationally, globally. They present information orally and in writing related to schools around the world.

Table 2 outlines the Summative Performance Assessment for this unit that includes tasks for all three Modes of Communication. The Interpretive Mode has three components: one focuses on Viewing, one on Reading, and one on Listening. The Presentational Mode offers two options: one is a polished, edited multimedia campaign, and the other is an "on-demand"

essay. In the Interpersonal Mode, learners discuss with others what they have learned in order to address the unit's essential question: why can't all young people go to school?

██████████████████████ with cultural competence and understanding.

The Cultures goal area includes two Standards connecting practices and products of the culture to underlying perspectives:

- **Relating Cultural Practices to Pers**pectives: Learners use the language to investigate, explain, and reflect on the relationship between the practices and perspectives of the cultures studied. Examples of Cultural Practices include how people greet each other, what families do on the weekend, and how people celebrate birthdays.
- **Relating Cultural Products to Pers**pectives: Learners use the language to investigate, explain, and reflect on the relationship between the products and perspectives of the cultures studies. Examples of Cultural Products include monuments such as the Pyramids in Egypt, literature such as *The Aeneid* by Virgil, and artwork such as the murals by Diego Rivera. Cultural Products also include items in daily life such as Italian ice cream, Japanese gardens, and Chinese lanterns.

The Cultures goal area is often referred to as the 3 Ps (Products, Practices, Perspectives) and a triangle is used to illustrate the relationship of a Practice to a Product and the underlying Perspective (Figure 2).

Table 2. Summative Performance Assessment for Thematic Unit on Education

Mode	Learners will:
Interpretive	• Watch a movie about a young girl in Sénégal who cannot go to school; identify reasons that prevent her from attending school. • Read an article about preparing for work and careers in the 21st century; identify reasons why it is important for all young people to go to school. • Listen to an appeal for support of an initiative to help young people stay in school; describe the main components of the initiative.
Presentational	• **Polished:** Work in groups to design a multimedia campaign to inform others of literacy rates around the world and ways that organizations are working to increase literacy rates globally. • **On Demand:** Respond to these questions in writing: What are reasons that all children cannot go to school? What are some possible solutions to this global problem?
Interpersonal	• Share ideas about the role and importance of education for all, and barriers to school attendance for young people locally, nationally, internationally. In small groups, discuss ways that the class could collaborate with a school in (X) to support the school's education program.

Figure 2. Culture Triangle

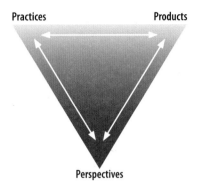

Table 3 shows the Cultures goal area as it is represented in the education unit template. Learners consider school as a *product* of the target culture, and going to school as a *practice* of the target culture. Learners are encouraged to ask questions about school and school attendance in order to gain insights into the importance that members of the target culture place on attending school. This *perspective* is developed through class discussions, readings, and interviews with native speakers from the target culture or those who have had extended experiences living in the target culture. The class might have a videochat with classes in the target country to ask their opinions on the importance of attending school.

It is important in discussing perspectives to open learners to the idea that there may be several plausible perspectives depending on who is offering the explanation (where they live within the target culture, their age, their life experiences). It is also important for learners to understand that cultural products, practices, and perspectives continue to evolve over time. The power of observation, withholding judgment, and ongoing exploration of the topic are lifelong skills all learners need in today's rapidly changing world. Failure to acknowledge that the meanings of products, practices, and perspectives change over time and with the source of the meaning may give rise to or reinforce stereotypes, resulting in cultural misunderstandings.

The second example of the Culture Triangle in Table 3 identifies a daily class schedule as a cultural product. The types of courses offered is the cultural practice. The variety of courses in a class schedule from the target culture might be compared to the variety on a schedule in the United States. This could prompt a discussion on the purpose of schools around the world giving insights into the perspectives that different cultures have concerning education.

GOAL AREA: CONNECTIONS – Connect with other disciplines and acquire information and diverse perspectives in order to use the language to function in academic and career-related situations.

The Connections goal area includes two Standards that emphasize how learners are able to build content knowledge by relating what they are learning in their language class to other disciplines.

- Making Connections to Other Disciplines: Learners build, reinforce, and expand their knowledge of other disciplines while using the language to develop critical thinking and to solve problems creatively. For example, Chinese language learners use their knowledge of how to determine percentages from math class to figure out the percentage of a person's salary that is spent on housing in Beijing.
- Acquiring Information and Diverse Perspectives: Learners access and evaluate information and diverse perspectives that are available through the language and its cultures. For example, French language learners watch or read a news report from France describing the attitudes of the French people towards their President. Learners are able to use this information not only to contribute to discussions in their French class but also to contribute to discussions in classes such as Political Science or Global Studies.

In the education unit, learners work with authentic texts comparing attitudes of people in the target cultures towards school. They may draw on background knowledge gained in Global Studies classes about literacy rates around the world to defend their ideas about the importance of school for all young

Table 3. Cultures Goal Area Represented in the Thematic Unit on Education

Cultures (Sample Evidence) *Indicate the relationship between the product, practice, and perspective.*	**Product:** School **Practice:** Going to school **Perspective:** Importance of school for all young people in (x)
	Product: Daily class schedule **Practice:** Required vs. elective courses **Perspective:** Purpose of school

Table 4. Connections Goal Area Represented in the Thematic Unit on Education

Connections (Sample Evidence)	Making Connections to Other Disciplines	Acquiring Information and Diverse Perspectives
	Social Studies: • Education as a right of the child (United Nations) • Global challenge of increasing literacy rates **English Language Arts and Literacy:** • Evaluation of the accuracy and validity of information from different Internet sources • Synthesis of information from a variety of sources • Sharing information and ideas with others through discussions	• Reading articles and viewing video clips from a variety of authentic sources about education and literacy rates around the world • Interviewing native speakers of the target language about their attitudes towards school

people. They use examples from the target cultures telling how education influences young people's lives to support their opinions. While this task is completed in the target language, it also addresses the English Language Arts Common Core Writing Anchor Standard 1: "Write arguments to support claims in an analysis of substantive topics or texts using valid reasoning and relevant and sufficient evidence" (Appendix E). At first glance, this Common Core Standard may seem out of reach for novice language learners. However, if the learners have the opportunity to interact with several authentic texts in a guided process, they can achieve this Standard. For example, learners may brainstorm why they think all young people around the world cannot go to school. Their next task is to read articles on the Internet about the topic, looking at headlines and introductory paragraphs to see what issues related to school attendance are addressed. They can then list the issues presented in the authentic texts to support their claims about why all young people cannot go to school. Table 4 shows the Connections goal area as it appears in the unit template. Notice that English Language Arts and Literacy is one of the disciplines highlighted.

░░░░░░░░░░░░░░░░░░░░░░░elop insight into the nature of language and culture in order to interact with cultural competence.

The Comparisons goal area includes two Standards that encourage learners to compare the language and culture they are studying to their own.

• **Language Comparisons: Learners** use the language to investigate, explain, and reflect on the nature of language through comparisons of the language studied and their own. For example, learners might compare the words (formal vs informal language) that people in the Arabic-speaking world use to greet each other among family, friends, and with new acquaintances. This Standard is not the "Grammar Standard." By this, we mean that this Standard does not ask learners to compare how to form the future tense in English and in the target language. Instead, this Standard draws attention to how language expresses culture. In the Arabic example, the choice of words to use to greet someone reflects the relationship between the people who are greeting each other.

• **Cultural Comparisons: Learners** use the language to investigate, explain, and reflect on the concept of culture through comparisons of the cultures studied and their own. For example, learners might compare the availability and popularity of public transportation in Germany to public transportation in their home towns.

Table 5 shows the Comparisons goal area as it appears in the unit template. In the education unit, learners explore the concept of *une année blanche* (literally, a white year) to understand how another culture and language convey a missed year of schooling. Learners make comparisons to their own lives by exploring reasons that their school year might be disrupted and schools closed. They consider the implications of passing or failing the *bac*, the exam given at the end of high school in Francophone countries, in comparison to the impact of exams given in the United States. They recognize that *passer* is a false cognate in the phrase *passer le bac* and means "to take the *bac*" and not "to get a passing grade on the *bac*."

Table 5. Comparisons Goal Area Represented in the Thematic Unit on Education

Comparisons (Sample Evidence)	Language Comparisons	Cultural Comparisons
	• *Une année blanche* (a missed year of school) • *Passer le bac* (to take the French exam at the end of high school)	• Reasons to attend/not attend school • Final exams in high school

██████████████ **municate and interact with cultural competence in order to participate in multilingual communities at home and around the world.**

The Communities goal area includes two Standards and recognizes the need for learners to communicate with their classmates and also with other speakers of the language beyond their classes. It encourages learners to take personal responsibility for their own learning.

- School and Global Communities: Learners use the language both within and beyond the classroom to interact and collaborate in the community and the globalized world. An example would be to establish a sister school relationship that includes opportunities for the learners to visit one another in person and/or virtually.
- Lifelong Learning: Learners set goals and reflect on their progress in using languages for enjoyment, enrichment, and advancement. An example is to have learners keep portfolios that document their personal language learning goals and evidence of progress towards meeting those goals.

Table 6 shows the Communities goal area as it appears in the unit template. In the Presentational task for the unit on education, learners prepare a multimedia campaign to inform people in their community about efforts to increase literacy rates around the world. They can also share their multimedia campaign beyond their community to sister schools around the world. In terms of lifelong learning, learners might be motivated to continue to support literacy efforts independently after completing the unit in class. Discussions in class during this unit about the importance of school might influence learners to set personal goals related to their plans for continuing their education after high school. Finally, this Standard encourages learners to adopt a routine of setting goals for learning, and then keeping track of their progress towards reaching those goals. In world languages, learners can document their progress towards greater proficiency in the language they are learning by using the NCSSFL-ACTFL Can-Do Statements explained later in this publication.

The 5 Cs—Communication, Cultures, Connections, Comparisons, Communities—guide the choice of content for a curriculum designed to build proficiency in the three modes of Communication *embedded in a cultural context*, and enriched by Comparisons, Connections, and Communities.

> Language-specific Standards are currently available in Arabic, American Sign Language (ASL), Chinese, Classical Languages, French, German, Hindi, Italian, Japanese, Korean, Portuguese, Russian, Scandinavian Languages, and Spanish at www.actfl.org/resources/world-readiness-standards-learning-languages.

What Other Resources Facilitate Curriculum, Unit, and Lesson Design?

ACTFL Proficiency Guidelines. The ACTFL Proficiency Guidelines were first published in 1986 and most recently revised in 2012. They assess how well a person uses a language independent of where, when, or how that person learned the language (see Appendix B). They explain "what individuals can do with language in terms of speaking, writing, listening, and reading in real-world situations in a spontaneous and non-rehearsed context" (ACTFL, 2012a). They include descriptions of proficiency at the Novice, Intermediate, Advanced, Superior, and Distinguished levels.

To receive a proficiency rating, learners must demonstrate that they can meet *all of the criteria* in a sustained fashion *all of the time* at a particular level as described in the Proficiency Guidelines. Official ACTFL proficiency ratings can only be awarded by ACTFL-certified proficiency raters.

NCSSFL-ACTFL Can-Do Statements. The NCSSFL-ACTFL Can-Do Statements (Appendix F) are based on the ACTFL Proficiency Guidelines and describe what learners can do at the Novice, Intermediate, Advanced, Superior, and Distinguished levels of proficiency. They are designed first and foremost to

Table 6. Communities Goal Area Represented in the Thematic Unit on Education

Communities	School and Global Communities	Lifelong Learning
(Sample Evidence)	• Inform others about literacy rates around the world and invite collaboration on a project related to education for all.	• Self-assess progress toward personal learning goals/can-do statements. • Consider the role that education plays in your life and set goals related to how to continue your studies and/or explore new learning opportunities.

help learners understand and set personal goals leading to greater proficiency. Teachers can use the Can-Do Statements to write communication objectives for curriculum, unit, and lesson plans. The Can-Do Statements are organized according to the three Modes of Communication and include three components: Proficiency Benchmarks, Performance Indicators, and Examples. The Proficiency Benchmarks broadly describe learners' progress towards proficiency from Novice through Distinguished levels. The Performance Indicators break each Proficiency level into Low, Mid, and High descriptors of performance, highlighting text types, contexts and content, and linguistic functions. The **Examples** reflect instructional contexts such as PK-20 classrooms, immersion and dual language programs, and adult education programs. These examples are intended to help learners and teachers write their own "customized" Learning Tasks that reflect the topics and content they are studying. The Can-Do Statements are not intended as

checklists of what learners need to demonstrate at each proficiency level. Multiple examples of evidence over time are required to demonstrate consistent language performance at a targeted level. Figure 3 shows the relationship among the three components of the NCSSFL-ACTFL Can-Do Statements.

It is important to remember that learners may demonstrate that they can perform tasks at a higher level of proficiency within an instructional setting than they might demonstrate in an unrehearsed proficiency situation. This is because in instructional settings, the contexts and topics for performance are familiar to the learners, their instructors, and others with whom the learners interact. Outside the instructional settings, learners will meet and interact with people who do not limit their interactions to topics that the learners have studied. Learners need to truly apply all the language and communication skills they have learned to these unrehearsed, spontaneous situations.

Figure 3. Sample Relationship Among Three Components of the NCSSFL-ACTFL Can-Do Statements

Presentational Communication
Novice Proficiency Benchmark

I can present information on both very familiar and everyday topics using a variety of practiced or memorized words, phrases, and simple sentences through spoken, written, or signed language.

Performance Indicators
How can I present information to give a preference, opinion or persuasive argument?

Novice Low	Novice Mid	Novice High
I can express my likes and dislikes, using practiced or memorized words and phrases, and with the help of gestures or visuals.	*I can* express my likes and dislikes on very familiar and everyday topics of interest, using a mixture of practiced or memorized words, phrases and simple sentences.	*I can* express my preferences on familiar and everyday topics of interest, using simple sentences most of the time.

EXAMPLES: Give a Preference, Opinion, or Persuasive Argument – Speaking or Signing

Novice Low	Novice Mid	Novice High
• *I can* ... *(customize with specific content)* • *I can* list places I like to go to see art or listen to music. • *I can* name sports I like or don't like.	• *I can* ... *(customize with specific content)* • *I can* tell where I like to go to see art or listen to music. • *I can* state my favorite free-time activities and those I don't like.	• *I can* ... *(customize with specific content)* • *I can* recommend places to experience a variety of art and music styles. • *I can* tell about others' likes and dislikes.

EXAMPLES: Give a Preference, Opinion, or Persuasive Argument – Writing

Novice Low	Novice Mid	Novice High
• *I can* ... *(customize with specific content)* • *I can* list places I like to go to see art or listen to music. • *I can* create a simpe chart of a few things I like and dislike.	• *I can* ... *(customize with specific content)* • *I can* write where I go to see art or listen to music. • *I can* write how much I like or don't like certain sports.	• *I can* ... *(customize with specific content)* • *I can* recommend places to experience a variety of art and music styles. • *I can* make a simple poster to campaign for a person or event.

Consider how Figure 4 depicts the differences between what learners can do in instructional settings (Performance) and what learners can do when they are not in an instructional setting (Proficiency).

When learners are in an instructional setting, they work with vocabulary and language functions in the context of a specific unit or topic. The learners benefit from practicing the targeted language in a series of activities that gradually build the learners' abilities to communicate in a broader variety of contexts on a greater variety of topics. Performance in an instructional setting builds towards greater proficiency where the learners can understand and use the language in unrehearsed, less predictable situations. Table 7 compares the ACTFL Proficiency Guidelines to the NCSSFL-ACTFL Can-Do Statements, showing how these two resources complement each other, supporting the pathway to greater proficiency.

Figure 4. Contexts for Performance and Proficiency

Performance	Proficiency
Within an instructional setting	Beyond the classroom
Based on specific instructional goals	Independent of specific instruction or curriculum
Familiar content and contexts	Broad content and contexts
Practiced vocabulary and functions	Spontaneous, unrehearsed

Table 7. Comparison of the ACTFL Proficiency Guidelines to the NCSSFL-ACTFL Can-Do Statements

	ACTFL Proficiency Guidelines	NCSSFL-ACTFL Can-Do Statements
Purpose	Describes what language learners can and cannot do with language at each Proficiency level regardless of where, when, or how the language was acquired.	Provides examples of how the learners might demonstrate what they can do to demonstrate Performance in each of the Modes of Communication at the various Proficiency levels.
Communication Skills	Speaking Listening Reading Writing	Interpersonal Interpretive Presentational
Levels	Novice Intermediate Advanced Superior Distinguished	Novice Intermediate Advanced Superior Distinguished
Contexts	Broad Unrehearsed, Spontaneous	Familiar topics and contexts Practiced, Familiar
Considerations	Context Content Global Tasks and Functions Discourse type Accuracy	Context Content Function Text type

How Can the 4 Cs of 21st Century Learning Facilitate Unit and Lesson Design?

21st Century Learning. 21st Century Learning or P21.org (formerly the Partnership for 21st Century Skills) is "a unified vision for learning to ensure student success in a world where change is constant and learning never stops" (Partnership for 21st Century Learning, 2016). Founded in 2002, 21 states have joined this initiative, along with the National Education Association, the American Federation of Teachers, and the National Board for Professional Teaching Standards among others. One of the components of 21st Century Learning is the Four Cs: Communication, Critical Thinking and Problem-Solving, Creativity and Innovation, Collaboration and Cross-Cultural Understanding. These skills are considered essential for success in daily life and in work in today's increasingly complex world. The *21st Century Skills Map for World Languages* was developed by hundreds of world language teachers under the leadership of ACTFL as part of the P21 initiative (Partnership for 21st Century Skills, 2011). The Skills Map is a collection of practical classroom examples of how to integrate world languages with the skills needed for success in the 21st century.

chosen the 4 Cs of 21st Century Learning—Communication, Critical Thinking and Problem-Solving, Creativity and Innovation, Collaboration and Cross-Cultural Understanding—to organize a language teacher's Instructional Repertoire. By Instructional Repertoire, we mean the tools teachers use to facilitate learning for the increasingly diverse population of learners in language classrooms. Instead of describing a long list of instructional tools, we have highlighted ones that suggest meaningful ways to build Intercultural Communicative Competence while, at the same time, developing 21st Century Learning skills. Teachers are encouraged to share components from this framework with learners to promote their growth and independence in taking more personal responsibility for their learning. Figure 5 represents the components of the Instructional Repertoire.

In the image of the Instructional Repertoire, the learner is in the center as a reminder that each learner has unique needs and interests, requiring differentiation of instruction for successful learning. Placing the learner in the center also indicates that the learner can use these instructional tools to become an independent learner. The imprint of the world on the mind of the learner highlights the connection between 21st Century Learning and the global contexts in which the learners communicate.

Figure 5. Instructional Repertoire for Language Teachers

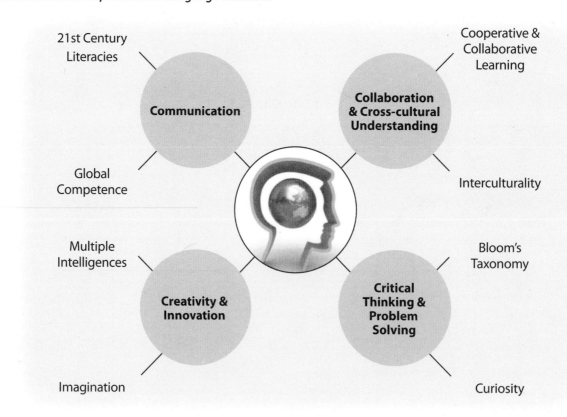

Each of the 4 Cs of 21st Century Learning—Communication, Critical Thinking, Creativity, and Collaboration—is presented individually in this section. However, these skills are interconnected with overlapping characteristics and real-world applications. Following a brief explanation of each C of 21st Century Learning, we share examples of how these skills can be integrated into world language unit and lesson planning.

Communication. "Communication competence involves mediated and digital communication, interpersonal, written and oral communication" (Partnership for 21st Century Learning, n.d.). We are highlighting 21st Century Literacies and Global Competence as two important subsets of Communication.

21st Century Literacies. Acknowledging that reading and writing are no longer sufficient literacy skills in today's world, the National Council of Teachers of English (NCTE) has expanded the definition of literacy to address the intensity and complexity of communication in a rapidly changing world. The NCTE definition of 21st century literacies (2013) states:

Active, successful participants in this 21st century global society must be able to:

- develop proficiency and fluency with the tools of technology;
- build intentional cross-cultural connections and relationships with others so to pose and solve problems collaboratively and strengthen independent thought;
- design and share information for global communities to meet a variety of purposes;
- manage, analyze, and synthesize multiple streams of simultaneous information;
- create, critique, analyze, and evaluate multimedia texts; and
- attend to the ethical responsibilities required by these complex environments.

The NCTE definition of 21st century literacies and the Partnership for 21st Century Learning both emphasize the effective use of print and digital media to build communication skills as consumers and as producers of information in a global context. The next sections show how 21st century literacies are reinforced through the three Modes of Communication.

Building Literacies Through the Interpersonal Mode. The Interpersonal Mode is two-way communication where the learners exchange ideas and information via face-to-face and virtual interactions, emails, social networking, and texting. NCTE Literacies that are reinforced and strengthened through the Interpersonal Mode include:

- building intentional cross-cultural connections and relationships with others so to pose and solve problems collaboratively and strengthen independent thought; and
- developing proficiency and fluency with the tools of technology.

The NCTE Literacies listed above are reinforced and strengthened in the 21st Century Learning characteristics that describe Communication. These characteristics are also descriptive of the Interpersonal Mode. Learners can:

- articulate thoughts and ideas effectively using oral, written and nonverbal communication skills in a variety of forms and contexts;
- listen effectively to decipher meaning, including knowledge, values, attitudes and intentions;
- use communication for a range of purposes (e.g. to inform, instruct, motivate and persuade);
- utilize multiple media and technologies, and know how to judge their effectiveness a priori as well as assess their impact; and
- communicate effectively in diverse environments (including multilingual). (Partnership for 21st Century Learning, n.d.)

The Common Core State Standards for English Language Arts and Literacy also underline the importance of these literacy skills among learners in Speaking and Listening Standard 1 (SL1): "Prepare for and participate effectively in a range of conversations and collaborations with diverse partners, building on others' ideas and expressing their own clearly and persuasively" (Appendix E).

Language learners can build literacy skills via the Interpersonal Mode by:

- exchanging ideas and information purposefully and with clarity;
- listening attentively to what participants in discussions and conversations say in order to respond or react appropriately;
- engaging other participants by inviting their perspectives on the topic;
- sharing ideas collected from a video clip or reading to determine if understandings are similar;

- monitoring participants' understanding, clarifying and elaborating as appropriate during a group discussion;
- playing a board game or card game that requires asking and responding to questions;
- interacting with people from around the world via technology;
- withholding judgment during the exchange of ideas and information, taking time to consider the perspectives of people from different cultural backgrounds;
- evaluating what others say, politely challenging the logic of their opinions and the accuracy of evidence they offer as appropriate;
- using follow-up questions and comments to clarify and expand on the topic; and
- adjusting nonverbal and verbal communication to the cultural context of the conversation.

All these skills can be encouraged among language learners by incorporating them into rubrics and scoring guides. For example, in addition to assessing use of vocabulary and comprehensibility, teachers could also add categories such as: "Demonstrates active listening," or, "Uses follow-up questions and comments to sustain a conversation." Categories such as these not only give learners ideas on how to be good participants in a discussion or conversation, they also send a message that these behaviors are valued. Other examples of rubrics and scoring guides are included in Chapter Four.

Examples of situations requiring Interpersonal skills are listed below and can be accomplished in face-to-face interactions or via technology using tools such as Skype, email, avatars, discussion boards, and videoconferencing to connect learners in your classroom with learners in classrooms in other places, locally, nationally, and internationally. Learners can:

- carry on a conversation about daily life and events;
- make plans (to meet someone, attend an event, to travel somewhere, host a videoconference, etc.);
- ask and respond to questions about a topic being studied in class;
- compare reactions to something or someone from pop culture;
- share insights gained from a movie or piece of literature;
- work with others to design and complete a task or project;
- participate in an interview about plans for the future, asking for more details and clarifications as needed;

- express and compare opinions and preferences about topics of interest; and
- participate in a panel discussion or debate on a topic currently in the news.

Building Literacies Through the Presentational Mode. The Presentational Mode is one-way communication via speaking, signing, or writing where the learners present ideas and information that they have rehearsed and polished for an audience. NCTE Literacies that are reinforced and strengthened through the Presentational Mode include:

- designing and sharing information for global communities to meet a variety of purposes;
- creating, critiquing, analyzing, and evaluating multimedia texts; and
- attending to the ethical responsibilities required by these complex environments.

The NCTE Literacies listed above are reinforced in the 21st Century Learning characteristics of Communication. These characteristics are also descriptive of the Presentational Mode:

- articulate thoughts and ideas effectively using oral, written, and nonverbal communication skills in a variety of forms and contexts;
- use communication for a range of purposes (e.g. to inform, instruct, motivate, and persuade);
- utilize multiple media and technologies, and know how to judge their effectiveness a priori as well as assess their impact; and
- communicate effectively in diverse environments (including multilingual). (Partnership for 21st Century Learning, n.d.)

The Common Core State Standards for English Language Arts and Literacy also underline the importance of these literacy skills among learners through several Writing, Speaking, and Listening, and Language Standards (Appendix E).

Language learners can build literacy skills via the Presentational Mode by:

- documenting ideas from a brainstorming session via a graphic organizer;
- using an outline to organize ideas and information for the presentation;
- planning and editing to produce a clear, organized, and informative presentation;

- demonstrating that, through choice of vocabulary, register, and topic, the learner is aware of the audience for the presentation;
- organizing an infographic about school in the United States to share with learners in another part of the world;
- preparing visuals that enhance understanding of an oral presentation;
- synthesizing information from several sources to present a new perspective on a topic;
- documenting the sources used in preparation of a written or oral presentation;
- writing a synopsis of an American movie for people in another country, including explanations of the cultural context;
- proofreading written texts for spelling, capitalization, punctuation, grammar;
- using evidence-based reasoning and arguments to support an opinion in a persuasive speech; and
- using technology appropriately to enhance understanding of the presentation.

Rubrics and scoring guides include categories from this list as appropriate to the task. For example, learners can be held accountable for creating an outline to help them organize their ideas for an oral or written presentation. The rubric or scoring guide may include a category about how the learner demonstrated attention to audience. The appropriate use of technology to create a product might be included in the evaluation.

Examples of Presentational tasks include:
- stories based on past experiences, real or imagined;
- cartoon strips illustrating an original story;
- news stories based on a current event;
- demonstrations of how to do something through a speech or through written instructions;
- brochures, leaflets, and flyers on a person, place, or event of interest;
- podcasts on a person, place, or event of interest;
- videos or live performances based on an original script;
- persuasive speeches or essays on a topic of importance locally, nationally, or internationally;
- researched reports based on findings from multiple sources; and
- websites or blogs on a person, place, or event of interest.

Building Literacies Through the Interpretive Mode. The Interpretive Mode is one-way communication via listening, reading, or viewing where the learners take in ideas and information from a wide variety of print, spoken, signed, or digital media. NCTE Literacies that are reinforced and strengthened through the Interpretive Mode include:
- managing, analyzing, and synthesizing multiple streams of simultaneous information;
- creating, critiquing, analyzing, and evaluating multimedia texts;
- attending to the ethical responsibilities required by these complex environments.

The NCTE Literacies listed above are reinforced and strengthened in the 21st Century Learning characteristics of Communication. This characteristic is descriptive of Listening in the Interpretive Mode:
- Listen effectively to decipher meaning, including knowledge, values, attitudes, and intentions.

The Common Core State Standards for English Language Arts and Literacy also underline the importance of these literacy skills among learners through Reading, Speaking and Listening skills (Appendix E).

Learners can build their Interpretive literacy skills by using pre-reading strategies/pre-listening or pre-viewing strategies in preparation for reading, listening to, or viewing the text. Learners will be more successful at interpreting texts when they:
- preview the type of text (e.g., newspaper, magazine, short story, news broadcast, song, or movie);
- preview the title and any visuals to begin to form ideas about the content;
- check the sources for the text to see if they are credible;
- list what is known about the topic and then make predictions about what the text is about; and
- read the first and last paragraphs of the text, make revisions to predictions as appropriate, and share with classmates.

To build literacy in reading:
- note the main idea of each paragraph in the margin;
- note connections of the ideas in the text to other texts or experiences;
- write a question or questions about the information presented on the page;

- underline words that are important to understanding the meaning of the text, trying to limit the number of words underlined to words that are essential to understanding the text; and
- reread the text after defining underlined words to gain deeper understanding of the text.

To build literacy when viewing a video clip:
- view the clip without sound the first time, making predictions about the content;
- view the clip with sound to modify predictions, add information;
- note images that are especially helpful and/or memorable in understanding the commentary; and
- note background sounds and music and how they facilitate understanding the message(s).

To analyze the text after reading, listening, or viewing:
- draw the main ideas and supporting details from a text to demonstrate understanding;
- create a timeline of events in the text;
- use graphic organizers to outline the main ideas and supporting details of a text;
- discuss the surface purpose for the text and writer's motivations;
- take what was learned from the text and draw conclusions that are not directly stated in the text but can be inferred; and
- conduct a Socratic seminar to analyze, synthesize, and evaluate points of view presented in the text.

It is important that teachers use multiple authentic texts to build learners' literacy skills in the Interpretive Mode. Interaction with authentic texts can create a sort of immersive learning experience for learners: they are hearing authentic language in their minds as they listen to music or a podcast, or read in the target language; they are seeing the target language in action as they watch and listen to video clips. Except in the case of "live" performances, learners can pause at any point while listening, reading, or watching to think about what the text communicated; they can reread a word, phrase, or even a page or two, or replay a segment to hear or view the language again.

Authentic texts are "those written and oral communications produced by members of a language and culture group for members of the same language and culture group" (Shrum & Glisan, 2016, p.84). Authentic texts are rich resources linguistically and culturally for language learners. They are models of how native speakers communicate their ideas. They reflect the culture of the person or people who created the text. They also reflect the attitudes of native speakers towards the topic of the text. As stated in the Connections goal area of the World-Readiness Standards: *Learners access and evaluate information and diverse perspectives that are available through the language and its cultures.* Authentic texts reflect the inextricable bond between language and culture. When selecting an authentic text, teachers need to keep the following considerations in mind:

- Identification of words and phrases that the learner can recognize is a first step in selecting a text. Determine if there are enough familiar words that help learners start to make meaning about the general idea of the text.
- Non-fiction is often easier to understand because the text is straightforward with a single focus. Charts, maps, drawings, and photos are frequently used to support explanations in the text. Learners may have background knowledge from other disciplines that facilitate understanding.
- Both non-fiction and fiction texts are more readable when there is a predictable sequence (beginning, middle, end), and when the "who," "what," "where," and "when" are clearly stated.
- Age-appropriate texts are intentionally designed to appeal to the interests, preferences, and life experiences of a specific group of readers, making the texts more accessible to that particular group.
- The format and genre of the text influence how easily a learner can engage with the text. Format includes such things as the use of bold-faced type or italics and headings and subheadings to emphasize the organization and/or important ideas, and visuals to support the written text. In terms of genre, readers will be more successful in understanding a text if they have had previous experiences with the genre they are reading. Transferability allows learners to use skills that they might have learned in an English Language Arts class to understand a text in the target language. For example, learners will be more successful reading a play in the target language if they had prior experience reading a play in English. Past experiences reading plays in the target language will also positively influence the learners' success in understanding another play.

- Learners benefit from background knowledge related to the cultural context of the reading. For example, when reading an *Astérix* comic book in French, learners will understand more about the story if they know about the storyline's connection to France's history.

- Short texts with visuals on familiar topics are more readable than ones without visuals and/or ones on unfamiliar topics. Comprehension increases when learners can read several short texts on the same topic that repeat key vocabulary items. Longer texts, especially with some visual support on familiar or unfamiliar topics, may be easier to understand if there are context clues and redundancy of key vocabulary.

Shrum and Glisan acknowledge that texts may contain vocabulary and structures that learners have not studied but state that the real difficulty is in the task that learners are asked to complete, not in the text itself. They recommend following the suggestion: "Edit the task, not the text" (Shrum & Glisan, 2016, p. 87). For example, think of how the front page of a newspaper might be interpreted by learners at different proficiency levels. Novice learners might be asked to identify the cities or countries where the front-page stories take place. Intermediate learners might select an article from the front page and identify the main idea. Advanced learners might read the same article in order to identify supporting details, and then analyze the writer's viewpoint. As a reminder, when learners have some background knowledge about the topic of the article, they will more easily understand the text.

Although the emphasis of this discussion is on authentic texts, we acknowledge that there are also semi-authentic texts and created texts. Semi-authentic texts are created by native and/or non-native speakers and are based on authentic texts but adapted for specific curricular goals. For example, a semi-authentic text might be a shortened version of an authentic story with visuals added and some key vocabulary glossed to facilitate comprehension. Created texts are texts designed by native and non-native speakers for non-native speakers; these texts are intentionally created for specific instructional goals. Stories in textbooks are often created texts that incorporate specific grammatical structures or vocabulary that are presented within a unit or chapter.

To summarize, it is important to provide continuous opportunities for learners to interact with a wide variety of texts. As in all instructional planning, teachers need to select texts based on the abilities of the learners, the instructional goal(s), and the amount of scaffolding that is provided.

> "Overall, readability and reading goals need to be set vis-à-vis the reader, not as a property of the text in its own right. And through reading an accessible authentic text, the reader is also likely to confront the stereotypes about a culture as well as those held by that culture. By learning to recognize ways authentic media reflect particular viewpoints, readers begin to engage in the practice of multi-literacies—explorations of self and others." (Center for Open Educational Resources & Language Learning, The University of Texas at Austin, n.d.)

Global Competence. Effective communication in a world language is a characteristic of global competence. In 2014, ACTFL issued a position statement on Global Competence:

> The ability to communicate with respect and cultural understanding in more than one language is an essential element of global competence. This competence is developed and demonstrated by investigating the world, recognizing and weighing perspectives, acquiring and applying disciplinary and interdisciplinary knowledge, communicating ideas, and taking action. Global competence is fundamental to the experience of learning languages whether in classrooms, through virtual connections, or via everyday experiences. Language learning contributes an important means to communicate and interact in order to participate in multilingual communities at home and around the world. This interaction develops the disposition to explore the perspectives behind the products and practices of a culture and to value such intercultural experiences. (ACTFL)

This position statement re-emphasizes the Communities goal area of the World-Readiness Standards: *Learners use the language both within and beyond the classroom to interact and collaborate in the community and the globalized world*. Communicating in the target language cannot be limited to pair and group work within the classroom. Connecting with native speakers in the community and beyond is no longer optional. Thanks to technology, classrooms in the United States can connect with classrooms around the world to collaborate on projects and to discuss topics of mutual interest. iEarn (iearn.org) is the world's largest non-profit organization connecting classrooms around the world to collaborate on projects designed to make the world a better place to live. Taking it Global, (TIGWeb.org, n.d.), connects young people around the world to discuss and problem-solve global issues. These are only two examples of many organizations that facilitate global connections.

There are more and more job opportunities for people who can demonstrate proficiency in more than one language and who possess cultural knowledge and understandings, sometimes called "cultural intelligence." ACTFL produced a series of articles about using languages in various careers and created a poster about desired proficiency levels for different jobs. Both are available at ACTFL.org. When designing instructional units, consider unit goals that might help prepare learners for certain careers. Motivation increases among learners when they see the relevance of what they are studying to their lives now or in the future.

As the position statement indicates, the ability to communicate in languages other than English also facilitates learners taking action to make a difference in the lives of people locally, nationally, and internationally. To that end, each year ACTFL sponsors the Global Engagement Initiative to recognize teachers and their students who are using their language skills to help others locally and internationally. For example, at Miami of Ohio University, Nohelia Rojas-Miesse developed a week-long program for pre-med students who speak Spanish to travel to Nicaragua to work with doctors there helping to deliver health-care services. Rojas-Miesse states that students return to the university motivated to continue learning Spanish and improve world health. In another project, two Spanish professors at Duquesne University guided their upper-level Spanish students in developing curriculum for a program for young immigrants. Upper-level Spanish students from Norman High School, Oklahoma, became volunteers to create lessons, curriculum, and materials to teach Spanish to 4th and 5th graders locally. Kristy Placido's Spanish classes at Fowlerville High School, Michigan, help fund the education of students in Antigua, Guatemala. Fundraising efforts have included a fair-trade craft market, and school-wide festivals.

World language teachers who purposefully plan their units and lessons to build global competence among their learners are sending a message to those learners, their parents, the school administration, and the community that learning to communicate in more than one language is a valuable and useful skill in today's world.

Critical Thinking and Problem-Solving. Many leaders in business, education, and government advocate for the development of critical thinking skills as a fundamental goal of education. Glaser in *An Experiment in the Development of Critical Thinking* (1972) stated that critical thinking required examining beliefs and supposed facts through the lens of evidence. In language classrooms that integrate 21st Century Learning skills, the opportunity is available for learners to use language purposefully to explore real-world topics of interest and importance. Learners can interact with a variety of authentic texts to gather evidence that supports their understanding of the people who speak the language they are learning and their related culture. The ongoing challenge for language teachers is how to develop critical thinking skills in learners who are operating linguistically at the Novice and Intermediate levels of proficiency.

Consider how 21st Century Learning, P21.org, describes these learners:

- reason effectively using various types of reasoning as appropriate to the situation;
- use systems thinking to analyze how parts of a whole interact with each other to produce overall outcomes in complex systems;
- effectively analyze and evaluate evidence, arguments, claims, and beliefs;
- analyze and evaluate major alternative points of view;
- synthesize and make connections between information and arguments;
- interpret information and draw conclusions based on the best analysis;
- reflect critically on learning experiences and processes;
- solve different kinds of non-familiar problems in both conventional and innovative ways; and
- identify and ask significant questions that clarify various points of view and lead to better solutions.

In designing units and lessons, Bloom's Taxonomy (Bloom, 1956) is an extremely helpful reference tool that gives examples of how to move from the lower-order thinking skills of remembering and understanding to the higher-level skills of analyzing, evaluating, and creating. In a language classroom, learners often spend a significant amount of time remembering and understanding the target language. When teachers actively apply ▪▪▪▪▪▪▪▪▪▪▪▪▪▪▪▪▪▪▪▪▪▪▪▪▪ beyond remembering and understanding to applying the language they have learned to real-world situations, analyzing and evaluating situations where the language is used, and ultimately creating a product that uses the language that they have learned.

A second concept that contributes to the development of critical thinking and problem-solving skills is curiosity. Curiosity motivates and sustains learners' interest in learning; it triggers the release of dopamine, which causes us to remember experiences in depth; it strengthens critical thinking skills (Ostroff, 2016).

The roles of Bloom's Taxonomy and curiosity in the world language classroom are discussed in the following sections. As you read, consider how you might integrate these ideas into your unit and lesson planning.

Bloom's Taxonomy. Bloom's Taxonomy, originally published in 1956 by a group of educational psychologists including Benjamin Bloom, was developed as a classification system of question types for professors to reference in order to encourage their use of higher-level questions designed to increase learning. In 2001 Loren Anderson, a former student of Benjamin Bloom, led a group of cognitive psychologists, curriculum theorists, and instructional researchers in the revision of the Taxonomy to reflect advances in learning theory and practices. The revised taxonomy uses verbs instead of nouns to show learners' thinking processes, and moves from lower-order thinking skills (remembering, understanding, applying) to higher-order thinking skills (analyzing, evaluating, creating). Figure 6 shows the levels of Bloom's Revised Taxonomy (Anderson, Krahthwohl, & Bloom, 2001).

Figure 6. Bloom's Revised Taxonomy (2001)

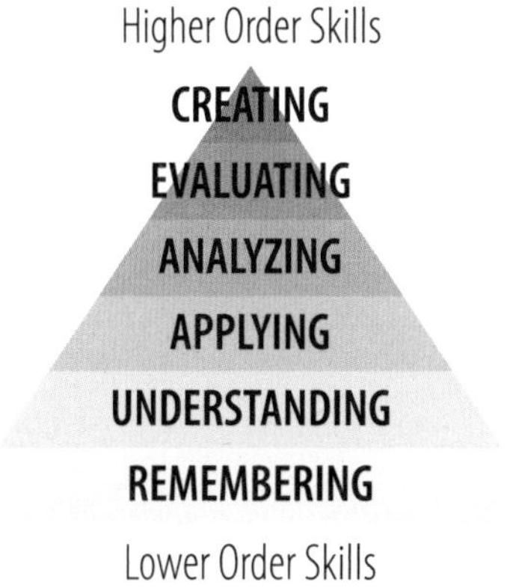

Higher Order Skills
CREATING
EVALUATING
ANALYZING
APPLYING
UNDERSTANDING
REMEMBERING
Lower Order Skills

Table 8 on the following page shows the levels of Bloom's Revised Taxonomy, and includes action verbs associated with each level and sample learning activities for the language classroom. The italicized words in the column of sample learning activities reflect suggestions for digital alternatives as proposed by Andrew Churches, a classroom teacher in Auckland, New Zealand, and a co-author of several books on the role of technology in the 21st century classroom.

The list of action verbs along with the sample activities in Table 8 are organized from lower-order to higher-order thinking skills. When planning units and daily lessons, language teachers are encouraged to utilize the full range of action verbs and suggested activities to facilitate learning. Novice language learners are as capable as Intermediate and Advanced language learners of analyzing, evaluating, and creating using the target language. For example, in a thematic unit about living in a city, Novice-level learners could:

- **locate** places in a city on a map of the city (*Remembering*);
- **compare** places in a city in (x) to those in the learner's city (*Understanding*);
- **dramatize** a day in the city of (x) (*Applying*);
- **categorize** places in the city that provide services and those that are businesses (*Analyzing*);
- **choose** places in a city in (x) and in the learner's city that make the cities special (*Evaluating*); and
- **design** a graphic that highlights places in city (x) (*Creating*).

Bloom's Taxonomy is useful in planning cognitively engaging and purposeful activities for daily lessons. It is also a helpful reference in selecting vocabulary that learners need in order to actively participate in those activities. For example, for learners to categorize places in a city that provide services and those that are businesses, they would need vocabulary to name and describe places that provide services such as "library" or "fire department." They would also need vocabulary that would allow them to name and describe businesses such as "grocery store" or "coffee shop." And they would need sentence stems such as, "Businesses include...." or, "Our city needs these services to make our city safe." When teachers plan lessons and units that reflect higher-order thinking skills, the need for certain vocabulary and grammatical structures becomes clear; the selection of vocabulary and grammatical structures is purposeful.

Table 8. Bloom's Revised Taxonomy
(Adapted from Andrew Churches's Bloom's Digital Taxonomy, edorigami.wikispaces.com)

Classification	Action Verbs		Sample Learning Activities
Remembering: Can the learner recall, recognize, or remember previously learned information?	Define Describe Find Identify List Locate Match Memorize Name Recall	Recite Recognize Record Relate Repeat Reproduce Retrieve State Tell Underline	• Exchange greetings, ask and respond to simple memorized questions. • Identify historic places in (city, country). • Label a picture, image. • Make a timeline. • Match an image to the written word. • Name (places in the city). • Recite a poem or saying. • Underline words that describe (x). **Digital alternatives** • *Bookmark* • *Highlight* • *List using bullet points* • *Search or Google*
Understanding: Can the learner explain or restate ideas and concepts?	Choose Cite examples of… Clarify Classify Compare Demonstrate the use of… Describe Discuss Explain Express	Illustrate Infer Interpret Outline Paraphrase Predict Report Restate Summarize Tell about…	• Compare (school schedules) in the target culture with those in the U.S. • Complete a graphic organizer. • Explain how to make or complete a task. • Illustrate the main idea(s) of a story or article or film. • Keep a journal discussing ideas or concepts presented in class. • Make inferences about a text based on knowledge of target culture. • Predict what a text is about based on visuals, title of the text. • Retell a story that was heard or read or viewed. **Digital alternatives** • *Annotate* • *Blog* • *Categorize* • *Comment* • *Conduct advanced searches* • *Tag* • *Tweet*
Applying: Can the learner use what was learned in a new way or situation such as a presentation, simulation, or interview?	Apply Change Choose Construct Demonstrate Dramatize Edit Experiment Illustrate Implement	Interview Make Modify Perform Present Produce Put into practice Share Solve Use	• Dramatize a day in the life of a student in the target culture. • Interview someone who has traveled or lived in the target culture. • Make a presentation about (traveling respectfully). • Proofread a text. • Simulate communicating with someone who speaks a language you don't know. • Suggest ways to collaborate with a school in the target culture. **Digital alternatives** • *Blog* • *Chat* • *Edit using online tools* • *Podcast* • *Skype* • *Text* • *Upload a presentation* • *Use PowerPoint* • *Videoconference* • *Vodcast*

Table 8. Bloom's Revised Taxonomy (continued)
(Adapted from Andrew Churches's Bloom's Digital Taxonomy, edorigami.wikispaces.com)

Classification	Action Verbs		Sample Learning Activities
Analyzing: Can the learner break information into parts and show the relationships among the parts?	Analyze Calculate Categorize Compare Conclude Contrast Correlate Critique Debate Deconstruct	Detect Diagram Evaluate Examine Integrate Organize Outline Question Subdivide	• Categorize lifestyle influences based on where one lives. • Contrast the importance of family in the target culture to the U.S. • Correlate cultural products to practices and perspectives. • Deconstruct a breakdown in communication between people from different cultures. • Design a questionnaire about (x) and analyze the results. **Digital alternatives** • *Diagram* • *Graphic organizer* • *Link* • *Mash* • *Online polls and surveys* • *Venn diagram*
Evaluating: Can the learner justify an opinion or judge the worth of information based on standards and criteria?	Assess Choose Critique Defend Determine Evaluate Judge	Justify Rate Reflect Test Validate Weigh	• Critique an issue that is in the news. • Design a rubric to evaluate a project. • Determine the accuracy of information on a website. • Keep a reflective journal about cultural encounters and your responses in those encounters. • Rate an oral presentation. • Self-assess language learning progress. • Write an editorial. **Digital alternatives** • *Blog* • *Chatrooms* • *Comments* • *Discussion board* • *Moderated thread* • *Posts* • *Reviews* • *Threaded discussion* • *Wiki*
Creating: Can the learner put together separate ideas or information to create a new product or point of view?	Assemble Compose Construct Create Design Develop Devise Hypothesize	Imagine Invent Make Modify Plan Prepare Produce Propose	• Create an infographic. • Design a website for a language class. • Imagine time traveling back to an historic event. • Invent a game that includes experiences living in a city in another country. • Propose a solution to a global issue discussed in class. • Write an original story. **Digital alternatives** • *Animation* • *Blog* • *Broadcast* • *Digital stories* • *Film* • *Online publishing* • *Podcast*

Curiosity. The *Merriam-Webster Dictionary* defines curiosity as the desire to learn or know more about something or someone. Learners who are curious ask a lot of questions: they have a strong "need to know more" about what they are learning. In other words, they are motivated intrinsically to actively participate in class activities that they believe will help them respond to the questions they have. A teacher who fosters curiosity provides space in lesson and unit plans for learners to explore topics of personal interest. This exploration may be related to the unit theme and essential question, or it may result from opportunities to choose a topic and create an essential question they want to pursue. The more ownership that learners have for the topic they are pursuing, the more engaged they become in participating in class activities related to the topic they are exploring.

Now let's look at three interrelated skills that strengthen curiosity's positive influence on learning: Questioning, Listening, and Reflecting. The unit plan highlights the importance of an Essential Question to guide learning throughout the unit. Questioning is not limited to that one overarching question. Critical thinkers ask good questions throughout the unit that spark interest and an exchange of ideas in the target language. Teachers can help learners ask good questions by drawing their attention to different kinds of questions. Jackson (2013) outlines three types of questions and their purposes in Table 9.

Fact questions can be used to verify that learners were able to find important details that they can use as a basis for further exploration of the topic. The example of a factual question (How many boys and how many girls graduated from high school in (x)?) will be used to explore differences in graduation rates around the world. The response to the factual question can serve as a springboard to a Personal Preference question: Why do you think boys stay in school more than girls? Personal Preference questions encourage a variety of opinions or possible responses with no judgment at this point about the accuracy of the opinion or judgment. Personal Preference questions can serve as a springboard to Interpretive Questions. In the example in Table 9, learners can research to find out why more boys graduate than girls in (x). They can further explore initiatives to encourage more girls to stay in school. A carefully planned sequence of questions encourages learner engagement, critical thinking, resulting in deeper learning.

The hierarchy of questions on the next page is inspired by the Oral Proficiency Interview (OPI) where the OPI tester moves from questions that require simple responses to ones that require extended explanations. We selected the image of a mountain as an analogy: the questions at the bottom of the mountain (hierarchy) require simple responses to concrete questions. As you move up the mountain (hierarchy), your view of possible responses is broadened because the questions become more open-ended. When you reach the top of the mountain (hierarchy), you can gaze out at a broad landscape with all sorts of possibilities. Your responses to questions are no longer words and phrases, but detailed accounts that reflect that broad landscape. We suggest that teachers recreate Figure 7 in the target language and post it in the classroom as a resource for learners to consult when they are asking questions in pair work and small group discussions.

Table 9. Kinds of Questions (Jackson, 2013)

Factual Retrieval	Personal Preference	Critical Inquiry
Fact Questions	**Imagine Questions**	**Interpretive Questions**
• have only one correct answer • provide an understanding of the details of a topic • good for checking for understanding • EXAMPLE: How many boys and how many girls graduated from high school in (X)?	• ask for some kind of opinion, belief, or point of view—no wrong answers • good for leading discussions • good as springboards to inquiry-based projects • EXAMPLE: Why do you think boys stay in school more than girls in (X)?	• have more than one answer but must be supported with evidence • effective for starting class discussions and for stimulating oral and written tasks • good for inquiry-based learning • EXAMPLE: How have initiatives for girls to stay in school impacted living standards around the world and graduation rates in (x)? What else has been impacted by the initiative?

Figure 7. Hierarchy of Questions

- What if...?
- Can you tell me about...?
- Can you describe...?
- How? Why?
- What? When? Where? Who?
- Either/or
- Which...?
- Yes/no

The following is an example of a hierarchy of questions for the education unit:

What if...?	**What if** all young people completed high school: how would the world be different?
Can you tell me about...?	**Can you tell me about** a class that was very valuable to you?
Can you describe...?	**Can you describe** a good education?
How? Why?	**Why** is school a basic right for all children?
What? When? Where? Who?	**When** does the school year begin in (X)? **Who** can go to school in (X)?
Either/or	Do you like science classes **or** history classes?
Which...?	**Which** class schedule do you prefer, the schedule from (X) or yours?
Yes/no	**Do** all students in (X) go to high school?

Another strategy to help learners practice asking good questions is "See – Think – Wonder" developed by Harvard Project Zero. In the first step, "See," the teacher asks learners to state what they see when they view an object, a photo, or a painting. Learners state what they see, which could range from colors and shapes to people, places, and things. In step two, "Think," the teacher asks learners to give their opinions about what they see (what do they think about it; what does it remind them of). In step three, "Wonder," the teacher ask learners: What do you wonder about? What are you curious about? What questions do you have about what you see? The ultimate goal is to help learners ask powerful questions that they can research, discuss, and explore in the target language. As learners are prompted via questioning to examine images closely, they develop their ability to interpret and understand visual texts and, by extension, the visual aspects of their surroundings. In "Visual Literacy: Reading Signs and Designs in the Foreign Culture," Morain (1976) states that, "Someone who is visually literate is able to recognize the natural and manmade symbols around one and interpret their meanings in the same way as those who live in that environment would interpret them" (p. 210). After expanding on this opening statement with multiple examples, Morain concludes the article with:

> The comfortable old folk adage holds that, "Seeing is believing." Unfortunately for cross-cultural understanding, it could more truthfully be stated, "Seeing is deceiving." Unless our students are made aware of signs and symbols in the unique context of the foreign culture, they will be handicapped in their efforts to interact intelligently and sensitively within that culture. We must teach now for visual as well as verbal literacy (p. 216).

Encouraging learners to be curious and ask good questions develops their interculturality, which will be discussed more fully later in this chapter.

The second skill that strengthens curiosity's positive influence on critical thinking and problem-solving is closely related to asking good questions. The second skill is good listening. People who ask good questions have to be good listeners. There is an adage that states: "Good conversations start with good listening." Good listeners:

- Show that they understand what the person is saying via body language (nodding head, leaning forward) and by verbal interjections (Yes! Hmmmm! I see!).
- Don't interrupt; they wait for the speaker to pause before asking clarifying questions.
- Use their own words to restate something that the speaker said to verify understanding and to value what the speaker's thoughts are (You said that....; you aren't sure that....).
- Share ideas that link to what someone else said.
- Ask good follow-up questions and add helpful comments.

Good listeners are curious. They think critically about what they have heard and how that helps them extend their knowledge and understandings. Their questions encourage clarifications, more details, more justifications, and more insights.

The third skill that strengthens curiosity's positive influence on critical thinking and problem-solving is reflection.

> "Reflective thinking is most important in prompting learning during complex problem-solving situations because it provides students with an opportunity to step back and think about how they actually solve problems and how a particular set of problem-solving

strategies is appropriated for achieving their goal." (University of Hawaii, n.d.)

Reflection is designed to build and solidify learning by asking learners to "replay" what they have read, heard, or discussed in order to summarize ideas, synthesize ideas from multiple resources and discussions, analyze information, draw conclusions, and ask more questions. The concept of reflection is prevalent in the World-Readiness Standards for Learning Languages (Appendix A):

- Cultures
    - Relating Cultural Practices to Perspectives: Learners use the language to investigate, explain, and *reflect* on the relationship between the practices and perspectives of the cultures studied.
    - Relating Cultural Products to Perspectives: Learners use the language to investigate, explain, and *reflect* on the relationship between the products and perspectives of the cultures studied.
- Comparisons
    - Language Comparisons: Learners use the language to investigate, explain, and *reflect* on the nature of language through comparisons of the language studied and their own.
    - Cultural Comparisons: Learners use the language to investigate, explain, and *reflect* on the concept of culture through comparisons of the cultures studied and their own.
- Communities
    - Lifelong Learning: Learners set goals and *reflect* on their progress in using languages for enjoyment, enrichment, and advancement.

The emphasis on reflection in the World-Readiness Standards implies that teachers need to include time for learners to reflect on both the language skills and cultural understandings that they experienced during the unit and lessons. Learners remember new knowledge, language patterns, and vocabulary when they take time to make connections to what they already know through reflection. Teachers might ask learners to give examples or explain how something they just learned relates to what they already know. Or, teachers might ask learners to suggest situations where they could use their new learning. Through reflection, learners can consider what they know and what additional information they need in order to respond to the essential question of a unit. Reflection documents how

learners' understandings of the target culture have evolved over time. Reflection is also about learners self-assessing what they can do in terms of understanding and communicating in the language they are learning. They can then set personal goals identifying which skills require more practice and which skills they want to develop next.

Reflection can take several forms. It might begin as a small group discussion where learners share their notes on a topic and clarify their understandings of what they have read, heard, and/or viewed. After the discussion, the instructor might give the learners time to write about the ideas that resonated with them during the discussions, and why those ideas are important to them. Another option is to have learners interview each other at the end of a lesson or unit or an especially significant learning activity to share understandings and ongoing questions. This requires integrating questioning skills with listening skills in ways that explore their partner's learning and their own learning. Journal-writing on a regular basis is another way to encourage reflection. Instructors might ask learners to respond to a question, describe an image, or react to a quote related to the unit of study. Portfolios provide a place for learners to keep their reflections on the progress they are making in learning another language and understanding other cultures. Those reflections are most effective when supported by samples of the learner's work that provide evidence of their progress. Lingua-Folio®, (LinguaFolio.uoregon.edu, n.d.), developed in tandem with the NCSSFL-ACTFL Can-Do Statements, is an example of how learners can document their progress in communication and cultural understanding. As the World-Readiness Standards emphasize, reflection is a critical component on the pathway to Intercultural Communicative Competence. Chapter Five includes more information on reflection.

Creativity and Innovation. "Creativity is about more than being able to develop an artistic product. To create or to innovate means to bring something into existence that did not exist before" (Crockett, Jukes, & Churches, 2011, p. 54). According to the World Economic Forum's Future of Jobs Report (January 19, 2016), creativity is one of the top three skills workers will need for 2020 and beyond, due to the preponderance of new products, new technologies, and new ways of working. Creativity includes the following dispositions according to 21st Century Learning at P21.org:

- Use a wide range of idea creation techniques (such as brainstorming).

- Create new and worthwhile ideas (both incremental and radical concepts).
- Elaborate, refine, analyze, and evaluate their own ideas in order to improve and maximize creative efforts.
- Develop, implement, and communicate new ideas to others effectively.
- Be open and responsive to new and diverse perspectives; incorporate group input and feedback into the work.
- Demonstrate originality and inventiveness in work and understand the real-world limits to adopting new ideas.
- View failure as an opportunity to learn; understand that creativity and innovation is a long-term, cyclical process of small successes and frequent mistakes.
- Act on creative ideas to make a tangible and useful contribution to the field in which the innovation will occur.

In order to encourage creativity and innovation, learners need opportunities to express their thoughts and ideas, and what they have learned in a variety of ways. Gardner's theory of Multiple Intelligences (1983) values different ways to demonstrate learning and solve problems. Gardner describes characteristics of learners according to the different intelligences he has identified, giving valuable examples of how to differentiate instruction to meet the needs of all learners. Multiple Intelligences Theory opens the door to creativity and innovation for both teachers and learners.

Multiple Intelligences. Gardner (1983) states that intelligence is the ability to solve problems, or to create products that are valued in one or more cultural settings. Gardner believes that all human beings possess the "8 ½" intelligences he has identified, but some intelligences are stronger than others in individuals (Gardner, 2011). Gardner refers to "8 ½" intelligences because he does not believe that Existential Intelligence fully meets the criteria he has established for designation as an intelligence. According to Gardner (2011), there are two key implications of the Multiple Intelligences Theory for education:

1. Personalization: It is important to use different types of activities that resonate with different learners in order to facilitate learning. Assessment must reflect how learners practiced the target language and, at the same time, ask them to apply that learning to different situations.
2. Pluralization – It is important to teach key concepts in multiple ways in order to reach more learners. Teaching may include asking learners to read something, listen to something, discuss an idea with others, write a personal example of a concept, or role play a situation that reflects the concept. According to Gardner, teaching a concept in multiple ways shows what it is like to be an "expert," to understand a concept through a variety of situations, and to apply what was learned in a variety of ways.

The 8½ intelligences identified by Gardner (1999) are presented in Table 10 on the following page and include characteristics of the learner and learning activities that are compatible to the intelligence identified.

The learner characteristics and learning activities outlined in Table 10 provide a wealth of ideas for purposeful practice of the target language. We know that learners need multiple opportunities to use new structures, patterns, and vocabulary in order to internalize them. We also know that "drill and kill" is not an effective strategy. By varying the types of activities, learners stay engaged and are more likely to remember the new language patterns and vocabulary. Drawing on a variety of learning activities across the intelligences is one way to accommodate the needs of diverse learners. If, for example, a learner is having difficulty remembering a linguistic pattern that is practiced orally in pair work activities (Interpersonal Intelligence), it could be helpful for the learner to physically construct the pattern using cards, each with a different word that is part of the linguistic pattern (Bodily-Kinesthetic Intelligence). Asking learners to help design different ways to practice and remember the target language using different intelligences encourages them to be creative while building their communication skills.

Table 10. Multiple Intelligences, Learner Characteristics, and Appropriate Learning Activities (Gardner, 1999)

Intelligence	Characteristics of Learner	Appropriate Learning Activities
Linguistic	• Has a good memory for names, places, dates, and trivia • Enjoys word games • Spells words accurately • Appreciates nonsense rhymes, puns, tongue twisters, etc. • Enjoys listening to the spoken word • Has a good vocabulary for his/her age • Communicates to others in a highly verbal way	• Large- and small-group discussions, lectures, debates • Books, worksheets, manuals • Brainstorming • Writing activities • Word games • Sharing time • Storytelling, speeches, reading to class • Talking books • Extemporaneous speaking • Journal keeping • Choral reading • Individualized reading • Memorizing linguistic facts • Recording one's words • Using word processors • Publishing (e.g., creating online newspapers, blogs, wikis)
Logical-Mathematical	• Asks a lot of questions about how things work • Computes arithmetic questions in his/her head quickly • Enjoys the challenges of math class • Finds math games and math computer games interesting • Enjoys playing chess, checkers, or other strategy games • Enjoys working with logic puzzles and brainteasers • Likes to experiment in a way that shows higher-order thinking processes • Thinks on a more abstract level than peers • Has a good sense of cause-and-effect relationships for his/her age	• Mathematical problems on the board • Design and conduct an experiment • Make up analogies to explain • Describe the patterns • Socratic questioning • Scientific demonstrations • Logical problem-solving exercises • Creating codes • Logic puzzles and games • Classifications and categorizations • Quantifications and calculations • Computer programming languages • Science thinking • Logical-sequential presentation of subject matter
Musical	• Remembers the melody of songs • Has a good singing voice • Plays a musical instrument or sings in a choir or other musical group • Has a rhythmic way of speaking and/or moving • Unconsciously hums to him/herself • Taps rhythmically on the table or desk as he/she works • Is sensitive to the environmental noises, like rain on the roof • Can easily imitate the voices and inflections of others	• Singing, humming, whistling • Playing recorded music • Playing live music on piano, guitar, or other instruments • Group singing • Mood music • Music appreciation • Playing percussion instruments • Rhythms, songs, raps, chants • Using background music • Linking old tunes with concepts • Creating new melodies for concepts • Music software

Table 10. Multiple Intelligences, Learner Characteristics, and Appropriate Learning Activities (Gardner, 1999) (continued)

Intelligence	Characteristics of Learner	Appropriate Learning Activities
Spatial	• Reports clear visual images • Reads maps, charts, and diagrams more easily than text • Daydreams more than peers • Enjoys art activities • Draws figures and pictures that are advanced for age • Likes to view movies, slides, or other visual presentations • Enjoys doing puzzles, mazes, "Where's Waldo?" or "hidden picture" or "I spy"- type activities • Builds interesting three-dimensional constructions for age (Legos) • Gets more out of pictures than words when reading • Doodles on workbooks, worksheets, or other materials	• Visualization • Photography • Videos, slides, and movies • Visual puzzles and mazes • 3-D construction kits • Art appreciation • Imaginative storytelling • Picture metaphors • Creative daydreaming • Painting, collage, visual arts • Visual thinking exercises • Using mind-maps and other visual organizers • Computer graphics software • Visual awareness activities • Optical illusions • Color cues • Telescopes, microscopes, and binoculars
Bodily-Kinesthetic	• Excels in one or more sports • Moves, twitches, taps, fidgets while seated for a long time in one spot • Cleverly mimics other people's gestures and mannerisms • Loves to take things apart and put them back together again • Has trouble keeping his/her hands off something new that they have just seen • Enjoys jumping, wrestling, or similar activities • Shows skill on a craft or good fine-motor coordination in other ways • Has dramatic way of expressing him/herself	• Field trips • Competitive and cooperative games • Physical awareness and relaxation exercises • All hands-on activities • Crafts • Use of kinesthetic imagery • Cooking, gardening, and other "messy" activities • Manipulatives—objects learners can hold in their hands • Virtual reality software • Communicating with body language/hand signals • Tactile materials and experiences
Interpersonal	• Seems to be a natural leader • Gives advice to friends who have problems • Seems to be people smart—attuned to others • Belongs to clubs, committees, or other organizations • Enjoys informally teaching other kids • Likes to play games with other kids • Has two or more close friends • Has a good sense of empathy or concern for others • Others seek out his/her company	• Cooperative groups • Interpersonal interaction • Conflict mediation • Peer teaching • Board games • Cross-age tutoring • Group brainstorming sessions • Peer sharing • Community involvement • Apprenticeships • Simulations • Parties/social gatherings as context for learning
Intrapersonal	• Has a realistic sense of his/her strengths and weaknesses • Does well when left alone to play or study • Marches to the beat of a different drummer in his/her style of living and learning • Has an interest or hobby that he or she doesn't talk about much • Has a good sense of self-direction • Prefers working alone to working with others • Accurately expresses how he/she is feeling • Is able to learn from his/her failures and successes • Has high self-esteem	• Set and pursue a goal • Independent study • Describe one of your personal values • Assess your own work • Self-paced instruction • Individualized projects and games • Private spaces for study • One-minute reflection periods • Interest centers • Personal connections • Options for homework • Choice time • Self-teaching programmed instruction

Table 10. Multiple Intelligences, Learner Characteristics, and Appropriate Learning Activities (Gardner, 1999) (continued)

Intelligence	Characteristics of Learner	Appropriate Learning Activities
Naturalist	• Has a strong affinity to the outside world, to the beauty in nature, or to animals • Enjoys subjects, shows, or stories that deal with animals or natural phenomena • May show unusual interest in subjects like biology, zoology, botany, geology, meteorology, or astronomy • Is keenly aware of his/her surroundings and changes in the environment • Has highly developed senses that help him/her notice similarities, differences, and changes in his/her surroundings • May be able to categorize or catalogue things easily • May notice things others might not be aware of • Likes to collect, classify, or read about things from nature — rocks, fossils, butterflies, feathers, shells, and the like	• Camping • Hiking • Scuba diving • Bird watching • Gardening • Climbing • Likes sitting quietly and noticing the subtle differences
Existential (NOTE: Gardner calls this the "1/2" in his list of Intelligences because it doesn't completely meet all criteria required to be an "intelligence".)	• The ability to be sensitive to, or have the capacity for concep- tualizing or tackling deeper or larger questions about human existence, such as the meaning of life, why are we born, why do we die, what is consciousness, or how did we get here • May have unique questions, insights, and perspectives about things spiritual or metaphysical • Children with a sixth sense or deep connections with earlier periods of time	• Discussion • Journaling • Reading

Imagination. In the language classroom, learners are constantly asked to tap into their imagination to place themselves in a context or situation within the target culture in order to make the communication pattern they are practicing seem real. Danesi (2003) identifies several meaningful contexts that engage learners' imaginations as they practice using the languages they are learning. Among them are:

- **cultural contexts** such as buying a train ticket or shopping in a market;
- **situational contexts** such as giving instructions to someone on how to prepare a certain food;
- **identification contexts** where, for example, a learner becomes a famous person from the target culture or, as in some classes, where the learners choose a new name from the target culture and take on a new identity;
- **information-giving** contexts where learners share information they have learned about the target culture with others, such as giving advice on what to see when someone is going to travel to a country that speaks the target language.

Another context that capitalizes on imagination is the story. Egan (1986) notes that the oral tradition of storytelling is how people preserved their history and culture over time. People remembered important events, people, traditions, and ideas because these elements were woven into imaginative stories. Curtain and Dahlberg (2016) suggest that teachers design lessons according to the qualities of a good story with a clear-cut beginning, middle, and end. Other strategies that storytellers use to engage the imagination and facilitate memory include:

- **images:** encouraging learners to generate images in the mind from words engages the imagination and strengthens memory of the words;
- **rhyme and rhythm:** creating rhymes and rhythms to remember words and phrases requires imagination;
- **jokes and humor:** certain jokes can help make language visible and greatly aid awareness and control of language;
- **play:** creating imaginary worlds where learners take on new identities and roles makes learning fun, lessening the stress/anxiety learners feel when attempting something new;
- **personalized narratives:** inviting learners to become part of a story as actors, narrators, and storytelling assistants builds interest and engagement.

A technique that capitalizes on imaginative storytelling in language classrooms is Teaching Proficiency Through Reading and Storytelling (TPRS), developed by Blaine Ray in 1990. TPRS attributes its success to the fact that the focus of instruction is on the learners, providing them with lots of positive feedback and encouragement as they are acquiring a new language (www.tprstories.com, 2017). Teachers personalize stories with the goal of maintaining the interest of the learners by making them characters and active participants in the stories. As the setting of a story is developed, the reader/listener is often transported to another place and time, allowing him/her to experience other ways of life and other cultures. The learners hear and practice the stories multiple times through a variety of creative repetitions in the target language.

Collaboration and Cross-Cultural Understanding. In today's globally connected world, learners can just as easily connect with peers in the same classroom as they can with peers around the world. Through the power of technology, learners can develop teamwork skills by working with peers from different cultures representing different perspectives on projects of mutual interest and importance. 21st Century Learning identifies the following skills as components of Collaboration and Cross-Cultural Understanding (Partnership for 21st Century Learning):

- Demonstrate ability to work effectively and respectfully with diverse teams.
- Exercise flexibility and willingness to be helpful in making necessary compromises to accomplish a common goal.
- Assume shared responsibility for collaborative work, and value the individual contributions made by each team member.
- Respect cultural differences and work effectively with people from a range of social and cultural backgrounds.
- Respond open-mindedly to different ideas and values.
- Leverage social and cultural differences to create new ideas and increase both innovation and quality of work.

Cooperative and Collaborative Learning. Working in small groups is a fundamental structure for world language classroom activities. For this publication, we define cooperative learning as learners working together in groups, most often within the same classroom, to practice their communication skills on a variety of tasks. We describe collaborative learning as learners making virtual connections with speakers of the language they are learning in order to share ideas and problem-solve. Prensky (2012) advocates teaching learners to

collaborate in online communities in order to be prepared for today's work world. He encourages groups of learners in one location to work on the same question or project with learners in another location, connected by technology.

Both cooperative learning and collaborative learning in online communities encourage learners to take ownership for their own learning, resolve conflicts, and improve interpersonal communication skills. What is important is that diverse perspectives come together that lead to greater understanding and possible solutions to the issues being discussed. Small groups of learners working together to answer a question, work on a project, or solve a problem foster purposeful and meaningful communication. The teacher can monitor the quality and quantity of language used among the learners along with on-task behaviors. In addition to the observations of the teacher, learners can evaluate their own participation, the participation of the group as a whole, and of individuals within the group.

Working in a small group cooperatively requires respecting these principles adapted from Johnson and Johnson (1999):

1. **Safe environment:** Learners must feel safe in sharing their ideas; there is no room for making fun of someone's ideas or dismissing them as unimportant.
2. **Clear objectives:** Learners need to know what the group is to accomplish via clear directions and clear evaluation criteria.
3. **Equal participation:** All learners are responsible for equal contribution to the work. No one can remain silent, and no one can be left out.
4. **Positive interdependence:** All learners are responsible for parts of the task that are required for the successful completion of the task. No one can be assigned to a task that is non-essential to the final product produced by the group.
5. **Individual accountability:** Each learner should self-assess his or her contributions to the task, and the group should honestly assess the individual contributions of each group member and the collaboration of the group as a whole.
6. **Resolution of conflicts:** Learners have learned procedures and protocols for resolving conflicts within the group.

Collaborative and cooperative groups need real-world topics or projects to pursue in order for the group work to be successful. For example, in a collaborative online project, learners in a Spanish class in the United States might connect to a class in Argentina to discuss the importance of education for all young people around the world. In preparation for the online collaboration, learners in both locations would need to research the topic, and then generate questions they would like to explore during the online collaboration. The two groups would then have to come to consensus on a final list of questions before the actual online discussion.

In a unit about healthy lifestyles, learners might work in cooperative groups to dramatize an ideal daily routine. Each group would have to come to consensus on what to include in the daily routine, how they are going to represent it, and what role each group member will play. To facilitate equal participation of all group members during the planning phase, the teacher could give each person a scoring guide to track his or her contributions to the group (Table 11).

Table 11. Scoring Guide for Cooperative Learning Group Project

	Yes	No
I suggested ideas for the storyline for the video.		
I added to other group members' suggestions for the storyline.		
I listened respectfully to other group members.		
Each member of the group has a speaking role in the story.		
Our group equally shared responsibilities for creating the storyline for the video.		
Our group cooperated to complete the outline for the story by the end of class.		

Interculturality. The concept of interculturality is a mindset, a way of being with the global community. Interculturality is multidimensional. It is manifested in how a person understands and responds to situations, actions, interactions, and experiences with people from different cultural backgrounds. Interculturality is influenced by a person's background knowledge and past experiences with different cultures.

In the classroom, interculturality is fostered when learners work in pairs and small groups, listening to one another's ideas with an open mind, being willing to work cooperatively with others. Collaborating with classrooms around the world to explore a mutual topic of interest gives learners the opportunity to hear opinions and perspectives that may be reflective of different cultural backgrounds and experiences.

A starting point for self-assessment of one's intercultural experiences is suggested by the Council of Europe. Learners can establish baseline data by rating the degree to which they agree with the following statements:

- I know that several languages are spoken in my country.
- I know which languages are spoken in my country.
- I can list several languages that are spoken in my country.
- I can recognize several languages when I hear them spoken.
- I can recognize the written form of several languages.
- I know people who live in another country.
- I know that people living in the United States have different cultural backgrounds.
- I like tasting dishes from different countries.
- I know and/or can sing songs from another country.
- I can give an example of a festival celebrated in another region/country.
- I can name several examples of regional cuisine from the United States.
- I can name several examples of cuisine from other countries.
- I have visited museums or seen films presenting the cultures of different countries.
- I know characters from stories, animated films, and cartoons from other countries. (European Language Portfolio Intercultural Experiences and Awareness, 2011)

Learners can document their growth in terms of interculturality through reflection and journaling about experiences they have had with people, places, situations, and experiences from other cultural backgrounds. The *European Language Portfolio* project (Little & Simpson, 2003) recommends that learners reflect on intercultural experiences using these four questions as guides:

1. Where, with whom, and in what context did the experience take place?
2. What kind of experience was it in terms of intensity?
3. What was my response? Did I merely reflect on the experience, or did it prompt me to some kind of action?
4. Why did I respond in the way I did?

Increasing their awareness of all the ways their lives connect to other cultures, and reflecting on their interactions with people from other cultures, is the first step in developing skills of interculturality among learners.

Summary. The Instructional Repertoire, organized around the 4 Cs—Communication, Critical Thinking and Problem-Solving, Creativity and Innovation, Collaboration and Cross-Cultural Understanding—of 21st Century Learning, gives language teachers a variety of tools to consider as they design unit and lesson plans with the overarching goal of engaging all learners purposefully in building their Intercultural Communicative Competence. Earlier in the chapter, the World-Readiness Standards for Learning Languages and the ACTFL Proficiency Guidelines were introduced as the foundation for curriculum design, and included a visual reminding us that effective curriculum, unit, and lesson design relates to the learner on a personal level (*Knowing Myself*), to where the learner lives locally, regionally, nationally (*Exploring Communities*), and to the learner's global connections (*Engaging with the World*). The next chapter will consider thematic unit design in more detail and will present a template for designing a Standards-based thematic unit.

Application

1. Your department has been asked to write a paragraph for the school newsletter explaining how languages are addressing the hyper-connected learner of the 21st century. What will you write?
2. You've been asked to define Intercultural Communicative Competence. What will you say? What examples will you share?

Reflection

1. How am I promoting the development of Intercultural Communicative Competence in my classroom? Are there specific ways that I might clarify this concept for learners and their families?
2. Do learners benefit from having an understanding of terms like proficiency and interculturality? Why or why not? How do I build awareness of these concepts in my classrooms?

Chapter 2 | Unit Design

To begin with the end in mind means to start with a clear understanding of your destination. It means to know where you are going so that you better understand where you are now so that the steps you take are always in the right direction.

— Stephen Covey

Why Is a Standards-Based and Text-Rich Approach to Unit Design Recommended?

Learners acquire language best in meaningful contexts. Authentic texts, those that are created by speakers of the language for speakers of the language, provide an ideal starting point for a thematic unit by establishing a meaningful context. Authentic written, spoken, or visual texts also guarantee that language is not separated from culture since authentic text embeds culture in the text itself. Mickan (2013) explains how even something as simple as a poster offering a reward for a lost dog tells us something about the culture of a people. That poster allows the reader to know that the culture values dogs, that dogs are part of the family, and that the relationship between an owner and pet is important as indicated by the offer of a reward. The language used in the poster is meaningful because it is embedded in a context that communicates a message. As learners develop a linguistic and cultural understanding of the text, they are more likely to want to discuss the text—creating optimum conditions for meaningful communication to occur. More importantly, learners are likely to retain what they are learning because what is being learned is contextualized and has meaning.

Why Are Themes Important in Unit Design?

Think back to when you were a child, or think about a child with whom you interact often today. You probably can recall a point in time where you or that child became curious about something. Interest in a topic may have been the result of something seen on TV, a gift or toy, or possibly an experience like a trip to the zoo. Suddenly, you were doing all that you could to learn more about that topic, consulting a variety of resources—reading, watching documentaries, talking to others, and visiting appropriate websites. Your knowledge of the topic increased, your vocabulary associated with the topic became increasingly more precise, and you found yourself asking more questions about the topic. The complexity of the text was not the determining factor; you were simply interacting with the text because of inherent interest or curiosity. Your interest may have continued, or it may have waned before moving on to other topics of interest. The conditions for motivation were met—mastery, autonomy, and purpose. You were attempting to learn all that you could about the topic, you had selected a topic of interest, and you knew why you were investigating the topic (Pink, 2009).

A thematic unit attempts to recreate this natural curiosity by allowing for exploration of a topic in greater depth. Thematic units allow for the development of topics that are organized around goals based on the World-Readiness Standards for Learning Languages and other relevant standards. Teachers gain increased control over the curriculum as they select topics that are likely to be of interest to their learners and materials that will introduce the topic in ways that invite learner inquiry. By design, thematic units incorporate a "less is more" approach, allowing learners to focus on fewer topics in depth rather than many topics superficially. Thematic units have the potential to alleviate some of the more commonly heard complaints about the general lack of time for in-depth study given the number of chapters required in a curriculum based on a textbook. Learners need time to process new information if they are to truly learn. They need time to connect new learning to prior knowledge and experiences, and they need adequate time to process new information through multiple, interactive experiences. They require an environment that addresses the brain's curiosity and need for novelty (Caine & Caine, 1990). Curiosity and novelty are needed to provoke exploration and engagement on the part of learners.

Project-Based Learning. Project-based learning (PBL) is designed to allow learners to be more engaged in their own learning by allowing them to work on real-world tasks that develop skills in critical thinking and problem-solving. PBL outlines design elements that must be included if a project is to be meaningful. Those elements include: Challenging Problem or Question, Sustained Inquiry, Authenticity, Student Voice and Choice, Reflection, Critique and Revision, and Public Product (Larmer, Mergandoller, & Boss, 2015). While a thematic unit might not address all aspects of PBL, there is clear overlap for many of the elements. Thematic units give learners increased time to consider a topic that is defined by a theme and an essential question. The essential question often frames a problem or issue that learners will be expected to solve or consider in depth. Emphasis on authentic texts and tasks invites inquiry and provides input that broadens learners' understanding and perspectives on the topic that they are exploring. The summative assessment tasks give learners the opportunity to apply what they have learned to the problem or the essential question that is driving exploration and learning. They then create a presentation to share with others, receive feedback on that presentation and, ultimately, reflect on their own learning.

In the unit on Education highlighted in Chapter One of this publication, the essential question, *"Why can't all young people go to school?"* poses a problem that learners are asked to address. Learners work collaboratively to design a multimedia campaign that will inform others of literacy rates around the world and ways that organizations are working to increase literacy rates globally. In the Interpersonal Mode, they discuss what they have learned in order to determine how the class might collaborate with a school in another country to support the school's education program. World language teachers who wish to implement PBL in their classes may find that the thematic unit design presented here supports many elements of PBL through the development of communication skills in a world language.

Thematic Unit Development. How many summers have teachers spent writing or rewriting curriculum when new textbooks or new materials were adopted? Thematic units are created independent of textbooks and other similar materials, so the emphasis is on revision and not on rewriting the entire curriculum. It can be disconcerting to lose the security of the predetermined scope and sequence of a textbook, and teachers may worry that learners need that type of structure. Yet research indicates that the use of thematic units is valuable for several reasons. Hale and Cunningham (2011) analyzed how first graders who had low literacy skills in English performed during a 10-week thematic unit called "All People Need Shelter." First graders read and wrote about a variety of shelters—igloos, *tipis*, castles, log cabins, and adobes. The group participating in the thematic unit showed statistically significant improvement through quantitative measures of vocabulary, reading level, and written expression. Teachers' and learners' comments were also positive in terms of motivation.

Thematic units such as this one on shelter allow for multiple entry points as learners engage in the topic. As teachers identify materials for the unit, they begin to pull together a collection of materials from different genres, media, and reading levels. Individual learners who have different interests and varying proficiency levels benefit from being able to learn about the topic using a variety of materials. These materials or text sets allow teachers to accommodate learners at their level, while still allowing each individual learner equal access to the topic. Additionally, learners benefit by reading about a topic in different genres, and the variety of texts also allows learners to consider different points of view on the topic (Lent, 2012). Thematic units also allow learners to explore both literary and informational texts, thus addressing one of the Common Core (CoreStandards.org) key considerations calling for learners to be able to read and comprehend a variety of complex literary and informational texts independently and proficiently.

"Less is More." The "less is more" aphorism is one of the nine principles of the Coalition of Essential Schools. It requires that learners be given the chance to develop solid understanding of concepts rather than simply taking time to explore numerous topics in a superficial way. The "less is more" principle reflects that learners need time to work with what they are learning in meaningful ways in order to retain the knowledge and skills (Cushman, 1994).

Research in vocabulary acquisition also supports the concept of "less is more." Vocabulary is key to learning a language, and the expanded amount of time on a topic allows for acquisition of new vocabulary by allowing learners time to acquire vocabulary in context before being required to use it in increasingly more complex tasks. Learning a new word is not just a factor of how many times a learner encounters a word (incidental learning), but is more a factor of how often the learner is able to use the new word in a meaningful context (intentional learning). Barcroft's (2004) fifth principle of effective vocabulary instruction states that there is a need to progress from less demanding to more demanding vocabulary-related activities. Clearly, teachers need time to create the contexts where learners can use and recycle vocabulary in meaningful ways (Barcroft, 2004; Selivan, 2010). Additional information on the selection of specific vocabulary will be shared when working with unit design later in this chapter.

What Is the Mindset for Thematic Unit Design?

A well-designed unit is the foundation for planning and delivering instruction. Based on the World-Readiness Standards for Learning Languages and the considerable library of research related to effective instruction, we suggest that units be designed around five basic principles. These principles are expansions of Helena Curtain's three requirements that units be cognitively engaging, intrinsically interesting, and culturally connected (personal communication, 2012). The units should be:

- Communicatively purposeful: Building toward proficiency
- Culturally focused: Developing interculturality
- Intrinsically interesting: Relevant to learners
- Cognitively engaging: Requiring critical thinking skills
- Standards-based: Reflecting goals for learning languages

Consider the education unit that was outlined in Chapter One. The essential question, "Why can't all young people go to school?" allows the learner to consider the topic from the perspective of self, the community, and the world. The theme is culturally focused, providing the opportunity to explore attitudes towards school and issues related to school attendance locally, nationally, and internationally. The essential question is framed as a global issue, allowing learners to apply what they are learning to address the problem of schooling in a creative way, and the performance tasks for the unit provide opportunities and purpose for meaningful communication. Finally, the unit is Standards-based, incorporating each of the goal areas for learning languages. Table 12 summarizes how the principles of the mindset for unit design are present in the unit on education.

What Are Global Themes for Learning Languages?

Thematic units shift instructional focus from language for the sake of language to the use of language to achieve meaningful goals. The theme creates a meaningful context allowing teachers to select texts that engage the learner in more complex thinking, allowing for a more sophisticated use of the language. Thematic units also offer a more natural setting for narrative structure and task-based organization of content (Curtain & Dahlberg, 2016). By working with themes in real-world contexts, learners are able to consider how the content of the thematic unit connects to their lives, their communities, and to the world. They use their communicative skills in the three modes to access and discuss new information and to share their learning with others. Figure 8 reintroduces the

Table 12. Mindset for Development of Thematic Unit on Education

Mindset	Sample Connections to the Unit
Communicatively Purposeful	• Essential question and unit goals ask learners to explore why all young people can't go to school
Culturally Focused	• Extensive use of authentic texts • Focus on school attendance, required/optional classes (products, practices, perspectives)
Intrinsically Interesting	• Choice in how information is shared with others • Theme has a strong personal connection and links to the community and world
Cognitively Engaging	• Research reasons why all young people cannot go to school • Evaluate global efforts to address school attendance
Standards-Based	• Communication: explore why all young people cannot go to school • Cultures: focus on education around the world • Connections: connect to Social Studies: educational systems • Comparisons: examine importance of school • Communities: collaborate with another school

visual of the curriculum framework as a reminder of how communication skills and intercultural skills develop through the 5 Cs, and adds Global Themes as the context for language learning in the 21st century.

Figure 8. Curriculum Design for Learning Languages in the 21st Century with Global Themes

Identity/Belonging

Challenges

Creativity

Discovery

Exploring Time and Place

Well-being

Copyright Clementi and Terrill 2013

Multidimensional themes allow learners to consider topics from a multicultural perspective, as the learners look first in the mirror to explore self and their immediate home environment, and then look out the window of the home to view other communities and the world. Learners use the mirror to reflect on their own experiences, and the window as they consider the perspectives of others. Themes invite learners to make connections and consider topics from different perspectives. The themes—Identity/Belonging, Challenges, Creativity, Discovery, Exploring Time and Place, and Well-being—can be tailored for use in all language learning program models and used to guide unit design in the 21st century. These themes invite teachers and learners to build Intercultural Communicative Competence by exploring a variety of topics through the lenses of self, community, and the world.

Let's consider how these Global Themes apply to the unit on education presented in Chapter One. The topic of education could be connected to several of the individual themes. For example, education could be connected to Well-being since a person's level of education can impact the quality of life. The unit could be part of Exploring Time and Place if the intent is to focus primarily on school as an institution in the past, present, and future, and its impact on society. Creativity or Discovery might be the theme if learners are asked to consider their school as a place that fosters both creativity and discovery, making

comparisons to other educational systems and offering suggestions for innovation based on what they learn. A class that wanted to focus on learners and the influence of peer groups might select Belonging and/or Identity as the theme. Perhaps the most important consideration is how relevant a unit theme and topic are to a particular group of learners. The curriculum mindset introduced earlier suggests that selection of a theme and topic be evaluated by asking the following questions:

- What is the cultural focus that allows for ongoing reflection on interculturality?
- How will learners communicate in purposeful ways?
- Why is this unit of study of interest to learners?
- How will they apply or transfer their learning to new situations?
- How does this unit address the World-Readiness Standards and other standards required by my school?

In the unit on education, the essential question, *"Why can't all young people go to school?"* presents an issue of global importance. Therefore, the theme of Challenges begins to frame the learning for the unit.

Additional Resources for Thematic Instruction. ACTFL, The College Board Advanced Placement (AP), and the International Baccalaureate (IB) offer additional resources for thematic teaching and learning. Learning scenarios for several different languages can be found in the *Standards for Foreign Language Learning in the 21st Century Revised 3rd Edition* (NSFLEP, 2006). These learning scenarios explain the context of a thematic unit and then name the Standards that are addressed in those units. Titles such as Buildings Tell a Story, Market Day, Moroccan Showcase, All in the Family, Immigration and Heritage, Photographs Have a Voice, Let's Stay Healthy, Birds Beyond Borders, The Legend of Corn, and Stereotypes and Prejudice suggest themes and topics that incorporate language, culture, and content. The curricula for both AP and IB language courses advocate a thematic approach to language learning by naming themes and suggesting contexts or topics that allow learners to explore each theme. Both use themes as the frameworks for their exams, and we encourage teachers in language programs connected to AP or IB to use those themes in their classrooms. Learners in those programs need to be familiar with and work frequently in the context of those themes. Table 13 includes the Global Themes outlined earlier and names the themes that are required by AP and those that are recommended for the IB. It's clear that the Global, AP, and IB themes are similar in nature. For example, each addresses the Global Theme of Identity/Belonging. AP highlights Personal and Public Identities, and Family and Communities. IB addresses similar concepts through Social Relationships. The themes share a common purpose. Their intent is to inform decisions about what to teach, ensuring that learners use language in ways that allow them to learn more about themselves, their communities, and the world.

The journal *Learning Languages* published by the National Network for Early Language Learning (NNELL) is a frequent source for thematic units. Previous issues are archived at NNELL.org. Titles such as The Mouse Marriage (Cai, 2010), Children and Art (Eddy, 2007), Adventures Through Time and Space (Eastburn, 2007), Insects: An Interdisciplinary Unit (Leger, 2007), and ¡Viva Colombia, Colombia Viva! A Fantasy Trip for the Five Senses (Ramirez, 2006) convey additional ideas for thematic units that are age appropriate for younger learners.

Table 13. Global Themes, Advanced Placement (AP), and International Baccalaureate (IB)

Global Themes	Advanced Placement (AP) Themes	International Baccalaureate (IB) Themes
• Identity/ Belonging • Challenges • Creativity • Discovery • Exploring Time and Place • Well-being	• Personal and Public Identities • Families and Communities • Global Challenges • Beauty and Aesthetics • Science and Technology • Contemporary Life	• Communication and Media • Global Issues • Social Relationships • Cultural Diversity • Customs and Traditions • Leisure • Health • Science and Technology

Essential Questions. A thematic unit is normally organized around an essential question that serves to focus both teaching and learning. Essential questions benefit teachers by helping to clarify and prioritize content that is truly important. Often teachers believe that everything they are supposed to teach is of equal importance and connected because it is all related to learning the language. An essential question focuses the unit and makes it easier to let go of content that has traditionally been taught, but is no longer relevant.

McTighe and Wiggins (2013) offer three connotations for the word "essential" and state that all three are valid in defining essential questions. The first type of essential question refers to a question that is important and timeless. These questions are broad in scope and can be discussed without ever arriving at a single answer. As understanding deepens, answers may change and become increasingly more nuanced. These questions promote learner inquiry and thinking and cause learners to learn how to learn. *"What is art?"* is a sample of an essential question that is important and timeless. The second type of question is considered to be "elemental" or "foundational" to a discipline. These questions surface frequently among experts and are often the subject of debate and research within a field of study. "What is interculturality and how do we assess it?" is an example of a question that is foundational to world language. The final category of essential questions allows for questions that are vital or necessary for understanding core content— the facts or skills that learners must learn in order to be able to transfer or apply the knowledge and skills that they are learning. "What literacy skills to I need to succeed as a global citizen?" prompts teachers and learners to think deeply about how language skills are used in the real world. We will focus on questions that are in the category of important and timeless for the development of thematic units in this publication.

Essential questions that are important and timeless benefit learners by inviting inquiry. They identify at the start of the unit what learners are going to explore, helping them focus on the knowledge and skills that they need in order to begin to formulate answers in the target language that address the unit question. This does not mean that essential questions need to be limited to what a learner can explicitly answer, but rather that the teacher must think carefully about how to help learners use the language that they already know in combination with what they are learning. Consider the essential question, *"What is art?"* Keeping in mind that this question does not have a specific answer, let's examine how a young child in kindergarten and a novice learner in middle school might answer the question. The kindergartner might respond with thumbs up or thumbs down when shown an image to indicate if the image represents art or not. The teacher might model, *"What is art?"* and then point to different examples saying, "This is art," or "This is not art." The child might then be able to point and say, "This is art." The novice high school learner might be able to answer in a more abstract manner saying, "Art is controversial, original, personal, beautiful, timeless." This type of response can only occur if the teacher predetermines and introduces key vocabulary through a variety of learning activities including authentic texts. In the education unit outlined in Chapter One, the Novice High or Intermediate Low learner might answer the question, *"Why can't all young people go to school?"* by saying, "Some young people don't go to school because of war in their country."

Essential questions allow for differentiation by asking all learners to consider the same question, even though the process for exploring and responding to the question may vary according to individual needs. For world language learners, an essential question is one that learners can answer in the target language. Therefore, teachers need to phrase the question so that all learners, regardless of proficiency level, can respond. Look again at the essential question, *"What is art?"* A learner with Novice level language skills could respond to this question by listing types of art: paintings, drawings, murals, statues, etc. Or that learner may describe art in short sentences: Art is creative; the drawings are interesting; the artist's style is unique, beautiful, etc. At the Intermediate level, learners might say that art tells a story in images. The learner then could describe the story represented in a painting or mural. At the Advanced level, a learner might respond with a researched presentation on a particular genre or artist. All learners are able to share ideas responding to the same essential question in the target language.

An effective essential question will also:

- **Provoke Critical Thinking.** Essential questions are open-ended, involve thinking, and do not have one right answer. Learners are not able to memorize or recall the answer to the question. They promote ongoing thinking about the question, and the question itself often sparks more questions than answers. Answers to the questions may change or expand in depth over time, and those answers require explanation and justification.
- **Foster Creativity.** Essential questions are provocative and can easily be revisited over time from different angles. They have the potential to hook students into wanting

to learn. They provide a sense of adventure and can be fun to explore.

- **Enhance Student Engagement.** Teachers are able to activate prior knowledge by allowing learners to begin the unit from their own past experience or understanding. Learners are able to make connections to their lives and to other disciplines. The question then allows for differentiation and personalized options. It allows learners to approach the question from their perspective and to demonstrate their learning in multiple formats. As stated previously, the question is framed so that learners can answer the question in the target language.
- **Be Relevant to the Learner.** Essential questions expand students' understanding of themselves in relation to their community and world in which they live. They deepen understanding of cultural products, practices, and perspectives. They challenge students to demonstrate that they understand the relationship between what they are learning and larger world issues.

Essential questions are not easy to write. It makes sense to craft an essential question as you begin to develop the unit, but essential questions are truly a genre of writing, and they will be improved by going through drafting, revising, and editing as the unit is developed (McTighe & Wiggins, 2013). The key components of essential questions are summarized in Table 14. Sample essential questions for each of the global themes at the Novice, Intermediate, and Advanced ranges can be found in Appendix G. As learners become familiar with the concept of essential questions, they can assist in the development of questions for a unit of study. Allowing learners to formulate their own questions is one way that teachers can cultivate curiosity in the classroom.

Table 14. Key Components of Essential Questions

Essential Questions			
Provoke Critical Thinking	**Foster Creativity**	**Enhance Learner Engagement**	**Relevant to Learner**
• Open-ended • No single right answer • Answers require explanation	• Provocative • Fun • Can be revisited	• Personalized • Activate prior knowledge • Connect to other disciplines • Differentiate • Can be discussed in the target language	• Expand understanding of self in relation to their community and world • Deepen understanding of culture

What Are the Steps in Designing a Thematic Unit?

Let's begin the process of creating a Standards-based thematic unit. The remainder of this chapter will guide you through the development of a thematic unit using the unit *A Balanced Lifestyle* as a model. The complete template is presented in this chapter in five sections:

- Section A: Language, Level and Performance Range, Theme and Topic, Essential Question, Unit Goals
- Section B: Summative Performance Assessment Tasks
- Section C: Connections to World-Readiness and Other Standards
- Section D: Toolbox—Can-Do Statements, Supporting Functions, Supporting Structures/Patterns, Priority Vocabulary
- Section E: Learning Activities/Formative Assessments, Resources, Technology Integration

Although it may be tempting to read quickly through the information that is presented here, we believe that it will be more beneficial to read a section, review the example, and then pause to consider a unit that you would like to develop. Before reading the rest of this chapter, you may find it helpful to review the completed unit for *A Balanced Lifestyle* (see Appendix H). You may also wish to print a copy of the blank template (see Appendix I). Both templates are also available online at www.actfl.org.

Language, Level and Performance Range, Theme and Topic, Essential Question, Unit Goals. The initial fields of the template ask for the language, level and performance range of the unit, the theme and topic, and the essential question that will frame the unit. The goals for the unit are then written in terms of what learners will know and be able to do by the end of the unit. Table 15 shows Section A of the unit template.

Language, Level and Performance Range, Theme and Topic, Essential Question. This thematic unit plan is designed for learners in the Novice range (Novice Mid to Novice High) who might be in a course that is often called French 1, Japanese 1, or Latin 1. While the example outlined here is specific to French language classes, it is a unit topic that transfers easily to other languages and one that could be adjusted for higher proficiency levels. It is also a theme that elementary, middle, and high school learners can explore and one that captures elements of topics that are often found in textbooks. The Global Theme of Well-being frames the unit. The essential question is open-ended and is likely to be revisited by individuals at different stages of their lives. From a language perspective, it is also a question that Novice learners can answer in the target language.

Unit Goals. The goals listed in Table 15 indicate the performance range that will guide the unit (Wiggins & McTighe, 1998). The goals address the World-Readiness Standards for Learning Languages and incorporate the three modes by creating a context and purpose for communication. The unit goals indicate what a successful learner will know and be able to do. They are written in ways that make the unit relevant to the learners' lives

Table 15. Unit Template Section A: Language, Level and Performance Range, Theme and Topic, Essential Question, Unit Goals

Language and Level / Grade	French – High School
Performance Range	Novice Mid/Novice High
Theme/Topic	**Well-being:** A Balanced Lifestyle
Essential Question	How do people here and in the (French)-speaking world describe a balanced lifestyle?
Unit Goals *What should learners know and be able to do by the end of the unit?*	Learners will be able to: • Describe their daily/weekly routines and categorize their activities in terms of relaxation, social life, physical fitness, academics, work (jobs or volunteer). • Compare their daily/weekly routine to their classmates' routines. • Explore several health and wellness websites in order to identify elements of a balanced lifestyle here and in (the French-speaking world). • Link with a classroom in the (French-speaking world) in order to learn about their daily/weekly routines. • Compare daily/weekly routines of young people in the US to the routines of young people in the (French-speaking world). • Create a definition for a "balanced lifestyle" for teenagers based on information from websites, readings, and interviews with teenagers in the (French-speaking world). • Make recommendations for a daily/weekly routine that reflects the definition developed in this unit. • Create a presentation for (the community) highlighting ways to encourage a balanced lifestyle.

and describe tasks that might occur in the real world. These goals do not indicate the vocabulary and structures that need to be learned. Those are considered later after the summative performance assessment tasks have been determined.

Consider the following questions as you review the unit goals created for the unit *A Balanced Lifestyle*:

- Are the goals relevant in today's world? Do they have the potential to engage the learner?
- Do learners acquire new knowledge and skills beyond (French) language and culture?
- Do the goals convey a purpose for communication in each mode?
- Do the goals integrate culture, language, and content?
- Do the goals provide an opportunity to use language beyond the classroom?

It's clear that the unit focuses on comparing lifestyles in different communities, allowing for the integration of the Cultures and Comparisons goals. The learners acquire information about health and wellness as part of a balanced lifestyle and are likely to address the Connections goal as they explore that topic. Finally, learners will present some of what they have learned beyond the classroom, allowing them to address the Communities goal area. Although the specifics of how each Standard will be addressed are not yet identified, the unit goals do integrate the 5 Cs of the Standards.

> ✔ **Pause to consider your unit.** Who are the learners? What is the performance range for the unit? What theme and topic will you address? What is the "working" essential question? What are the unit goals?

Summative Performance Assessment Tasks. Just as the goals for the unit are organized around the World-Readiness Standards, so are the summative performance assessment tasks. With the unit goals in place, it is important to identify how those goals will be assessed. Understanding by Design (1998) stresses the need to begin with the end in mind, and therefore summative assessment tasks immediately follow the unit goals in the template. They are real-world performance tasks that allow learners to demonstrate how well they can apply the goals to real-world tasks or situations. The tasks also give learners the opportunity to address aspects of the essential question. The alignment between the summative performance assessment tasks and the essential question and goals of the unit creates the connections recommended for an Integrated Performance Assessment (IPA) (Adair-Hauck, Glisan, Troyan, 2013).

Learners must know at the beginning of the unit how they will demonstrate learning by the end of the unit, and they must know how their work will be assessed. Knowing where they are headed in terms of performance allows learners to focus their attention in ways that guide their efforts to meet the performance goals of the unit. The performance tasks are not intended to take place on the last day of the unit. Instead, they are integrated throughout the unit and happen when the teacher determines that the learners are ready to demonstrate what they know and are able to do. Ways of assessing and providing feedback on these tasks will be discussed in Chapter Four. Table 16 shows the summative performance assessment tasks for the unit (Section B), followed by an explanation of the tasks for each mode of communication.

Table 16. Unit Template Section B: Summative Performance Assessment Tasks

Summative Performance Assessment Tasks	Interpretive Mode		
• These tasks allow learners to demonstrate how well they have met the goals of the unit. • The tasks follow the format of the IPA, but are integrated throughout the unit. • The template encourages multiple Interpretive tasks. • The Interpretive tasks inform the content of the Presentational and Interpersonal tasks. • The tasks incorporate 21st Century Learning.	Read a blog written by a teenager where he discusses his activities. Demonstrate comprehension by completing a graphic organizer based on information found in the text.	Watch a commercial for a product that promises to make life easier or less stressful and identify audience, purpose, and message.	Read a schedule of a top athlete to determine how he spends the hours in his day. Decide which elements are part of a balanced lifestyle and which elements, if any, are missing.
	Presentational Mode		**Interpersonal Mode**
	Polished - Create a presentation based on multiple sources of information highlighting ways to promote a balanced lifestyle for teenagers. Share the presentation with another French class. **On demand** - Write a paragraph explaining how balanced your lifestyle is, making simple comparisons to balanced lifestyles in the target culture.		In pairs or small groups, learners share what they have learned about their lifestyle and the lifestyle of teenagers in (the French-speaking world) in terms of balance. Compare daily routines, making and responding to suggestions to adjust their lifestyle.

The Interpretive Assessment Tasks. As stated previously, learners benefit from a text-rich environment that promotes the acquisition of language from meaningful contexts. Mickan (2013) explains the importance of text, defining it as any communication spoken, written, or visual involving language. Mickan states:

> Texts comprise meaning potential. At the very heart of our language experience is the need to create our own meanings in response to texts. Texts set up opportunities for communication about content—for consent, for exploration of ideas, and for contestation. Each interaction with texts involves processing the meanings of what is going on at a particular moment. We appraise and assess what we read, what we write, what we hear and say. In so doing, we declare, develop, and define personal interpretations. Text encounters are opportunities for action—for expression of points of view, for argument, for dispute—and for negotiation, agreement, affirmation, and confirmation. Texts are ideal for direct engagement of learners in discussions, as they constitute discourse resources for formulation of individual and group ideas. (p. 39)

The unit template encourages multiple Interpretive assessment tasks in order to address reading, listening, and viewing. The Interpretive tasks for the unit *A Balanced Lifestyle* convey that learners will be expected to read, listen to, and/or view a variety of texts. They will read a blog on activities, watch a commercial based on quality of life, and read the schedule of a top athlete.

The Presentational Assessment Tasks. The Presentational tasks for this unit address the unit goals and help learners frame answers to the essential question. The tasks are spoken , signed, and/or written tasks that allow learners to showcase what they have learned. Presentational "polished" tasks offer opportunities for learners to collaborate with peers in the classroom and with others in communities beyond the classroom using available technology tools to create final products. Quality Presentational tasks move beyond written , signed, and spoken tasks that simply require learners to reproduce what they did during the unit. These tasks offer learners the opportunity to solve problems and to provide evidence of their ability to take what they have learned and create a new product. The audience for the performance moves beyond just the teacher and the learners in the class. This public performance increases the stakes and raises the bar, often resulting in a higher quality performance. The *"polished"* task asks learners to create a wellness promotional piece that can be shared with others, either locally or globally, using web-based tools. This task is designed to give learners the time they need to draft, revise, and edit the presentation. There is also an option for an *"on demand"* task. This can be given in addition to the polished task, or in some cases, the *"on demand"* task may be used instead of the polished task as evidence of what the learners can do independently without feedback and editing. The "on demand" task asks learners to write an explanation of how balanced their lifestyle is while making some comparisons to the lifestyles of the target culture.

The Interpersonal Assessment Task. The Interpersonal task asks learners to engage with others in communication that is unrehearsed, and that calls for active negotiation of meaning. Learners engage in oral or written communication to exchange information. To build the Interpersonal skill, teachers create opportunities for learners to work with the content from the unit in ways that allow for meaningful conversation. The Interpersonal task for this unit gives learners the opportunity to reflect on their own life and to discuss the balance in their lives, as they consider what they learn from their peers and what they have learned about teenagers in other parts of the world.

✅ **Pause to consider your unit.** What authentic materials do you intend to use? You may want to search for authentic texts that will anchor the unit before going much further. What will your performance assessment tasks be for each mode? Do the assessment tasks address the essential question of the unit? Do your tasks target the appropriate performance level for the unit? Use this as an opportunity to make certain that your performance assessment tasks ask learners to perform at the higher levels of Bloom's Taxonomy.

Which Standards are Addressed in a Thematic Unit?

Integration of Standards. With the theme, topic, essential question, unit goals, and summative assessments in place, the next section of the template shows how the World-Readiness Standards and other Standards that may be required by a school or district are reflected in the unit plan. For this publication we have chosen to narrow our focus to 21st Century Learning and the Common Core State Standards for English Language Arts and Literacy, which were discussed in the Instructional Repertoire presented in Chapter One. Table 17 details Section C of the unit template showing how the World-Readiness

Standards, 21st Century Learning, and Common Core are represented in the thematic unit.

The World-Readiness Standards for Learning Languages were explained in detail in Chapter One, with examples given for the unit *Challenges: Education*. Here, we will explain how the World-Readiness Standards are integrated into the unit *A Balanced Lifestyle*.

Cultures. Teachers begin this section of the template by identifying the cultural products, practices, and perspectives within the context of the unit. The template allows for two examples, although units will include several more. Keep in mind that culture is a natural component of authentic texts—thus authentic

Table 17. Unit Template Section C: Connections to World-Readiness and Other Standards

Cultures (Sample Evidence) *Indicate the relationship between the product, practice, and perspective.*	**Product:** Café **Practice:** Stopping with friends for coffee **Perspective:** It's not the coffee, it's the conversation. **Product:** School year calendar **Practice:** Regular breaks, holidays **Perspective:** Balance	
Connections (Sample Evidence)	**Making Connections to Other Disciplines**	**Acquiring Information and Diverse Perspectives**
	Health and wellness: Compare recommendations for healthy lifestyles. **Media Studies:** Consider impact of media on lifestyle considerations like diet and exercise.	· Differences in school schedules · Importance of vacation and family time · Tradition of *"Fermature annuelle"* (annual closing) in France
Comparisons (Sample Evidence)	**Language Comparisons**	**Cultural Comparisons**
	la joie de vivre (joy of living), *métro, boulot, dodo* (subway, work, sleep), *Ne t'en fais pas!* (Don't worry!), *La détente* (relaxation)	Work time/leisure time Meal time with/without family Weekend activities
Communities (Sample Evidence)	**School and Global Communities**	**Lifelong Learning**
	Share information on wellness with community.	Self-assess progress toward personal learning goals/can-do statements. Examine personal lifestyle and make adjustments as needed.
Connections to Other Standards	· **21st Century Learning: Collaboration.** Work together to design materials to promote balance. · **21st Century Learning: Creativity.** Create a persuasive piece that can be shared with others. · **21st Century Learning: Critical Thinking.** Evaluate your lifestyle in terms of balance from an American and a (French) perspective. · **Common Core: Reading 1.** Read closely to determine what the text says explicitly and to make logical inferences from it; cite specific textual evidence when writing or speaking to support conclusions drawn from the text. · **Common Core: Language 4.** Determine or clarify the meaning of unknown and multiple-meaning words and phrases by using context clues, analyzing meaningful word parts, and consulting general and specialized reference materials as appropriate. · **Common Core: Writing 6.** Use technology, including the Internet, to produce and publish writing and to interact and collaborate with others. · **Common Core: Writing 7.** Conduct short as well as more sustained research projects based on focused questions, demonstrating understanding of the subject under investigation. · **Common Core: Speaking and Listening 1**. Prepare for and participate effectively in a range of conversations and collaborations.	

texts selected for a unit provide rich resources for exploring the products, practices, and perspectives of another culture.

The two samples from the unit *A Balanced Lifestyle* capture aspects of culture that are relevant to the unit theme and address specific unit goals. The concept of having a coffee with friends at a local café allows learners to consider the role the café plays in other cultures. Learners might view a clip from a movie, commenting on what they observe in a café scene—who is there, what they are doing, the position of tables and chairs, etc. They might consider the time of day, the length of time the person is there, and whether they are alone or with friends. Learners might then compare that experience to one in their own lives, noting similarities and differences. Learners might work together to identify a place in their community that is similar to the café. The second example deals with school year calendars. Learners consider the cycle for vacations in the schools, making comparisons to the school calendar in their community. As learners compare schedules, they consider why different calendars exist and what those calendars say about lifestyles. They might then work together to create the ideal school year calendar for their community, taking into consideration the limitations and benefits of such a calendar.

> ✔ **Pause to consider your unit.** Consider how the authentic texts you have selected embed cultural information. What products, practices, and perspectives will you highlight in your unit?

Connections. The Connections goal area highlights the importance of learners using the target language to learn content from other disciplines while considering the perspectives that other cultures bring to that content. Learners are not just learning language; they are using their language skills to learn about a variety of topics.

The essential question for the unit guides the learning that will take place in the classroom. Remember the essential question for this unit: *"How do people here and in (the French-speaking world) describe a balanced lifestyle?"* In this unit, learners connect to the content of other disciplines as they learn more about healthy lifestyles and look at the ways that media in different cultures influences consumers. Learners are encouraged to independently explore related topics of personal interest. They might read information on the importance of sleep and compare the amount of sleep they typically get with their peers

in other cultures. They might then propose solutions that address the need for more sleep. Learners will consider different attitudes toward work and leisure, discussing, for example, the fact that Paris is often considered empty in August with so many people on vacation for the entire month. They might interview their parents to learn more about their vacation schedules at work and why a month-long vacation may or may not be possible. Table 17 shows how the content of the unit addresses the Connections goal area.

> ✔ **Pause to consider your unit.** What other disciplines are connected to your unit theme and topic? Are learners studying aspects of the topic in other classes? Are there aspects of the topic that are perceived differently depending on where someone lives?

Comparisons. The Comparisons goal area allows learners to develop a greater understanding of their own language and culture while learning about others. It promotes reflection at the beginning of language instruction, allowing learners to develop skills needed to compare and contrast elements of language and culture without making judgments. As one exchange student said frequently at the beginning of a home stay when asked what she thought about something: "It's neither bad nor good, just different."

Comparison of language is more than the comparison of linguistic structures; language comparisons allow learners to consider how words convey meaning. In the sample unit, learners consider language expressions that are unique to the target culture and not easily translated into another language, and determine how or if that information is conveyed in their culture. They might look at store hours or signs stating, "Annual Closing," and compare that information to the advantages and disadvantages of what occurs locally. Comparison of culture allows learners to make comparisons to their own cultures and to other cultures where the language is spoken. In today's diverse classrooms, it may also be an opportunity to bring in the cultural background of learners from other cultures. The suggested topics for this sample unit deal with elements that are part of learners' lives, but learners may also identify other cultural elements that they wish to explore. Learners might design a survey using a web-based survey tool asking peers in another country to share facts and personal information about the structure of a typical teenage day. That same survey might be administered to learners of the target language in a nearby community, allowing for analysis of the results across cultures. Table 17 indicates the types of comparisons that could be made in the unit.

> ✓ **Pause to consider your unit.** What resources do you have that will allow you to make comparisons based on evidence in texts? What words and expressions are native speakers likely to attach to this topic?

Communities. The Communities goal area promotes involvement with both the target language and target culture communities. It is also the goal area that envisions how learners will use their skills beyond the classroom and for the rest of their lives. Access to technology has made it much easier to achieve this goal, allowing learners to reach beyond the walls of the classroom using technologies like Skype to discuss particular issues when working in the Interpersonal Mode, reading blogs of native speakers when working in the Interpretive Mode, and by having learners post their work to a wiki or blog when working in the Presentational Mode.

The sample unit asks learners to examine a problem and offer solutions. The research may be done by interviewing learners in the target culture and/or by inviting guest speakers from a local target language community. Learners may participate in a community fair or may share their findings and solutions online or by writing a letter to the editor of a target language paper or online journal. Learners can be challenged to demonstrate their personal growth and learning regarding interculturality by keeping a reflective journal where they comment on what they are learning, and the cultural and linguistic insights that they are acquiring as they interact with others in the target language. They may also be encouraged to set a personal learning goal or wellness goal based on what they have learned in the unit. Table 17 indicates how learners will apply and share their learning with others.

> ✓ **Pause to consider your unit.** How will learners extend their learning beyond their classrooms? How will what they have learned impact their lives? How will they be given the opportunity to self-assess their learning with regard to unit goals?

21st Century Learning. This unit incorporates the 4 Cs of 21st Century Learning. Communication is the foundation for all learning experiences in the unit. Learners collaborate in the Interpersonal Mode and use *critical thinking skills* to discuss balance in their lifestyles. In the Presentational Mode, they *collaborate* and use their *creativity and critical thinking* to design the necessary materials to promote a more balanced lifestyle. The tasks in all three modes ask learners to *think critically and solve problems* as they analyze authentic texts in the Interpretive Mode, evaluate lifestyles in terms of balance during group discussions, and seek solutions to a wellness issue in their community. Table 17 includes examples of how 21st Century Learning is incorporated throughout the unit.

Common Core State Standards. As outlined earlier, there are strong connections between the Common Core State Standards for English Language Arts and Literacy (Appendix E) and the expectations found in the World-Readiness Standards for Learning Languages. Learners demonstrate college and career readiness through achievement of the Standards. The same is true of language learners who demonstrate what they are able to do as they engage in the summative performance assessment tasks for the unit. The types of performance required by the summative assessment tasks can be easily aligned to the ELA Common Core Anchor Standards for Reading, Writing, Speaking and Listening, and Language. Consider the performance assessment tasks for *A Balanced Lifestyle*. The selected Common Core State Standards capture how learners will advance their literacy skills as they complete the required performance assessment tasks. Interpretive tasks align with the Anchor Standards for Reading. Presentational tasks align with the Anchor Standards for Writing. Interpersonal tasks are reflected in the Anchor Standards for Speaking and Listening.

> The document Alignment of the World-Readiness Standards for Learning Languages with the Common Core State Standards can be found at: www.actfl.org.

> ✓ **Pause to consider your unit.** Determine how your performance assessment tasks address other standards that are required by your school or district.

What is the Purpose of the Language Toolbox?

Toolbox. The toolbox section of the template pulls together the elements that explain what learners need to know and be able to do in order to meet the expectations of the unit goals and to successfully complete the summative performance assessment tasks. Table 18 shows the components of the Toolbox and gives a brief overview indicating the role that each element plays in the design of the unit.

Let's consider how each component of the toolbox is integrated into the sample unit plan. Table 19 provides detail on Section D of the unit template, showing how each of the toolbox components is addressed in the sample unit *A Balanced Lifestyle*.

Can-Do Statements. As explained in Chapter One, the NCSSFL-ACTFL Can-Do Statements (Appendix F) consist of Proficiency Benchmarks, Performance Indicators and Examples. Teachers may find examples relevant to the unit

A Balanced Lifestyle in the document, but it is important to remember that the examples in the actual Can-Do document are simply examples. Therefore, it is likely that teachers will have to create their own Can-Do Statements, ones that are

Table 18. Unit Template: Toolbox Components

Can-Do Statements	Unit-specific statements based on the NCSSFL-ACTFL Can-Do Statements
Supporting Functions	Key functions identified in the context of how they will be used in the unit
Supporting Structures/ Patterns	Grammatical structures or sentence patterns required by the function
Priority Vocabulary	Vocabulary that is essential to communication about the unit topic
Key Learning Activities/ Formative Assessments	A representative sample of learning experiences that show how learners will prepare for the summative assessment tasks
Resources	Specific resources that will be used in the unit
Technology Integration	Suggestions of how learners might work with technology to meet unit goals

Table 19. Unit Template Section D: Toolbox — Can-Do Statements, Supporting Functions, Supporting Structures/Patterns, and Priority Vocabulary

Toolbox		
Can-Do Statements		
Interpretive	(Reading + Listening) I can understand when someone talks about their daily routine. (Reading + Listening) I can understand simple illustrated instructions for exercises to do to stay in shape. (Reading) I can understand a short interview where an athlete shares his daily routine to stay in shape. (Listening) I can understand people as they describe their daily routines.	
Presentational	(Speaking + Writing) I can present information about the elements of a balanced lifestyle. (Speaking + Writing) I can present information comparing lifestyles in France and the U.S. (Writing) I can keep a diet and exercise journal to track what I do to stay healthy.	
Interpersonal	• I can ask and answer questions about what I do each day to be healthy. • I can share how often I do certain activities each week. • I can exchange information about what people in (country) do to be healthy.	

Supporting Functions	Supporting Structures/Patterns	Priority Vocabulary
Compare *lifestyle routines*	*plus que, moins que, aussi que* (more than, less than, as…as)	• expressions of time • adverbs of frequency • days, months • time • feelings *Une bonne hygiène de vie* (a healthy lifestyle) *Un régime équilibré* (a balanced diet) *La détente* (relaxation) *S'entraîner* (to exercise) *Se détendre/se dépêcher* (to relax/to hurry) *Être détendu/être stressé* (to be relaxed/to be stressed)
Describe *your daily schedule*	*(le) lundi…* (on Mondays)	
Ask and answer questions *about daily routines*	*oui/non* (yes/no), *ou* (either/or), *quand* (when), *à quelle heure* (at what time)	
Express frequency *saying when and how often you do certain things*	*tous les jours* (every day) *une fois par semaine* (once a week), *rarement* (rarely)	
Express needs *saying what you need to do to be healthy*	*Il faut / Il me faut* (It's necessary/I need)	
Express opinions *about daily activities, schedules*	*Il est important de, Il est bon de* (It's important to/ it's good to)	
Make suggestions *about ways to be healthy*	*Tu devrais / Vous devriez* (You should) *Il te/vous faut* (You need to)	

relevant to the goals of the thematic unit. Can-Do Statements provide clear direction to learners by identifying different communication tasks that will be accomplished prior to the end of the unit. These tasks equate to the individual training goals that someone who wants to run a marathon must accomplish prior to running the actual event. Learners are able to measure progress and feel success as they meet the expectations for each Can-Do Statement. The unit *A Balanced Lifestyle* targets the Novice Mid/ Novice High performance range, and the Can-Do Statements for the unit will fall within that range. These statements make clear what learners will be expected to do in each mode during the unit.

Supporting Functions. Language functions describe how we use language in our daily lives. They convey the purpose for speaking or writing by identifying the basic task that a person must be able to do in order to communicate effectively in a given situation. A list of possible functions has been created to make it easier to identify appropriate functions that relate to unit goals (see Appendix J). The list is divided into six broad categories: describing people, places, things, how and how well something is done; asking and responding to questions; expressing feelings and emotions; expressing advice, opinions, preferences; telling and retelling stories, and sequencing; expressing hopes, dreams, future plans. We believe that these six functions are fundamental to making progress in communication skills. Within each category are related functions, those functions that are similar to the six broad functions listed above. Finally, within each category is a progression from simple to more complex ways to express the functions. Teachers can intentionally plan instruction that moves learners to greater facility within the six functions, thus building their communication skills. The functions for this unit were determined by looking carefully at the unit goals and performance assessment tasks. For example, learners are expected to be able to compare their routines with those of others. In order to do that, they will need to be able to *"ask and answer questions about daily routines."* The broad category of the function is *"ask and answer questions."* This broad function is one that is likely to be recycled in all units. The specific descriptor, *"about daily routines,"* clarifies how this function will be addressed in this unit.

> **✓ Pause to consider your unit.** What Can-Do Statements will be part of your unit? What language functions are needed to allow learners to meet the goals of the unit? Be sure that these statements reflect language as it will be used in the real world and that they are specific to the theme and topic of this unit.

Supporting Structures/Patterns. Once the language functions for the unit are in place, the related grammatical structures or language patterns are identified. This is done to make certain that structures and patterns have a communicative purpose, allowing the focus on form to occur within the context of a text. Language learning should never be driven by grammar instruction alone, and language instruction must avoid manipulating grammatical structures out of context. Learners who only know grammar will struggle to be able to use the language in meaningful ways (Shrum & Glisan, 2010). Glisan and Donato (2017) identified this focus on form as a high-leverage teaching practice, stressing that the selection of a form is not the same as selecting a grammar point to be covered each day or as a focus of a unit. Instead, there is a deliberate effort to cause learners to notice a form when listening to, reading or viewing texts. As learners notice and discuss the uses and meaning conveyed by the form, they come to understand how that form is used to convey a more precise message. Moeller and Ketsman (2010) discussed the prevailing theories regarding grammar instruction and reported on various studies that examined effective practices on the teaching of grammar. Based on their findings, they then created several activities designed to illustrate the principles of best practice. They recommend that such activities:

- allow learners to complete a task before working in pairs to construct and explain the grammar rule;
- allow learners to see examples of rules in context before being asked to analyze and apply the pattern in a new context; and
- require that learners complete tasks that require them to focus on both form and meaning.

For example, learners need to express frequency, saying how often they do certain activities. In order to be able to do this, they will need to know some adverbs of frequency and will need to know how to use these adverbs to communicate with others about their activities. The teacher begins by selecting a text that includes examples of adverbs of frequency. Learners work with the text to demonstrate understanding, discuss how the adverb of frequency is used in context, and then have the opportunity to complete a task that requires learners to use adverbs of frequency in a meaningful context. By connecting supporting structures and patterns with the supporting functions, grammar becomes an integral part of the communicative process.

Vocabulary Building. Learners of a world language need words in order to communicate. ". . . while without grammar very little can be conveyed, without vocabulary nothing can be conveyed" (Wilkins pp.111–112, 1972). Vocabulary is more than single words. It includes lexical phrases or chunks of language that convey a unified meaning. Vocabulary is retained more successfully in the memory of learners when it is presented and recycled multiple times in meaningful contexts and connected to prior learning. Opportunities to practice new vocabulary need to be intentionally included in lesson plans every day. As learners engage in a thematic unit, they encounter multiple texts on the same topic and/or longer texts that explore the topic in depth.

Priority Vocabulary. Traditionally, vocabulary was learned from lists, and there were often too many words on the list for vocabulary acquisition to take place. Strong learners were able to memorize the words for a test, but often forgot them quickly. Learners seemingly understand the cycle of memorizing and forgetting, since it is not uncommon to hear older learners say, "Quick give me the test, before I forget!" These learners had memorized lists of words without being able to use the words in any meaningful context. The days of the week were taught as a list, and learners recited and wrote the seven days of the week, scoring well if they knew all seven in the correct order. The communicative approach requires that vocabulary be used in meaningful ways. Today's learners are far more likely to learn to use the days of the week in the context of a communicative function. If learners are trying to find out who has the busier schedule on a certain day in the sample unit, one learner might begin by asking, "What are you doing *on Saturday?*"

The selection of priority vocabulary is influenced by the choice of authentic texts for a thematic unit. The amount of vocabulary that can be acquired is limited by the amount of time available for the unit and by the age of the learner. The concept of priority vocabulary requires that teachers select words and phrases that will be used purposefully and frequently during the unit, and those that are likely to transfer to other situations. In the unit *A Balanced Lifestyle*, learners will need words and phrases associated with activities and sports, and words to indicate how often they engage in certain sports and activities. In order to understand authentic texts, they will also need to become familiar with activities and sports that people in the target cultures do.

Learners may read another text that discusses times when peers feel "relaxed" or "stressed" or "tense" or "overwhelmed." The nuance of these words may be critical to understanding the main idea and supporting details of a text. These same words are also extremely useful in describing the learners' own perceptions of how balanced their lifestyles are. Heritage speakers who already know common words used in daily speech benefit from learning the more precise and academic vocabulary found in authentic texts. Authentic texts may also include vocabulary that learners will understand in context, but are not likely to add to their active vocabulary. These words would not be part of the priority vocabulary. For example, the learners may read about a "sedentary lifestyle" but would not learn this expression as part of their active vocabulary. To determine which words to include in the list of priority vocabulary, teachers need to consider how frequently the learners will encounter and use the word both within and beyond the unit of instruction.

Learners also need words that allow them to express concepts in culturally authentic ways. All languages have words and phrases that do not translate easily into other languages. They are terms that convey a precision of meaning and often bring a cultural perspective that is unique to the language. The term *"joie de vivre"* which translates literally as "joy of living" conveys a much deeper meaning in French culture that goes beyond "joy of living." It encompasses an attitude and value embraced by the French, and is important to their concept of a balanced lifestyle.

To determine priority vocabulary, begin by searching for authentic texts related to the unit theme and essential question. Evaluate these texts for vocabulary that is repeated within a text and across texts to help select the priority vocabulary that learners really need to understand and to exchange information about the unit topic. Wilfong (2013) suggests that the following questions be considered when selecting vocabulary.

- **Representative:** Is the vocabulary critical to understanding the topic and texts? Include idioms, as these can often mislead learners if they interpret them literally.

Idioms also contribute to learners' ability to express ideas as a native speaker would. Include adverbs and adjectives that change the meaning of a phrase. Phrases such as "disorganized routine" or "restless sleep" may cause confusion if they are not clearly understood.

- **Repeatability:** Will the vocabulary be used again and again and again during the unit and afterwards? Select words that are high-utility academic and non-academic: words that are going to appear in texts frequently, and that learners need to use frequently.

- **Transportability:** Is the vocabulary needed for discussions and/or writing assignments? Determine if the learners need to be able to use the vocabulary actively (I can retrieve and use the word "almost instantly") or passively (I can recognize the word in context).

- **Contextual:** Can learners use context to figure out the meaning of a word? Determine if learners can determine or infer meaning from context clues.

- **Structural:** Can learners use root words, prefixes, or suffixes to figure out the meaning of the word? Determine if the word needs to be taught, or if learners can determine the meaning of a word by breaking it apart.

- **Cognitive load:** Can learners fit these words into their brains this week? Teachers can have a greater impact on vocabulary by giving students repeated exposures to 5-10 useful new words every week, rather than by drilling them on 20 or more words at a time. Teachers are often dismayed to realize that learners who did very well on the more traditional vocabulary quiz fail to recall those same words in future lessons. Researchers have found that it usually takes 10-15 exposures for new words to stick in people's minds, and those words stick better when used in context as they speak or write, rather than when studying new words as part of a list. Instead of relying on isolated words or phrases, give learners sentence starters with important vocabulary imbedded to help learners improve how they express themselves orally and in writing. In the unit *A Balanced Lifestyle*, learners might be asked to respond to this question: How do I create balance in my day? The teacher might provide a series of sentence starters to help learners form their thoughts while using new vocabulary:
  - When I am feeling too much stress, I….
  - No matter what, I find time to….
  - I always try to ignore….

The questions and comments outlined above cause teachers to limit the number of words that can be taught. Teachers should not feel pressured to create thematic lists of vocabulary in an effort to provide all words relevant to a topic. As stated previously, a thematic unit is not a list of associated vocabulary words. Prior vocabulary lists may have included every possible sport or every possible family member, but it was nearly impossible for most learners to acquire and retain all those words. Instead challenge learners to develop their own personal vocabulary. For example, a learner who is passionate about skateboarding would add that word to a personal vocabulary list. That learner then becomes responsible for communicating the meaning of personal vocabulary to classmates who may not know the words. This requires learners to use a variety of communication strategies to explain the words, a skill that is extremely useful in the real world. In Chapter Four, we will discuss the role that personal vocabulary plays when assessing learners in the Interpersonal and Presentational Modes.

The priority vocabulary section of the template highlights those words that are truly essential to successful communication within the context of the unit. These words are connected to the unit goals, allowing learners to understand and express ideas related to the unit topic and essential question. The number of words considered "priority" is limited, so that learners have multiple opportunities to use the words so that they become part of the learners' active vocabulary.

> ✓ **Pause to consider your unit.** Look carefully at the unit Can-Do Statements and the unit functions. What grammar or patterns will learners need? What vocabulary words will they need? Are there words and expressions that will allow them to work with the authentic text that will anchor the unit? Are there cultural expressions or idioms that native speakers would use when discussing the unit topic?

Key Learning Activities/Formative Assessments. The template has followed a backward design model, allowing teachers to think through the desired results and the acceptable evidence that would serve as proof that learners had achieved the goals of the unit. The final stage of backward design focuses on the learning experiences and instruction that will allow learners to meet the expectations of the unit. Learning experiences are focused and purposeful, formative in nature, and set high expectations (Dougherty, 2012). Both teacher and learners understand the relationship of individual activities in terms of meeting unit goals. Activities that are isolated and not clearly connected to unit goals need to be eliminated.

Formative assessment is assessment *for* learning. It is an intentional part of unit and lesson design that partners teachers and learners in gathering and evaluating evidence of learning in order to improve performance (Moss & Brookhart, 2012). By viewing learning activities as formative assessments, teachers gain valuable information about their instruction, and learners receive timely feedback on aspects of their work while there is time to adjust. Therefore, the unit-planning template does not separate learning activities from formative assessments.

This section of the unit template allows teachers to identify a few key learning activities/formative assessments. The sample activities reflect what teachers might do at the beginning, middle, and end of the unit, and they are intentionally grouped to show how learners might work in all three modes to strengthen their language skills. The first column in Table 20 describes the key learning activity/formative assessment with sufficient detail to give a general sense of what might be done. The second column asks for a simple explanation of how the activity supports a learning goal for the unit. The third column asks for the mode(s) of communication being used. This column allows teachers to see at a glance that there is a good balance of the Interpersonal, Interpretive, and Presentational

Modes, but also provides the opportunity to think through ways that an activity might be expanded or reshaped to practice a different mode. Table 20 shows section E of the unit template and provides four sample learning activities/formative assessments. Additional examples of learning activities/formative assessments are described in the complete template (see Appendix G). Resources for the unit and opportunities for integration of technology are also addressed in Section E of the template.

Resources and Technology Integration. It can be challenging to think of resources and technology as the final considerations in unit design, especially if a teacher is moving from a situation where the textbook and accompanying ancillaries and technology pieces have been the curriculum. As you begin the development of a unit, take time to search for resources that will provide a strong foundation for the unit. With your theme and topic in mind and a preliminary essential question, it is critical that you search for text that will support the unit and inspire your thinking. The song *Ma Vie au Soleil* (My Life in the Sun) was a starting point for the design of this entire unit. As stated in Chapter One, it is critical that learners have multiple opportunities to interact with a wide variety of texts. Authentic texts allow learners to have increased access to content that is designed for native speakers. The link between culture and language in authentic text ensures that learners acquire and use language in an authentic context. Such materials are also

Table 20. Unit Template Section E: Learning Activities/Formative Assessments, Resources, and Technology Integration

Learning Activity/Formative Assessment *(Sample activities are listed from the beginning to the end of the unit.)*	How does this activity support the unit goals or performance tasks?	Mode of Communication
Watch video clip of Song – *Ma Vie au Soleil* (My Life in the Sun), list activities that relate to *métro, boulot, dodo* (subway, work, sleep) and activities that relate to a more relaxed lifestyle.	Explore elements of a balanced lifestyle.	Interpretive
Use *Libération* magazine headline and article on stress at school. Have learners complete graphic organizer with statistics from article and then compare to their own situations.	Impact of school on lifestyles	Interpretive Interpersonal
Read article on how French teenagers spend free time. Design survey questions to use with learners studying French. Create graphic organizer to compare school results to those in article. Discuss results in groups.	How French teens spend free time and make comparisons	Interpretive Interpersonal Presentational
Work in groups to create a multimedia presentation that explains *métro, boulot, dodo* (subway, work, sleep) in the context of a teenager's life in the U.S.	Product that explains the lifestyle of a US teenager to French teens	Interpersonal Presentation
Resources	**Technology Integration**	
Ma Vie au Soleil – https://www.youtube.com/watch?v=NqyOJ7oUnbl http://www3.sympatico.ca/serge.richard2/ http://www3.sympatico.ca/serge.richard2/page5.html Additional resources available at: http://clementi-terrill2012.wikispaces.com	Teachers can create a safe, free space for learner blogs and more: http://kidblog.org	

likely to be of higher interest to learners and, as a result, they may be more likely to search out additional resources on subjects of interest. A few resources for the sample unit are listed in Table 20. A detailed resource list and appropriate links are available at www.actfl.org. Keep in mind that a list of generic resources is not all that helpful. Curriculum documents in the past may have simply listed materials and resources in a generic manner—textbook, workbook, video, songs, etc. Instead, use this section of the template to identify specific instructional resources that will be integral to the unit.

Technology. Technology integration requires that teachers think of how to best use available resources within and beyond the classroom. Resources like Skype allow learners to communicate easily with native speakers beyond the walls of the classroom. Technology tools allow learners to create new products in ways that can be easily shared with others, allowing for communication and collaboration beyond the classroom.

Technology Integration. Technology integration is more than just the tools that teachers and learners will use throughout the unit. Technology integration incorporates the definition of literacy from the National Council of Teachers of English referenced earlier, and includes the definition created by the Center for Media Literacy:

> Media Literacy is a 21st century approach to education. It provides a framework to access, analyze, evaluate, create, and participate with messages in a variety of forms—from print to video to the Internet. Media literacy builds an understanding of the role of media in society as well as essential skills of inquiry and self-expression necessary for citizens of a democracy (Center for Media Literacy).

Technology has made it both easier and more challenging to create content. Computers have certainly allowed writers to write differently. Multiple drafts are possible, material can be copied and pasted, editing programs make proofreading easier, and design programs make it much easier to produce quality final products. Computers now allow for multimedia components to be incorporated, and writers can access a variety of spaces where text can be composed and shared. Tools exist to allow the writing process to be collaborative and interactive. Today's learners must be able to manage and use all of these tools well if they are to create and share content (DeVoss, Eidman-Aadahl, & Hicks, 2010). The unit template includes space to suggest how technology might be integrated within the unit.

> ✓ **Pause to consider your unit.** Identify your resources and consider the role that technology will play in your unit. Consider carefully the authentic text that you will use to launch the unit. Find texts that can be used in a variety of ways. Try to organize the learning activities/formative assessments in ways that make sense, showing how learners will make progress toward a specific goal.

The unit template that has been described in this chapter was designed in a way that hopefully caused teachers to reflect on each section. The questions and prompts found in the shaded areas of the template were used to explain the purpose of each section and to call attention to what needs to be considered when developing a unit. As curriculum units are shared with others, it may be helpful to provide a unit overview, a "unit-at-a-glance." Table 21 shows an overview for *A Balanced Lifestyle*. Note that the content of the Toolbox has been consolidated to save space, and that the sections for Learning Activities/Formative Assessments, Resources, and Technology Integration are not part of the overview. The overview captures Stages 1 and 2 of Backward Design. Teachers and learners can easily see the goals of the unit and how those goals will be assessed. The content of the Toolbox provides further guidance on what learners will need to know and be able to do during the unit of study.

Table 21: Thematic Unit Overview

Well-being: A Balanced Lifestyle
Novice Mid/High
How do people here and in the (French)-speaking world describe a balanced lifestyle?

Unit Goals

Learners will be able to:
- Describe their daily/weekly routines and categorize their activities in terms of relaxation, social life, physical fitness, academics, work (jobs or volunteer).
- Compare their daily/weekly routine to their classmates' routines.
- Explore several health and wellness websites in order to identify elements of a balanced lifestyle here and in (the French-speaking world).
- Link with a classroom in the (French-speaking world) in order to learn about their daily/weekly routines.
- Compare daily/weekly routines of young people in the US to the routines of young people in the (French-speaking world).
- Create a definition for a "balanced lifestyle" for teenagers based on information from websites, readings, and interviews with teenagers in the (French-speaking world).
- Make recommendations for a daily/weekly routine that reflects the definition developed in this unit.
- Create a presentation for (the community) highlighting ways to encourage a balanced lifestyle.

Summative Performance Assessment Tasks

Interpretive
- Read a blog written by a teenager where he discusses his activities. Demonstrate comprehension by completing a graphic organizer based on information found in the text.
- Watch a commercial for a product that promises to make life easier or less stressful and identify audience, purpose, and message.
- Read a schedule of a top athlete to determine how he spends the hours in his day. Decide which elements are part of a balanced lifestyle and which elements, if any, are missing.

Presentational	Interpersonal
Polished – Create a presentation based on multiple sources of information highlighting ways to promote a balanced lifestyle for teenagers. Share the presentation with another French class. **On demand** – Write a paragraph explaining how balanced your lifestyle is, making simple comparisons to balanced lifestyles in the target culture.	In pairs or small groups, learners share what they have learned about their lifestyle and the lifestyle of teenagers in (the French-speaking world) in terms of a balance. Compare daily routines, making and responding to suggestions to adjust their lifestyle.

Can-Do Statements

Interpretive	• (Reading + Listening) I can understand when someone talks about their daily routine. • (Reading + Listening) I can understand simple illustrated instructions for exercises to do to stay in shape. • (Reading) I can understand a short interview where an athlete shares his daily routine to stay in shape. • (Listening) I can understand people as they describe their daily routines.
Presentational	• (Speaking + Writing) I can present information about the elements of a balanced lifestyle. • (Speaking + Writing) I can present information comparing lifestyles in France and the U.S. • (Writing) I can keep a diet and exercise journal to track what I do to stay healthy.
Interpersonal	• I can ask and answer questions about what I do each day to be healthy. • I can share how often I do certain activities each week. • I can exchange information about what people in (country) do to be healthy.

Supporting Functions	Supporting Structures/Patterns	Priority Vocabulary
• **Compare** *lifestyle routines* • **Describe** *your daily schedule* • **Ask and answer questions** *about daily routines* • **Express frequency** *saying when and how often you do certain things* • **Express needs** *saying what you need to do to be healthy* • **Express opinions** *about daily activities, schedules* • **Make suggestions** *about ways to be healthy*	• *plus que, moins que, aussi que* (more than, less than, as … as) • *(le) lundi…* (on Mondays) • *oui/non* (yes/no), *ou* (either/or), *quand* (when), *a quelle heure* (at what time) • *tous les jours* (every day) *une fois par semaine* (once a week) *rarement* (rarely) • *Il faut / Il me faut* (It's necessary/I need) • *Il est important de, Il est bon de* (It's important to/it's good to) • *Tu devrais / Vous devriez, Il te/vous faut* (You should/you need to)	• expressions of time • adverbs of frequency • days, months • time • feelings *Une bonne hygiène de vie* (a healthy lifestyle) *Un régime équilibré* (a balanced diet) *La détente* (relaxation) *S'entraîner* (to exercise) *Se détendre/se dépêcher* (to relax/to hurry) *Être détendu/être stressé* (to be relaxed/to be stressed)

Summary. Let's consider how the unit A *Balanced Lifestyle* addressed each component of the thematic unit mindset. The unit is culturally focused and considers personal lifestyles, communities, and world perspectives. It is intrinsically interesting and gives learners the opportunity to focus on their own health and well-being. The performance tasks allow for meaningful communication in each mode, and the tasks are cognitively engaging. Learners consider an issue from different perspectives and propose solutions. Finally, it is Standards-based, addressing each of the 5 Cs in a meaningful way. This unit is based on the mindset for effective thematic unit design, providing learners with purposeful and meaningful practice to build their communication skills toward increased proficiency. Remember, proficiency and the World-Readiness Standards guide all curriculum and unit decisions. In the next chapter, we propose a template for lesson planning to facilitate implementation of the thematic unit on a daily basis.

Application

1. You are convinced that curriculum should be designed around thematic units. What would you say to convince your colleagues who are worried about the change?

2. You are mentoring a young teacher and have just observed a lesson using dated materials that did not appear to be of interest to several learners. How might you use the thematic unit mindset to help her reflect on her lesson?

3. What examples would you share to help colleagues understand the concept of interculturality?

Reflection

1. How did a recent unit of mine address each principle of the thematic unit mindset? Are there changes that I might make when I teach the unit again? Why would I make those changes?

2. How do the units I teach connect to the Global Themes or the AP/IB Themes? How might I use those connections to strengthen my units?

Chapter 3 | Lesson Design

I never teach my pupils; I only attempt to provide the
conditions in which they can learn.

— Albert Einstein

What Does the Educator Need to Consider to Create a Learner-centered Classroom?

A teacher may complain that she is working harder than her students. She realizes that she spends hours each week preparing lessons that will engage learners, lessons that are designed to keep learners involved and focused on the objectives. Then, during each class period she acts as the orchestra conductor for the class, directing learners from one activity to the next. At the end of the lesson, the teacher is exhausted and realizes that she had found and created the necessary materials, presented all of the new information, and led the discussions. The challenge for this teacher is to create a more learner-centered classroom. The National Capital Language Resource Center offers the following definition of a learner-centered classroom:

> Learner-centered instruction encourages students to take responsibility for their own language skill development and helps them gain confidence in their ability to learn and use the language. Teachers support students by devoting some class time to non-traditional activities, including teaching learners how to use learning strategies, how to use available tools and resources, and how to reflect on their own learning (NCLRC, 2003).

In addition to the concepts of self-assessment and reflection presented in Chapter One, the learner-centered classroom requires an understanding of:

- motivation;
- self-efficacy;
- differentiation; and
- brain-based learning and its implications for lesson design.

Motivation. In today's globally connected world, knowing how to communicate in more than one language is a real-world skill. No longer do you have to depend on travel to have the opportunity to meet and converse with someone who speaks a language that is not your own. You can quickly connect with people around the world virtually. Yet, even with this "instant access" to speakers of other languages, there is still a need to convince learners, parents, administrators, and community members that the skills that are acquired through learning a language are vital in a world where, according to many Americans' perceptions, everyone speaks English. That mindset of "English is all that I need" reduces motivation or can make it disappear. This is a significant issue because research shows that "motivation is a consistently strong predictor of successful language learning" (Center for Open Educational Resources & Language Learning, The University of Texas at Austin).

In trying to address this issue and understand why people study languages, Gardner and Lambert (1972) identified two types of motivation to learn languages: instrumental and integrative. Learning a language with the goal of getting a job, getting into college, meeting a graduation requirement, or receiving a promotion is identified as instrumental motivation. The second type of motivation, integrative, is when the learner is personally motivated to learn a language in order to become acquainted with people who speak the language studied and its related culture. Following Gardner and Lambert's work, Graham (1984) identified a third type of motivation: assimilative. In this type of motivation, the learner has a strong desire to become a member of the culture that speaks the language the learner is studying. Pink (2009) also recognizes the importance that motivation plays in learning. He comments that getting an "A" in French class is simply an achievement or performance goal, and one that would be indicative of instrumental motivation. He considers it far more important that learners have learning goals such as the integrative or assimilative goal of learning to speak French in order to meet and become acquainted with people whose native language is French. By placing an emphasis on learning for personal reasons, learners are more likely to become lifelong learners.

Horowitz (2008) suggests that the types of motivation defined by Gardner and Lambert may not be compelling for everyone given the attitudes that many Americans have towards learning languages other than English. The following classroom strategies, based on suggestions by Horowitz (2008), may more effectively motivate learners once they are in a world language classroom:

- Help learners set personal goals: identify reasons that are personally relevant to their lives and future plans; set realistic and attainable communication goals facilitated by tools such as LinguaFolio®.
- Discuss attitudes about the target language and culture: distinguish between stereotypes and generalizations related to the people who speak the target language; have learners document their experiences with other languages and cultures and the people who speak other languages as evidence of their growing interculturality.
- Connect to native speakers and authentic materials: share a wide variety of authentic materials with learners; introduce learners to native speakers within your community and in locations around the world via technology to make the language "come alive."

Concerning the actual daily routine in a language classroom, the following strategies help create a positive, productive, and pleasant atmosphere, motivating learners to continue their study of another language. These strategies are based on research conducted by Dörnyei and Csizér (1998) and on recommendations made by Shrum and Glisan (2016):

- Conduct the class in the target language, making sure that the language is comprehensible to the learners: use visuals, gestures, acting, facial expressions, props, drawing, and be ready to repeat, rephrase, simplify, and slow down your speech as needed.
- Encourage learners to use the target language with one another continuously including during unstructured times.
- Share the daily learning objectives at the beginning of class, and refer to them during class as appropriate so that learners know the purpose for the activity or task; check for understanding frequently and adjust plans accordingly, moving more quickly or more slowly as needed.

- Give clear instructions, and model how to complete the activity or task successfully.
- Teach learners how to ask for clarification when they don't understand something using phrases such as: repeat please; I don't understand; slow down please; what does (x) mean; can you explain this (again).
- Create a friendly atmosphere where learners are comfortable taking risks with the language and making mistakes as they try to create meaning with the target language.
- Make pair and small group work part of the regular classroom routine, assigning communicative tasks that are purposeful and meaningful.
- Provide opportunities for learners to help set the agenda concerning what they are learning and how they will demonstrate what they have learned.
- Make learning fun: "The role that fun plays with regard to intrinsic motivation in education is twofold. First, intrinsic motivation promotes the desire for recurrence of the experience…Secondly, fun can motivate learners to engage themselves in activities with which they have little or no previous experience" (Bisson and Luckner, 1996).

These factors are critical in terms of building relationships and creating the classroom climate that is essential to building a strong learning community in the classroom.

Self-efficacy. Self-concept of ability or self-efficacy is also important when considering how students learn. Learners need to believe that participation in new learning experiences will lead to success rather than failure. They need to know that they are capable of setting and achieving short-term, realistic goals. The teacher's role is to give learners strategies that allow them to meet their goals. This is critically important, especially for older learners who may have acquired behaviors that cause them to be failure-avoidant rather than success-oriented. When older learners begin to feel that they are not able to do something, they may begin to engage in behaviors to avoid failure—not trying, procrastinating, denying that they tried, and reporting false effort; behaviors that are often seen as "failure with honor" (Ames, 1990; Marzano 2006). Teachers enhance self-efficacy and increase success-oriented behavior when they make certain that learners know what they are supposed to learn and create learning experiences that help learners achieve these goals. Marzano (2006) reports that learners credit their success to four possible attributes—ability, luck, task difficulty, and effort. Learners who believe that ability plays a role in success may be quick to believe that others succeed because they have greater ability. Those who rarely feel success may be too quick to say that they were lucky or that the task was just easy on those occasions when they succeed. Those who attribute their success to individual effort are more likely to see the relationship between their effort and their level of success. Therefore, many learners need help to see the correlation between effort and achievement. Marzano (2006) suggests that learners have the opportunity to reflect frequently on the amount of effort they put into a task and the results they achieve on that task.

Dweck (2010) states that learners are more likely to value effort if teachers emphasize challenge and not success. Learners must encounter meaningful learning tasks that challenge each learner in some way. The focus on challenge promotes a growth mindset as learners begin to realize that their ability increases over time as a result of their hard work. Creating a cycle of success based on meaningful work is critical if learning is to occur, but this does not mean lowering expectations. Learners who expect to succeed without effort are more likely to give up when they are asked to work hard. Tasks that lack challenge may foster a fixed-mindset belief with an expectation that being smart means doing something easily. Teachers hold the expectation that all learners will succeed by accomplishing meaningful and challenging tasks that are aligned to the goals of the unit. Differentiation greatly increases the chance of meeting individual learner needs as they work toward those goals.

Differentiated Instruction. Differentiation means tailoring instruction to meet individual needs. Whether teachers differentiate content, process, products, or the learning environment, the use of ongoing assessment and flexible grouping makes this a successful approach to instruction (Tomlinson, 1999). Based on Tomlinson's suggestions for differentiation, language teachers can differentiate:

CONTENT

- Using a variety of texts on a topic at different levels of complexity;
- Using images to accompany step-by-step instructions;
- Making available videos that explain new concepts for learners to view on their own time;
- Providing videos and websites related to the content of the unit;
- Supplying key vocabulary to accompany interpretive tasks;
- Supplying word banks when completing writing tasks;

PROCESS

- Offering the option for learners to work alone, in pairs, or small groups to complete a reading or writing practice assignment;
- Providing help sessions or tutors to work with learners individually or in small groups;
- Leading a "think aloud" to model the steps in reading a text;
- Varying the length of time to work on a task;

PRODUCTS

- Allowing learners to complete a task at their proficiency level;
- Letting learners choose the medium they will use to demonstrate that they have met the unit goal;

LEARNING ENVIRONMENT

- Creating a "help desk" bulletin board with suggestions of websites and other resources to practice the language;
- Organizing the resources in the classroom so that they are easily accessible to all learners;
- Providing quiet space to work without distractions; and
- Providing space for learners to work together in pairs or groups.

Motivation, self-efficacy, and differentiation are key pieces that inform decisions teachers must make about how to best support individual learners. All three require teachers to be thoughtful, recognizing that what applies to one learner is not likely to be true of another. Let's consider one additional factor that cannot be overlooked when planning for learning—the brain. How can we use what we know about how the brain learns to enhance learning?

Application of Brain-Based Learning Principles. Since teachers are trying to facilitate learning, they are in essence trying to change the brain every day. The more they know about how the brain learns, the more successful they can be (Sousa, 2006). Brain research provides insights into how individuals learn, when they are learning best, and their capacity for learning new items. The research also stresses how individuals move information from working memory into long-term memory, providing critical considerations for learning and retention. Careful attention to these concepts can enhance the effectiveness of a lesson and cause more students to meet the learning objectives of the individual lesson.

The brain seeks novelty, and an environment that contains mainly predictable or repeated stimuli lowers the brain's interest in the outside world and tempts it to turn within for novel sensations. Lessons that are not cognitively engaging almost always guarantee that some learners will look for other distractions and are more likely to attempt to text, to daydream, or disrupt others. Teachers who use multisensory activities during a learning episode are more likely to engage the learner, resulting in increased retention of new material (Sousa, 2006). Himmele and Himmele (2011) explain that a total-participation mindset is essential for ensuring high levels of learner engagement, and they stress that learning experiences need to be designed to be high cognition and high participation. Teachers who are engaged in facilitating the learner-centered multisensory classroom focus on lesson goals with an emphasis on what learners will do. Learners work in pairs, in groups, or alone depending on the task, and the classroom atmosphere is purposeful, noisy, and busy at appropriate times. Learners assess their own learning, and both learners and the teacher provide feedback (NCLRC, 2003).

Brain research suggests that teachers pay close attention to the primacy–recency effect, which states that individuals learn best what they learn first and last. Therefore, teachers should generally plan to do what is most important at the start of the lesson and should make certain to close lessons in ways that allow learners to consolidate their learning and demonstrate progress toward lesson objectives. Consequently, teachers should limit the amount of input given at one time by opting instead for a cycle of input followed by guided and independent practice. Subsequent cycles allow for additional input, followed again by guided and independent practice. Figure 9 suggests what a typical 20-minute cycle might look like in terms of a learning experience for an adolescent or adult.

The age of the learner also determines how much information can be processed at one time. Research suggests that the number of minutes involved in the cycle approximates the age of the learner, but a cycle never lasts more than 20 minutes. An adolescent or adult can normally process items in working memory intently for 10 to 20 minutes before mental fatigue or boredom occurs and the individual's focus drifts (Sousa, 2006; Curtain & Dahlberg, 2016). Schmoker (2011) suggests that teachers focus on working with small, ordered steps, allow time for thinking, and practice new learning by talking or writing. This deliberate process respects the limits of memory and average attention span and allows the learner to process the new information every few minutes. The lesson-planning template is designed so that teachers can plan an instructional sequence that is chunked in ways that allow learners to progress in small ordered steps, giving learners time to use new information as it might be used in the real world (Sousa, 2006). Frey and Fisher (2011) also advocate for an instructional framework that gradually shifts responsibility to learners. Lessons begin with a focus lesson, followed by guided instruction. During guided instruction the teacher has the opportunity to provide feedback while providing additional input. Learners are then given the opportunity to consolidate their understanding as they work with peers to apply new learning. Finally, each lesson includes an opportunity for learners to apply what they have learned on their own. As responsibility gradually shifts to the learner, learners are asked to demonstrate their understanding and are receiving feedback on their work. This cycle is often referred to as, "I do it," "We do it," "You do it together," and, "You do it alone." As learners are engaged in doing the work, the teacher is receiving feedback on how to adjust future lesson cycles or lessons. Although the concepts of primacy-recency and gradual release of responsibility serve as guidelines for making instructional decisions with regard to lesson format, it would be nearly impossible to follow a rigid structure, given the need to change and adapt to learners' needs during the lesson. As the lesson template is explained, we will explore the implications of this learning cycle in more detail.

Mindset for Lesson Plan Design

What Design Elements Should Be Considered When Planning a Lesson? A good lesson seems effortless, but its success is determined by how carefully an educator attends to those elements

Figure 9. Primacy–Recency Learning Cycle Adapted from Sousa (2006)

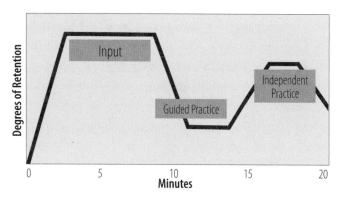

that provide structural support for the lesson while maximizing potential for learning. Three critical factors are:

- 90%+ use of target language;
- comprehensible input; and
- planning for transitions.

90%+ Use of Target Language. Learners come to our classes with an expectation that they will be able to use the language they are learning; our challenge as teachers is to create the classroom environment that will allow this to happen. ACTFL published a position statement stating that teachers and learners should use the target language at least 90% of the time at all levels of instruction during instructional time and, when feasible, beyond the classroom (ACTFL, July 2012). ACTFL's position statement reflects a well-established position in second language acquisition: Target language input and interaction are essential to acquisition and the development of communicative competencies. By setting the goal at 90% or more, ACTFL's position statement also recognizes that there are times when use of English may be beneficial to the learner (LeLoup, Ponterio, & Warford, 2013).

While the transition to a culture of teaching in the target language may prove to be challenging, it is critical that learners have the opportunity to hear and use the language purposefully throughout the class period. The decision to use English should be a conscious one with a clear pedagogical purpose. Experts in the field advocate for judicious use of English to avoid having learners feel that everything of "importance" will be stated in English (Curtain & Dahlberg, 2016). This means that teachers must be careful and systematic about what will be said in English. Limited translation to support comprehension of new vocabulary or structure can have a place, but it cannot be the routine, or learners will quickly realize that they can simply wait for the translation (LeLoup et al., 2013).

Adherence to the 90%+ guideline does mean that teachers have a few minutes each day when they can use English if necessary, and teachers may want to consider how they and learners will signal a switch from the target language to English. Some use signs designating the language that is to be spoken, and others require that both the teacher and learners ask for permission in the target language to use English before switching. Many advocate for using English only to establish lesson objectives, posting those Can-Do Statements in English and in the target language in the room in order to ensure that all learners understand what they are expected to be able to do. As learners advance in proficiency, those objectives are posted in the target language. Clementi (in Crouse, 2012) advocates for giving students articles on cultural topics to read in English as homework assignments to allow learners to explore cultural topics at a deeper cognitive level, so that the resulting target language discussions that occur in class can be held at a simpler linguistic level while still allowing for a deeper understanding of the topic.

Comprehensible Input. Consider how challenging it is to listen to a radio program in a language that you do not understand well. You are a motivated learner and are determined to improve your language skills, but you quickly realize that you are not able to maintain your focus. The same thing is likely to happen when watching a film in another language. Even the visuals can't hold your attention for long. This also happens when reading a text that is not comprehensible. Learners who encounter any type of text that is too challenging, including lectures or comments made by the teacher, are likely to give up in frustration. They hold low expectations for themselves, believing that they are incapable of processing the text. These low expectations develop as learners attempt to struggle with a text that is simply too challenging, and then they lose interest in the topic due to lack of comprehension. Lent (2012) identifies this as a cycle for failure. Stephen Krashen's Input Hypothesis states that acquisition occurs only when learners receive an optimal quantity of comprehensible input (i+1) (Shrum & Glisan, 2016).

Giving instructions for an activity is one area where teachers may be tempted to resort to English in order to save time and guarantee comprehension. Instead, the teacher may opt to use the target language at a level slightly beyond what learners understand (i+1), but model what is being said by engaging in the activity with a learner in front of the class. Learners are hearing the directions in the target language, but they are also being given visual support to make the language more comprehensible (LeLoup et al., 2013).

As teachers work to make input comprehensible, they need to remember that the key factor is to ascertain that learners can complete the task that accompanies the authentic text. Learners who are able to extract meaning from an authentic text will build confidence in their ability to work with authentic texts in order to complete meaningful tasks. Young children rarely understand every word that they encounter, but still attend to the message to get the main idea. Teachers may believe that if they revert to translation in an effort to make certain that learners understand everything, they are accelerating the learning process. In fact, this may cause a learner to be hindered in his ability to process a text that is of interest, but slightly beyond his comprehension level. Comprehensible input must not be confused with total comprehension. Even the youngest learner will sit on a parent's lap and listen to a story that is beyond what she can completely comprehend. In summary, input must be comprehensible, and it must be meaningful for learning to occur. As stated previously, use of the target language with attention to the learners' comprehension is a contributing factor to creating a classroom environment that is positive, productive, and pleasant. Table 22 provides a summary of visual, verbal, and non-verbal cues that may be used to make input more comprehensible (Fortune, 2012).

Table 22. Making Input Comprehensible (Fortune, 2012)

Visual Support	Verbal Cues	Non-verbal Cues
• Visuals and props • Graphics • Realia • Pictures • Graphic organizers	• Exaggerated pronunciation • Slower than normal speech • Purposeful pauses • Intonation or tone of voice • Slowed speech for emphasis • Key word emphasis and repetition • Paraphrasing (saying it in an easier way)	• Gestures • Facial expressions • Pantomime • Demonstration • Routines • Context clues

Lesson Transitions. One additional aspect of lesson planning is the need to manage transitions. There is no way to capture transitions on an actual lesson plan template. They occur at the start and end of class and at times during the lesson when there is a shift in learning activities. They occur when class is interrupted when the principal comes to the door with a question. The sample lesson plan has six transitions, and there could be more depending on adjustments that have to be made during the lesson. Managing transitions becomes a mindset for teachers, and can be the determining factor in whether a lesson proceeds smoothly or results in too much downtime with the teacher constantly having to bring the learners back to attention. Hunter and Hunter (2004) coined the term "sponge activities" to designate activities that would soak up the wasted minutes that could be used productively for review or reflection. These sponge activities allow teachers to use every available minute to reinforce learning. While it is possible to plan sponge activities that are lesson-specific, it is also possible

to work from a set of activities that can be easily adapted to meet any situation. Consider the following activities:

- Answer a question from different perspectives.
- Brainstorm as many words as you can for this image/concept.
- Complete a sentence frame.
- Complete an admit or exit slip.
- Draw and caption a summary.
- Interview your partner to find out (x).
- Provide definitions by using circumlocution.
- Read and identify the most important word or main idea.
- Read and write a title for (x).
- State your opinion of (x).
- Take turns describing (x).
- Think of three things to say about (x).
- Write a tweet that summarizes (x).
- Write a five-word description of the story.
- Write a question for a future quiz.
- Write questions you would like to ask.

Table 23 shows how sponge activities might be used to manage transitions in order to make every available minute count.

Table 23. Transition/Sponge Activities in the Classroom

The teacher says...	Learners:
While I take attendance...	Write two questions to find out how busy your partner is.
While I pass out the graphic organizer...	Think of ways to complete the following sentence, "I have fun when I..."
While I answer this student's question...	Engage in conversation to discuss weekend plans with your partner.
While I find the picture...	Tweet what you like to do.
We have one minute left...	Use circumlocution to see how many of the following words you can get your partner to say.

Lesson Plan Design

Backward Design. The lesson plan template that is used here is certainly not the only way to think through the lesson planning process, but it is designed to capture the more important concepts of a well-designed lesson by using the backward design process. Teachers:

- identify desired results by determining the objectives for the lesson;
- determine acceptable evidence and know how individual learners will provide that evidence; and
- plan learning experiences and instruction.

Identify desired results: The objectives for the daily lesson are derived from the unit goals. The lesson plan template begins the backward-design process by asking that the teacher refer back to the unit plan to make note of the unit theme and essential question. This ensures that the focus of the lesson is on the unit goals and begins the process of creating a clear focus for the lesson. This step is important to avoid creating a lesson that is just a series of activities designed to engage the learner. Learners in the classroom of a teacher who plans lessons by simply thinking through a list of activities might see a list such as the one that appears in Figure 10.

Figure 10. List of Activities

```
1. warm up
2. video and worksheet
3. write about picture
4. activities 3, 4, and 5
   (p. 260)
5. vocabulary game
6. homework
```

The agenda conveys the activities for the day, but it fails to state in clear terms what learners will be able to do with the language as a result of those activities. It's not enough to just use the language; the language must be used in ways that allow learners to make progress toward the daily communicative objective. Language educactors may find the following questions to be helpful when creating objectives or identifying desired results:

- Why are you doing this activity? What is the purpose?
- What will learners be able to do as a result of the lesson that they couldn't do at the start of the lesson?
- Does this objective require learners to use language as it is used in the real world?

All lessons must have clear learning objectives to ensure that meaningful learning and effective teaching occur. Learners need to know how they will know when they have achieved the daily objective and how they will demonstrate their learning. Once the daily objectives or Can-Do Statements have been determined, they are:

- posted so that learners can see the objectives throughout the lesson;
- referenced so that learners are continually aware of what they are supposed to be able to do; and

- assessed so that the learners know where they are with regard to the objectives.

Determine acceptable evidence. Planning a lesson requires that educators think like assessors (Wiggins & McTighe, 1998). As assessors, educators select activities that allow learners to demonstrate their progress toward specific lesson objectives. Both educators and learners know how they will measure progress toward those objectives. The following questions may be helpful when deciding the type of evidence that will measure individual learning:

- What is sufficient proof that learners are meeting the daily objectives?
- What will I ask learners to do that will provide concrete evidence of who really understands?
- How will each individual learner know that they have met the lesson objective before the end of class?
- What are available tools that can help me document learner progress more precisely and efficiently?

Educators who design effective lessons make a conscientious effort throughout the lesson to ensure that all learners are progressing in each segment of the lesson before moving on to the next one. The educator continually conducts formative assessment at each stage of the lesson to see how learners are progressing. Strategies that elicit performance in each mode while checking for understanding include:

Interpretive
- Acting out or drawing the sequence of events or scene that is described.
- Identifying and explaining the most important word or sentence.
- Signaling—thumbs up/thumbs down, true/false.
- Signaling by using web-based tools such as Poll Everywhere.

Interpersonal
- Calling on a sampling of learners randomly to ask/answer a question.
- Exchanging information in line-up or inner–outer circle.
- Using the strategy of think–pair–share, think–write–pair–share.

Presentational
- Creating an A–Z word list on a topic.
- Completing an exit slip.
- Processing using quick write or quick draw.

- Responding to a question according to an assigned number (numbered heads together).
- Responding in a journal.
- Writing responses on dry erase boards.

These constant checks for understanding provide critical feedback to the learner, while allowing educators to determine what is needed later in the lesson or in subsequent lessons. Learners benefit from lessons that are focused on clear learning objectives and those that are delivered in short instructional "chunks" or segments punctuated by multiple cycles of guided practice and formative assessment. The cycle of guided practice with multiple checks for understanding allows learners to know how well they are meeting lesson objectives (Marzano, 2007; Schmoker 2011). Learners provide evidence of and assess their own learning and are therefore better prepared for subsequent lessons. Refer back to Figure 9 to see how the primacy–recency learning cycle supports the cycle of input, guided practice, and formative assessment.

Plan learning experiences and instruction. Teachers may be tempted to plan by selecting activities with the sole purpose of making class more enjoyable. Injecting an element of fun into a lesson is important, but this must also be purposeful, helping learners build their communication skills. For example, a teacher may decide that she wants learners to work with new vocabulary and decides on a game of bingo or flyswatter. These games are fun and may help learners acquire vocabulary, but they cannot be played in isolation. They need to be connected directly to other activities that ask the learners to use vocabulary that they practiced in the game for meaningful communication. If, during a game, learners practiced vocabulary related to what you see on a street from the target culture, they might work in pairs, each person with a slightly different image of a street scene. They must ask and answer questions about similarities and differences between the images in an information gap activity. Learners use the new vocabulary in a context

where that vocabulary might be used in real-life situations, and the activities become "minds-on" rather than merely "hands-on." The following questions may be helpful when determining learning experiences:

- How will the activities I've chosen address the lesson objectives?
- Do I have the resources I need to support lesson objectives?
- "What do I know about language learning in general that leads me to believe that my choices will be effective?" (Duncan & Met, 2010, p. 8)

Each lesson is structured so that teachers and learners focus on the daily lesson objectives. They require teachers to reflect and consider carefully what the next steps will be to advance learning, while recognizing that not all learners will advance at the same rate.

Planning for Instruction. Table 24 provides a summary of what might occur at each stage of backward design, showing this teacher has a clear understanding of what learners in her classroom are expected to be able to do by the end of the lesson.

Learners know that they will watch a video, and they understand what they are supposed to do as a result of that activity. They understand that they will talk about balance in terms of their lives (*identify desired results*). Learners will demonstrate comprehension of new vocabulary by classifying their daily activities as obligations or options and will then write individually about their lives (*determine acceptable evidence*). Finally, a specific learning experience is described, showing how learners will begin to acquire the skills needed (*plan learning experiences*). There is a clear connection between the activities and the way the teacher is checking for understanding. This lesson vignette also illustrates how formative assessments take place when the learners create individual charts with obligations, pair to discuss the charts, pair to classify the activities, and

Table 24. Lesson Plan Summary Showing Elements of Backward Design

Lesson Element	Application in lesson:
Daily objectives	Learners can: • name obligations and optional activities that create balance in daily life based on authentic video *Ma Vie au Soleil* (My Life in the Sun); and • ask and answer questions about what they do to create balance in their lives.
Learning activities	Learners create an individual chart of obligations and optional activities. They pair to discuss what is on each chart and to determine who has the more balanced lifestyle.
Checks for understanding	Learners work in pairs to classify activities as obligations or optional activities. Individually, learners write simple sentences that convey obligations and optional activities.

write simple sentences about those activities. A more detailed lesson plan will be presented later in this chapter.

Lesson Planning. Lesson planning is where theory and good ideas meet the demands of individual learners in the classroom. Each lesson is a carefully sequenced set of tasks designed to allow learners to reach the targeted learning objectives of that lesson. Writing a lesson plan is like putting a complicated jigsaw puzzle together. The picture on the box shows you the final result, but the pieces have to be sorted, manipulated, and nudged into place. Teachers might think that they have their plan perfectly organized, but all teachers know that learners have a way of causing a change in plans at any given moment for a multitude of reasons. It is the well-prepared teacher who can easily abandon one plan in favor of another in such a way that learners still meet the targeted objectives.

The Lesson Template

The lesson plan template is a tool for organizing thinking. It allows a teacher to identify the learning objectives of the lesson, indicating activities that connect clearly to the stated objectives. The individual lesson becomes part of a plan for meeting unit goals. The intent of such a plan is to allow teachers to develop a way of thinking that will support student learning. Table 25 on the following page shows a completed lesson plan for *A Balanced Lifestyle*. The lesson plan is divided into sections, and each section will be explained in detail in the narrative that follows the lesson plan. Although it may be tempting to read quickly through the lesson plan, we believe that it will be more beneficial to read each section of the narrative for the information and examples that will be provided. Then pause to consider a lesson that you would like to develop and begin to draft that lesson as each component part of the lesson plan is presented. You may also wish to print or download a copy of the blank template (Appendix K), which is also available online at www.actfl.org.

Section A: Initial Steps in Lesson Plan

Section A of the lesson plan template shown in Table 25 is designed to provide an overview to the lesson and to place the lesson in the context of a specific unit. Specific lesson objectives are stated, and the modes of communication that will be stressed during the lesson are identified. The lesson objectives may come directly from the unit goals, or teachers may find it necessary to unpack the unit goals into more manageable steps. Each lesson has clear communicative and cultural objectives in one or more of the modes of communication. The communicative and cultural objectives allow for the integration of the other goal areas—Connections, Comparisons, and Communities—as appropriate to each lesson. Like the thematic unit template, the lesson plan template also provides an opportunity to connect an individual lesson to other Standards.

The sample lesson plan shown here is for the second day of the unit *A Balanced Lifestyle*. The first day of any given unit is designed to hook the learners, to frame the unit, and increase student interest in the topic. Day One of this unit might focus on headlines that deal with quality of life or with short media clips conveying information about lifestyle balance. Learners may complete a quick poll to determine the percentage of the class who feel stressed before looking at data on the number of teens from other countries reporting that they feel stressed. Using the first day of a unit in this way also allows a teacher to activate prior knowledge and allows learners to make connections to their own lives and to what they are learning in other disciplines. It can also be a day where learners generate questions addressing topics of interest to them, allowing them to become more engaged in the unit of study. Allowing learners to ask questions activates their curiosity, giving them more control over their own learning.

> ✅ **Pause to consider Section A of your lesson plan.** Complete the fields that come from the unit plan. What are the lesson objectives? Do they reflect real-world communication? How does this lesson connect to other standards? You may find it easier to return to certain fields as you plan the lesson details.

Table 25. The Lesson Template

Section A: *Initial Steps in Lesson Plan*

Target	Novice Mid/ High	Grade	9-12	Date	xxx	Day in Unit	2	Minutes	50

Theme/Topic	**Contemporary Life:** A Balanced Lifestyle
Essential Question	*How do people here and in (the French-speaking world) describe a balanced lifestyle?*
Daily Topic	Subway, work, sleep – *Métro, boulot, dodo*

STANDARDS			LESSON OBJECTIVES
What are the communicative and cultural objectives for the lesson?	**Communication *and* Cultures**	*Which modes of communication will be addressed?* ✔ Interpersonal ✔ Interpretive ☐ Presentational	**Learners can:** • Name obligations and activities that create balance in daily life based on authentic video *Ma Vie au Soleil* (My Life in the Sun). • Ask and answer questions about what they do to create balance in their lives.
If applicable, indicate how this lesson connects to other standards.	**Connections**		
	Comparisons		Language: *métro, boulot, dodo* (subway, work, sleep)
	Communities		
	Other Standards		**Common Core: Speaking and Listening (SL1)** Prepare for and participate effectively in a range of conversations and collaborations with diverse partners, building on others' ideas and expressing their own clearly and persuasively.

Section B: *Gain Attention/Activate Prior Knowledge*

Lesson Sequence	Activity/Activities What will learners do? What does the teacher do?	Time How many minutes will this segment take?	Materials/Resources/Technology Be specific. What materials will you develop? What materials will you bring in from other sources?
Gain Attention/ Activate Prior Knowledge	• The teacher displays a variety of images depicting wellness and stress. • Learners look at the images and list activities that they consider to be chores or obligations, as well as those that are done by choice or are of interest.	5	• Images depicting wellness/stress • Images of various activities, preferably images that learners have used in previous units

Section C: *Provide Input (Cycle 1)*

Provide Input	• Learners are given a set of statements concerning the video content. • The teacher reads each statement, taking time to develop comprehension. • Learners are asked if they agree or disagree with the statements. • Learners are asked to find proof for or against each statement as they work with the video. The video is shown first without sound. Learners have time to individually note proof for and against based on visual images. • Learners also list any words they expect to hear in the video.	10	• Video *Ma Vie au Soleil* (My Life in the Sun) • Proof for/proof against activity page.

Section D: *Elicit Performance and Provide Feedback (Cycle 1)*

Elicit Performance/ Provide Feedback	• Learners indicate by signaling thumbs up or down if they have proof for or against each statement after watching the video. • They pair to share their comments on proof for/proof against statements. They compare their ideas with their partner's and each adds details to their individual lists. • The teacher asks two or three learners to share their responses and then calls on volunteers. • The teacher then asks learners to share words or phrases that they anticipate hearing in the video based on what they saw.	10	

Section E: *Provide Input, Elicit Performance and Provide Feedback (Cycle 2)*

Provide Input	• The teacher introduces the concept of *métro, boulot, dodo* (subway, work, sleep). • Learners watch the video for a second time, with sound on, identifying words on their lists that connect to the concept of going to work or working. • The teacher shares a prepared list of activities drawing from those in the video and from those suggested by learners during the warm-up. Learners review and learn new sentence and question frames—What do you do? I do/don't…, Do you like…? I like/don't like…, Do you want? I want/don't want…, Do you have to…? I have to, don't have to—while working with the list of activities.	10	• Images depicting *métro, boulot, dodo* (subway, work, sleep) • Prepared list of activities based on video
Elicit Performance/ Provide Feedback	• Learners work individually to complete a graphic organizer, writing simple sentences about things they do that relate to the routine of work and things they do for fun. • Learners pair and rotate in inner-outer circles to see what they have in common.	10	• Graphic organizer – work, fun, and overlap for both

Section F: *Assess Performance/Closure*

Closure	Learners are given an image of *métro, boulot, dodo* (subway, work, sleep). They write down any words or sentences that they associate with the images. These are collected and may be used as future prompts for discussion.	5	• Image representative of *métro, boulot, dodo* (subway, work, sleep)

Section G: *Enhance Retention and Transfer*

Enhance Retention & Transfer	• Learners consider the concept of balance in their lives. They take an online quiz, *Test your stress smarts*. They consider how they might comment on their results in French in class. • Alternatively, learners read part of an online article about health and well-being of teens around the world. They consider how they might share some of what they learned in French in class.		• Articles or references in English or French to enhance awareness of the importance of a balanced lifestyle

Section H: *Reflection/Notes to Self*

Reflection/ Notes to Self	• What worked well? Why? • What didn't work? Why? • What changes would you make if you taught this lesson again?

Section B: Gain Attention/Activate Prior Knowledge. Begin by presenting and posting the daily objectives so that learners know what they are expected to be able to do by the end of the lesson. Posting the daily objectives in English and the target language ensures that all learners clearly understand the objectives. Ideally, the answer to the common question, "What did you do in class today?" would be, "I learned to…." and learners would restate a version of the objectives.

The first few minutes of a lesson are critical in terms of how learners will engage. The primacy–recency cycle is shown again in Figure 11 as a reminder that learners learn best what happens first. Figure 11 also shows the connections between the stages of the lesson plan template and the primacy–recency learning cycle by giving an indication of the amount of time that would ideally be spent on each part of the lesson. This is a learning cycle that can be repeated multiple times within a lesson depending on the length of the lesson. The sample lesson is for a 50-minute class, and two learning cycles will be presented for this particular lesson.

Figure 11. Primacy–Recency and Connection to Gain Attention/Activate Prior Knowledge, Provide Input, and Elicit Performance and Provide Feedback

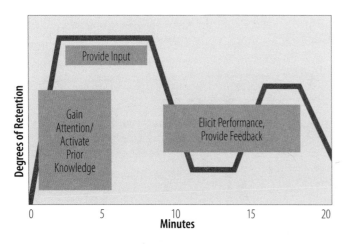

The brain does not process all of the stimuli that it encounters. Therefore, teachers must strive to capture or "hook" the learner's attention using the opening activity or "warm-up" to set the stage for what will follow. Table 25 shows how this lesson is designed to gain the attention of the learners while activating prior knowledge. Lesson activities are written primarily in terms of what learners will do, there is an indication of how long the activity might take, and finally, the materials needed are listed.

The lesson for Day Two of *A Balanced Lifestyle* begins with images designed to capture the interest of the learners. Prior knowledge is activated when learners generate previously learned vocabulary that connects in some way to those images. As learners become invested in the images and react to the activities, they are more likely to pay close attention since the material is meaningful to them (Willis, 2006). Because the first few minutes of class are so important, it can be helpful to remember to begin class with an activity that:

- gains the attention of the learner;
- engages each learner;
- is doable and achievable as a warm-up, takes no more than five minutes; and
- connects in some way to what will happen next.

Since the beginning of class is prime learning time, avoid beginning class by:

- collecting or checking homework;
- holding individual conferences with learners while other learners wait to begin;
- passing back papers while learners settle in and talk; or
- starting a class with administrative duties.

The warm-up activity sets the stage for what follows, and learners will use the images and the vocabulary that they have generated in other parts of the lesson. This ensures that the working memory of learners is not overloaded prior to the introduction of new material (Sousa, 2006).

Section C: Provide Input (Cycle 1). The primacy–recency cycle in Figure 11 shows that learners are most attentive and learn best at the beginning of the learning cycle, and it is where teachers should do what they believe to be most important. Teachers may find it helpful to ask the question, "What is the most important thing that I intend to do today to enhance learning?" The activities selected for this part of the lesson reflect the answer to that question.

The sample lesson plan incorporates the video *Ma Vie au Soleil* (My Life in the Sun) by Keen'V to introduce the theme of the unit. Learners see a businessman who is tired of work and abandons that lifestyle in favor of life on an island. Table 25 outlines what teachers and learners do during the input part of the lesson. The input portion of the sample lesson begins by using an authentic text. Authentic texts provide insights into the target culture and allow learners to process correct models of language in a real-world context. Unfortunately, teachers may dismiss authentic texts, thinking they are too challenging for learners even though this is not a key consideration in selecting texts in one's first language. Consider choosing a book for a young child. Imagine that the child has a deep interest in dinosaurs even though she is not yet reading. You would not pick up a book only to set it aside because the vocabulary was too complex or because a certain grammar structure appeared in the text. Instead, you would select a text that is interesting and use a variety of strategies to make the information comprehensible. Identify texts that allow learners to be immersed in the language by listening, reading, and/or viewing, that are intrinsically interesting, cognitively engaging, culturally connected, and communicatively purposeful. Zyzik and Polio (2017) caution that learners cannot be motivated by texts that they do not understand, even if they are of high interest. They state that it is not the authentic text that is in and of itself motivating. Rather, it is the process of understanding the text that builds confidence and results in increased motivation. When selecting authentic texts, look for a text that is accessible to the learners, but do not have an expectation that learners need to understand everything. The key is to create tasks that allow learners to interact with the text in meaningful ways.

In this lesson learners will be asked to process the text first by interpreting the visuals without hearing or reading the actual text. They will consider what they see in terms of the proof for/proof against statements that they have discussed before seeing the video. Based on what they see, they will note proof for and against each statement. They will also make note of any vocabulary that they believe they will hear when the video is played with sound.

Section D: Elicit Performance/Provide Feedback (Cycle 1). Learners need time to process and apply the information that was shared during the input part of the lesson. A key feature of effective lessons is the conscientious effort that is made by the teacher throughout the lesson to ensure that all learners are meeting the objectives of each segment of the lesson before moving on to the next segment. As learners practice, the teacher conducts formative assessment by checking to see that learners are able to demonstrate their learning (Schmoker, 2011). This segment of the lesson plan is designed to allow learners to apply what they are learning in meaningful ways. As learners process new learning, teachers monitor and provide feedback on individual performance. Input followed by performance and feedback creates a cycle of guided practice and checking for understanding (Marzano 2007). Practice is likely to be more effective if teachers use strategies that allow

learners to demonstrate individual learning. The following questions may be helpful when selecting activities:

- Does the activity ask each individual learner to contribute equally?
- Is there a way to assess individual learner performance at the end of the activity or by the end of the lesson?
- In the Interpretive Mode, do learners have a guided task to complete as they read, listen, or view individually and silently?
- In the Interpersonal Mode, are learners given the opportunity to speak or write without rehearsing?
- In the Presentational Mode, do learners have the chance to write their own thoughts before and/or after sharing with others?

At this stage of the lesson the teacher has presented a small amount of material, allowing the learners to think and process that material individually before working with a partner to extend their learning by talking and writing about the new material. The focus is off the teacher and on what learners are able to do with the language. The teacher has a chance to gauge where learners are and what they may need before the next step in the lesson. This mid-lesson feedback is critical since it allows learners to work to achieve the lesson objective and then to receive information that lets them know if they are on track or need to make adjustments. With clear objectives, learners are more likely to seek and listen to feedback. They will know what they know and what they don't know (Brookhart, 2012; Hattie, 2012; Wiggins, 2012). In summary, effective lessons incorporate small, ordered steps; periodic thinking reviews; and practice by talking or writing.

Learners have only seen the video without sound at this point in the lesson. The teacher does a quick thumbs up/thumbs down to see if learners have found proof for or against the statements that were presented before seeing the video. Before sharing as a whole class, learners work with partners to compare results and exchange evidence for and against based on what was seen in the video. The teacher first asks a few students who did not volunteer and then a few students who volunteer, asking them all to share their evidence in support for or against each statement. Finally, the teacher asks students to share words and phrases that they expect to hear in the video. Section D of Table 25 provides details about what teachers do to elicit performance so the learner can receive feedback on that performance.

> ✔ **Pause to consider the first learning cycle of your lesson plan.** How will you start the lesson? What is most important in terms of lesson objectives? What will learners do to work with the new material? How will you structure an activity to allow for feedback?

The first learning cycle—gaining attention/activating prior knowledge, providing input, eliciting performance, and providing feedback has been completed at this point in the lesson. Since this is a 50-minute class, there is time for an additional learning cycle that begins with another opportunity for input. It's not necessary to repeat the "gain attention" aspect of the lesson, because this is often accomplished by changing the type of work that learners will do.

Section E: Provide Input, Elicit Performance, and Provide Feedback (Cycle 2). The lesson plan continues with a second cycle of input, performance, and feedback. In this lesson, learners will again work in the Interpretive Mode initially, but will then move to the Interpersonal Mode to discuss personal opinions. After seeing the video for the second time, there is a short period of direct instruction that connects to the objective of the lesson. Direct instruction is still a critical component of a lesson when a teacher needs to present new information. This lesson template allows for direct instruction, but also recognizes the need to pause frequently to allow learners to process and use the new information in meaningful ways.

The teacher begins the second input cycle by explaining the concept of *"métro, boulot, dodo"* (subway, work, sleep) using visual images. The learners then watch the video with sound and make note of words on the lists they created earlier in the lesson that relate to the concept of work. The teacher then introduces sentence and question frames that learners will use to discuss what they do. They will discuss the activities that they worked with at the beginning of class by asking and responding to questions about what they like, want, and have to do. Section E of Table 25 describes the second cycle of input.

Elicit Performance/Provide Feedback. It is important that the second input stage is followed by another opportunity for learners to again have a chance to apply what they are learning while receiving feedback.

Learners work individually to complete a graphic organizer stating what they do for fun and for work. They then have the opportunity to move, forming inner–outer circles so that they can rotate and discuss their activities using newly acquired question-and-answer patterns with random partners. Section E of Table 25 also shows how learners move from input to performance as they demonstrate their understanding of the new material.

> ✔ **Pause to consider the second learning cycle of your lesson plan.** What additional input do learners need? How will they use what they are learning? How will you monitor learning and provide feedback?

Section F: Assess Performance/Closure. The teacher was able to assess learner performance on the second objective of the lesson during the inner–outer circle discussions. That discussion activity provided an opportunity for formative assessment on the daily objective: "Ask and answer questions about what they do to create balance in their lives." As learners engaged with multiple partners, the teacher had the opportunity to help individuals or to listen for common problems that could be addressed in the next lesson. The last part of the lesson is designed to capture information on how well each individual learner met the first objective of the lesson.

Section F of Table 25 describes the closure activity that addresses the second objective requiring learners to write words and phrases that they associate with an image. In the last few minutes of class, learners are asked to write any words, phrases, or sentences that they associate with the visual that was shared earlier depicting, *"métro, boulot, dodo"* (subway, work, sleep). These exit slips are collected from each learner, allowing the teacher to see who has met the daily objective: "Name obligations and activities that create balance in daily life."

Section G: Enhance Retention and Transfer. We have elected not to use the word homework as a label for this section in an effort to call attention to the fact that work done outside of class serves a specific purpose. Homework is most often a way to reinforce the learning that occurred in class, while giving learners the opportunity to demonstrate that they are able to apply what they have learned to other situations. It is important that both teachers and learners agree that this work is appropriate and purposeful. As such, homework is an opportunity for formative assessment allowing learners to demonstrate that they are able to apply what they have learned in class.

Since teachers have been assessing and monitoring learner performance throughout class, they need to decide near the end of the lesson what learners could do to reinforce and possibly extend the objectives of the lesson. Vatterott (2009) explains that there are four purposes for homework: pre-learning, checking for understanding, practice, or processing. When homework is given as a pre-learning activity, the work serves to introduce the topic or may be given to stimulate interest in the topic. It may be used to find out what learners already know and may invite learners to create questions that they have about the topic. It may also be used as preparation for the next day of learning. A teacher may challenge learners to be ready to do a specific task when they enter class the next day: "Be ready to identify three things you do to keep balance in your life." Checking for understanding is a valuable way to gauge learning and is a critical step before learners move to practice. Practice has traditionally been the most common reason for giving homework. There is danger in this type of homework if it is assigned before the teacher has proof that learners understand the new learning. Learners may become frustrated and fail to complete the homework, or they may complete the homework following an incorrect pattern. The repetition of an incorrect answer may cause students to "learn" that answer as though it were a correct response. Finally, processing homework allows learners to extend their learning in new ways. Learners apply what they have learned to new situations or extend their own learning through enrichment opportunities. Often this type of work is a short- or long-term project, which may be the presentational performance assessment task for the standards-based unit.

Section G in Table 25 gives two options for extending learning. The sample lesson plan uses homework as a pre-learning activity by suggesting that learners do some reading in English in order to have a better understanding of the issues that relate to a balanced lifestyle. They will take a personal stress test and are asked to consider comparisons on the health and well-being of teens from around the world. As teachers strive to use the target language at least 90% of the time in class, there is a need to find ways to engage learners at higher cognitive levels when dealing with topics that may be new to them. There is also a need to find ways to allow learners to explore content and culture at the appropriate cognitive level. Using English outside of the classroom is one way to meet this goal. Learners are being given the chance to enhance their understanding of the topic by accessing information in English at home. They are taking responsibility for their own learning and are doing work that

may have previously been done in class, thus increasing the amount of class time that is available for interaction with peers in the target language. This type of assignment meets tenets of the flipped classroom (Bergmann, Overmyer, & Wilie, 2012). Alternatively, learners could have been asked to apply what they learned during the lesson by using the target language to:

- check for understanding by expanding the visual representation of *métro*, *boulot*, *dodo* (subway, work, sleep), adding words and/or images that captured elements of their personal lifestyle;
- practice by working with the graphic organizer started during class and using that information to create sentences describing their work-related and fun activities; or
- process by writing questions they might ask on a future survey to determine how balanced the lifestyles of their peers in another country are.

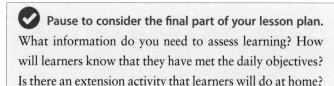 **Pause to consider the final part of your lesson plan.** What information do you need to assess learning? How will learners know that they have met the daily objectives? Is there an extension activity that learners will do at home?

Section H: Reflection/Notes to Self. Teachers encounter numerous decision points as they plan and deliver lessons. Danielson (2009) points out that many decisions teachers make become routine and that those decisions are made quickly and automatically based on previous experience. She also states that there are other times when teachers benefit from the opportunity to step back and self-reflect in order to address more substantive issues. It would be impossible to reflect on all of the questions that follow for each lesson. Instead, select those questions that seem most appropriate in order to develop the habit of reflection or draft a question that captures what you want to focus on in any given lesson.

- What worked well? What didn't work? How do you know?
- How would you adapt this lesson, or how did you adapt this lesson during the day if it was taught more than once? Why would you make or did you make those changes?
- Did all learners learn? How do you know? What will you do to adapt for those who are not learning?
- Consider some of the key factors in lesson planning as you reflect on/revise the lesson. How was the lesson:
  - goal focused?

- learner-centered?
- brain-based?
  - How did the lesson provide opportunities for:
    - critical thinking and problem solving?
    - creativity?
    - collaboration?
    - communication?
    - assessment/feedback?
  - How was this lesson part of a unit that is:
    - communicatively purposeful?
    - culturally focused?
    - intrinsically interesting?
    - cognitively engaging?
    - standards-based?

The Busy Educator's Planbook

Educators have very limited time to write such detailed lessons on a consistent basis, but all educators benefit by engaging in the process from time to time. Detailed planning makes the process more routine and allows teachers to create their own shorthand that conveys a powerful lesson in a few words. Figure 12 shows what might appear in the lesson plan book of an experienced educator. When asked for detail, this teacher would be able to give significant detail, explaining all that went into the design of what looks to be a simple plan.

Figure 11. Educator Plan Book

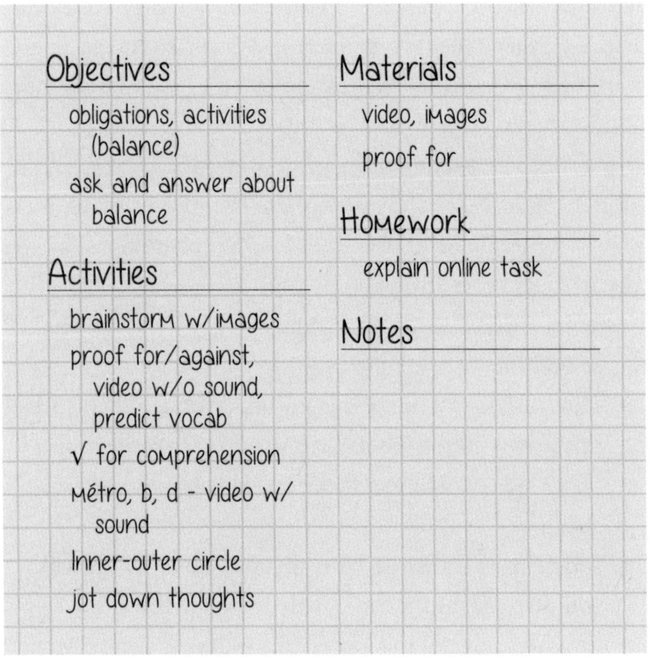

Additional Sample Lesson Plan

A lesson titled Agriculture in China's Regions is part of a unit guided by the question: *"How does where I live influence what I eat?"* (Appendix L). The lesson allows learners to communicate primarily in the Interpersonal Mode as they focus on the regions and agricultural products found in China. It is an example from a series of 30-minute lessons written for a third grade classroom with novice learners, and we have included it here to give an example of how this template might apply to an elementary content-related classroom. Notice that with the shorter class period, there is only one learning cycle of gain attention, provide input, elicit performance, and provide feedback.

Summary. Each day, educators interact with learners as individuals, manage the classroom, design learning experiences that allow learners to meet lesson objectives, and devise strategies that allow for feedback. Most educators are thinking constantly, making countless instructional decisions throughout the lesson. The lesson plan template presented in this chapter is designed to help busy educators organize their lessons in ways that help all learners achieve the lesson objectives. In Chapter Four, we will discuss assessment *of* and *for* learning.

Application

1. A new teacher has come to you concerned because she is always running out of time to finish her lesson plan. What questions would you ask? What strategies might you suggest to help her out?
2. Administration has just asked that all instructors avoid doing homework-related activities at the beginning of class. What information would you share with colleagues who are resistant to this change?

Reflection

1. What am I doing to promote learning goals that address integrative or assimilative motivation? What do I say when learners state that they are taking the class because it is required for college?
2. What are the benefits of applying the primacy–recency learning cycle in my lessons?
3. What aspects of the lesson-planning template do I consider when planning lessons?
4. How might I use some of the strategies presented in this chapter to involve learners more in the learning process, thus making the class more learner-centered?

Chapter 4 | Assessment of and for Learning

Self-assessment is essential for progress as a learner; for understanding of selves as learners, for an increasingly complex understanding of tasks and learning goals, and for strategic knowledge of how to go about improving.

— D.R. Sadler

How Do We Document and Assess Learning?

With curriculum, unit, and lesson planning aligned to the overarching goal of building learners' Intercultural Communicative Competence, assessments of and for learning must also be aligned to this goal. Wiggins and McTighe define assessment in *Understanding by Design, Expanded 2nd Edition* (2005): "Assessment is the giving and using of feedback against standards to enable improvement and the meeting of goals" (p. 6). Formative and summative assessments must be designed with the mindset that these assessments provide evidence of progress in understanding and communicating respectfully in the target language. You may be wondering how to determine if the assessments you design target the appropriate level of challenge and proficiency for your classes. The response is a combination of your professional judgment and the following ACTFL resources:

- ACTFL Proficiency Guidelines
- NCSSFL-ACTFL Can-Do Statements
- ACTFL Performance Descriptors for Language Learners: Parameters and Qualities of Performance

Let's discuss each of these resources and how they guide the design of assessments.

ACTFL Proficiency Guidelines: The ACTFL Proficiency Guidelines (Appendix B) provide a detailed explanation of what a language user can and cannot do at each proficiency level— Novice, Intermediate, Advanced, Superior, Distinguished— regardless of where, when, or how the language was acquired. The Proficiency Guidelines serve as the pathway of growth in communication skills for language learners. The ACTFL Proficiency Pyramid (Figure 13) visually represents this pathway,

showing how, as learners move from Novice to Superior levels of proficiency, the pathway widens to accommodate the increasing number of topics that the learners can discuss, and deepens to accommodate the increasing complexity of the language.

Figure 13. ACTFL Proficiency Pyramid

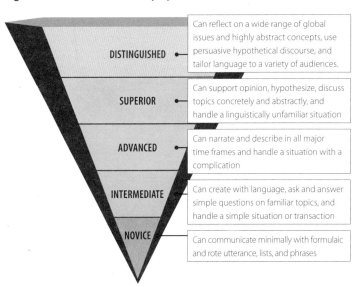

Novice learners use words, phrases, and short memorized sentences and questions to communicate about very familiar topics. Intermediate learners begin to create with language, expressing their thoughts and ideas in strings of sentences; they gradually increase the number of topics they can discuss and the amount of detail they can provide. Advanced learners are "storytellers," as they express their ideas and provide rich details in paragraph-length narration. Although the Proficiency Guidelines include Superior and Distinguished levels, for the purposes of this publication, we are focusing on Novice, Intermediate, and Advanced levels of proficiency.

NCSSFL-ACTFL Can-Do Statements. The NCSSFL-ACTFL Can-Do Statements (Appendix F) align with the ACTFL Proficiency Guidelines but are written in language that is accessible to learners. The Can-Do Statements convey what learners can understand and produce in the language they are learning at the Novice, Intermediate, Advanced, Superior, and Distinguished levels in the Interpersonal, Interpretive, and Presentational Modes of communication. As outlined in Chapter One, the NCSSFL-ACTFL Can-Do Statements are designed especially for the language learner. Sharing the Can-Do Statements with learners as they begin their sequence of language study helps them understand how their abilities to understand and communicate in the language they are learning will increase with practice over time from the single words and short memorized sentences of a beginner all the way to sophisticated presentations on abstract concepts by a highly accomplished speaker. The Can-Do Statements help learners set realistic personal goals related to what they want to be able to understand and say in the language they are learning, and then self-assess their progress toward achieving those goals. Learning a language is like learning to play a musical instrument or a sport. It takes time and consistent, meaningful practice to improve.

The NCSSFL-ACTFL Can-Do document serves as a resource to help both learners and teachers write specific Can-Do Statements for each unit of instruction. Each mode and level includes sample Can-Do Statements for a variety of programs, including immersion, K–8 programs, high school, and post-secondary programs. Using these sample statements, learners and teachers can write level-appropriate Can-Do Statements to reflect the theme and topic that they are studying. Let's use the example of a unit about a balanced lifestyle to show the relationship between the model statements and the "customized" ones for this unit. The essential question is: "*How do people here and in the French-speaking world describe a balanced lifestyle?*" The Can-Do Statements are modeled after Can-Do Statements written for Novice Mid/Novice High learners. Table 26 shows the Performance Indicator, the Examples of Can-Do Statements based on the Proficiency Benchmarks, and the "customized" versions for the balanced lifestyles unit. Notice that some of the Can-Do Statements are at the Novice

Table 26. Model Can-Do Statements and "Customized" for Balanced Lifestyle Unit

MODE	Level & Performance Indicator	Examples of Can-Do Statements	"Customized" Can-Do Statement Based on the Example
Interpretive	**Novice High** I can understand familiar questions and statements from simple sentences in conversations.	I can understand questions about someone's social schedule.	I can understand when French teenagers talk about their daily routines in France.
Presentational	**Novice High** I can present on familiar and everyday topics, using simple sentences most of the time.	I can present basic information about things I have learned using phrases and simple sentences.	I can present information comparing lifestyles in France and the U.S.
	Novice Mid I can present information about myself, my interests, and my activities using a mixture of practiced or memorized words, phrases, and simple sentences.	I can list my classes or work activities and tell what time they start and end.	I can keep a diet and exercise journal to track what I do to stay healthy.
Interpersonal	**Novice Mid** I can request and provide information by asking and answering a few simple questions on very familiar and everyday topics using a mixture of practiced or memorized words, phrases, and simple sentences.	I can ask and answer questions about school, food, or hobbies in an online conversation.	I can compare my diet and exercise routines to those of a French teenager.
Interpersonal	**Novice High** I can request and provide information by asking and answering practiced and some original questions on familiar and everyday topics using simple sentences most of the time.	I can exchange information about things to do in my town.	I can ask and answer questions about what people do each day to be healthy.

Mid level, and some are at the Novice High level because the unit is written for Novice Mid/Novice High learners. All Can-Do statements suggest appropriate communication tasks to meet the targeted performance level.

We remind teachers and learners that the Can-Do Statements are not meant to be checked off based on a single performance in a single unit. Learners need to provide multiple examples of successfully completed tasks at a targeted level from a variety of units to demonstrate solid performance at that level.

Teachers may find that the complete NCSSFL-ACTFL Can-Do Proficiency Benchmarks, Performance Indicators, and Examples found at the ACTFL website under Publications is useful, not only for learners, but also when working with parents and administrators. It makes clear that communication skills are multidimensional, involving Interpretive listening and reading, Presentational speaking and writing, and Interpersonal two-way interactions. The examples that follow the Performance Indicators are designed to show that a learner may have, for example, stronger listening skills than writing skills, and that all of the skills develop over time.

A portfolio, either electronic or paper, gives learners a tool to monitor their language learning progress and set appropriate goals for continued progress. One model designed specifically for world language learners is LinguaFolio®, which is an online portfolio based on the NCSSFL-ACTFL Can-Do Statements. Research conducted by Moeller, Theiler, and Wu (2012) found a significant relationship between learners' ability to set personal goals and their language achievement. In another study conducted by Ziegler and Moeller (2012), beginning language learners at the university level showed increased intrinsic motivation, increased task-value, and more accurate self-assessment of learning. Other studies related to the European Language Portfolio showed similar results.

ACTFL Performance Descriptors for Language Learners: Parameters and Qualities of Performance. With the pathway to proficiency in mind, ACTFL provides additional guidance in identifying appropriate criteria for assessing performance: Parameters of Performance and Qualities of Performance (ACTFL Performance Descriptors for Language Learners, 2015). The Parameters of Performance include three domains: Functions, Contexts and Content, and Text Type. These domains guide curriculum and assessment decisions as teachers seek to determine the themes and topics of a curriculum and how to

set increasing expectations of performance, moving learners to greater levels of proficiency. Curriculum is designed to allow learners to expand the number of topics about which they can communicate and the types of situations where they can successfully interact. Carefully designed tasks require learners to understand and use language functions with increasing complexity and demonstrate their ability to do so by using increasingly sophisticated text type in increasingly diverse contexts drawing on increasingly varied content. Table 27 provides an overview of the Parameters of Performance.

Let's consider each of the domains addressed by the Parameters of Performance in more detail.

Functions. Language functions are key to developing competency in another language. They represent the kinds of communication that learners can understand and use. The Toolbox of the unit template identifies the supporting language functions that learners will use as they work to accomplish the goals of the unit. Consider the supporting functions that were identified for the *Education* unit (Appendix D):

- **Compare** *various components of school systems/schedules.*
- **Describe** *attitudes toward attending school.*
- **Express opinions** *on the importance of school.*
- **Ask and answer questions** *to learn more about schooling in other cultures.*

The language function "ask and answer questions" explains what learners will do with the language. The remainder of the statement conveys the context within this particular thematic unit.

We have identified six key language functions (Appendix J) that we believe occur at all levels of language learning:

- Describing people, places, things, how and how well
- Asking and answering questions
- Expressing feelings and emotions
- Expressing advice, opinions, preferences
- Telling and retelling stories, sequencing
- Expressing hopes, dreams, possibilities

The concept of working with key language functions will be discussed in more detail in Chapter 5.

Contexts and Content. The second domain in Parameters of Performance is Contexts and Content. In designing unit and lesson plans, teachers need to introduce different contexts in which the learners communicate. For example, communicating with classmates in the classroom may provide the first context in which learners understand and use the target language. Gradually learners are introduced to other contexts, which may require that they use their imagination to transport themselves to a city in a country where the target language is spoken. Or the context may be a Skype exchange with a classroom in another country. Content is based on the themes, topics, and essential questions explored in each unit of instruction. The consideration of theme and essential question ensures that even when a topic such as food is included in multiple levels, the actual content of the unit will be different. Elementary learners who engage with the topic of food may consider where food comes from, as they discuss plant growth, farmers' markets and world biomes. Middle school learners may consider whether they eat to live or live to eat while discussing meals and snacks and comparing food pyramids from around the world. Finally, high school learners may consider food in the context of the slow food movement, as they discuss the implications of using pesticides, antibiotics, and genetic engineering on food. At each level, learners are expressing preferences and opinions about food, but the content allows them to address the topic of food from multiple perspectives. Remember that the Proficiency Pyramid is three-dimensional: moving from the Novice level to the Intermediate and beyond means that the pyramid gets broader and deeper, symbolic of the quantity of language that learners have to acquire in order to move from one level to the next.

Text Type. The third domain in Parameters of Performance is Text Type. When we think of text type, we often think first about how much language learners will produce. It is important for teachers to design tasks in ways that allow learners to produce the type of language that is appropriate for their anticipated performance range. While it may be appropriate for a novice learner to describe using phrases and very simple sentences, an intermediate learner must have a task that requires an extended description, sharing his or her thoughts and ideas in several sentences.

Of equal importance to the type of language that learners produce is the input that they receive. Krashen (1982) hypothesizes that language production is predicated on the quantity of language that learners hear and read:

> Acquisition occurs only when learners receive an optimal quantity of comprehensible input that is interesting, a little beyond their current level of competence ($i + 1$), and not grammatically sequenced, but understandable using background knowledge, context, and other extra-linguistic cues such as gestures and intonation. Note that the "i" refers to the current competence of the learner, and the "1" represents the next level of competence that is a little beyond where the learner is now (Shrum and Glisan, p. 15).

Krashen's $i + 1$ hypothesis emphasizes that comprehensible input is essential for language acquisition to take place. Glisan and Donato (2017) identify making the target language comprehensible as one of six high-leverage teaching practices that

Table 27. ACTFL Parameters of Performance

Domain	Parameters of Performance	Examples
Functions	What types of communication can the learner understand and use? Functions are the global tasks the learner can perform in the language.	Ask questions Describe Retell a story Give an opinion
Contexts and Content	What are the contexts (situations) in which the learner can communicate? Contexts are situations within which the learner can function. What are the topics that the learner can understand and discuss? Content is the topics which the learner can understand and discuss.	Oneself Family and friends Community Interests Professions Global issues
Text Type	What types of texts can the learner understand and produce? Text type is that which the learner is able to understand and produce in order to perform the functions of the level.	Words Phrases Sentences Questions Strings of sentences Paragraphs

research shows have a significant positive effect on language acquisition.

Research and theory indicate that effective language instruction must provide significant amounts of comprehensible, meaningful, and interesting talk and text in the target language for learners to develop language and cultural proficiency. Further, according to brain-based investigations, learners constantly ask themselves two questions in the face of new ideas or information: "Does this make sense?" and "Does this have meaning?" (Sousa, 2011, p. 52). Learning experiences that are comprehensible (i.e., make sense to learners) lead to improved retention (Maquire, Frith, & Morris, 1999). In this regard, meaning is an essential criterion for bringing about understanding and learning (Sousa, 2011). Therefore, it should come as no surprise that one high-leverage teaching practice that is essential for all foreign language teachers is the use of the target language during instruction in ways that make meaning clear and do not frustrate or de-motivate learners. (Excerpted from *Enacting the Work of Language Instruction: High-Leverage Teaching Practices* by Glisan and Donato (2016) in *The Language Educator*, March/April 2017, page 51).

Keeping the three Parameters of Performance—Functions, Content and Context, Text Type—in mind, teachers can plan purposeful learning experiences that move learners along the proficiency continuum.

Qualities of Performance. Now let's consider the Qualities of Performance. The Qualities of Performance describe how and how well the learners can communicate in the target language. Table 28 shows the four domains for the Qualities of Performance: Language Control, Vocabulary, Communication Strategies, and Cultural Awareness.

Let's expand the definition of each of these Qualities of Performance:

Language Control: Language control refers to errors that affect the meaning or intent of the message. It includes the level of detail that a learner can accurately understand (comprehension). It also refers to how well the learner is understood when speaking or writing in the target language (comprehensibility). Comprehensibility may be impacted by grammar, pronunciation, and word choice.

Vocabulary: Vocabulary refers to both the quantity of words that a learner can understand and produce, and the quality of the words in terms of sophistication. As learners build their proficiency, they are able to understand and communicate on an increasing number of topics. At the same time, their vocabulary moves from general language to specialized or sophisticated language that more accurately reflects the learner's thoughts. Teachers need to monitor learners as they practice expressing their thoughts and ideas, noting gaps in what they try to say or write. Learners can also take ownership for their vocabulary by adding words that they need in order to express their ideas. This is the role of personal vocabulary. We suggest that they record these words in their journals with examples of how they are using them. Teachers can give feedback through the journals related to the appropriate use of the word that the learner selected.

Communication Strategies: Communication Strategies are the strategies that learners use to understand the target language. They may include using background knowledge, context clues, cognates, word roots, and resources such as dictionaries. Communication Strategies also include strategies that leaners use in spoken interactions. They may include asking for clarification, repetition, explanation, rewording and rephrasing, and using circumlocution.

Table 28. Qualities of Performance

Domain	Qualities of performance	What it describes
Language Control	How accurate is the learner's language?	The level of control the learner has over certain language features or strategies to produce or understand language
Vocabulary	How extensive and applicable is the learner's vocabulary?	The parameters of vocabulary used to produce or understand language
Communication Strategies	How does the learner maintain communication and make meaning?	The strategies used to negotiate meaning, to understand text and messages, and to express oneself
Cultural Awareness	How is the learner's cultural knowledge reflected in language use?	The cultural products, practices, or perspectives the learner may employ to communicate more successfully in the cultural setting

Cultural Awareness: Cultural Awareness refers to how the learners use knowledge of the target language culture to communicate with respect for the values and practices of that culture. It also includes attention to, for example, appropriate gestures and proximity, choice of language register, and culturally appropriate expressions.

The Qualities and Parameters of Performance highlight the key characteristics that distinguish the performance of learners at the different levels of proficiency.

Formative and Summative Assessments

Assessments can be broadly divided into two categories: *formative* and *summative*. Formative assessments, introduced in Chapter 2, are assessments *for* learning and take place throughout the daily lessons of a unit, providing helpful feedback to both teacher and learners. This feedback tells learners how well they know and understand the content of the lesson. Teachers use this feedback to make adjustments to lesson plans and pacing as appropriate: slowing down to allow more practice; re-teaching using different types of explanations, examples, and learning activities when learners have not grasped a concept; or moving forward more quickly when learners demonstrate that they are comfortable with the new concepts. Formative assessments provide valuable insights about individual learners' strengths and challenges in meeting the goals and objectives of a lesson or class, opening the way for differentiation of instruction to meet the needs of all learners. (See Chapter 3 for more information on differentiation.) Since formative assessments are assessments for learning and not final measures of specific unit goals, they do not have to be graded. They are practice sessions similar to orchestra or choir rehearsals, or scrimmages in a sport, intended to give feedback to the learners on how well they know and can use the language, and where more practice is needed. Keeping a record of the formative assessments is helpful in showing learners the relationship between practice and final performance, but it is the final summative performance assessment that shows what learners know and can do related to the unit goals and objectives.

Summative assessments in world language classrooms are performance-based assessments of learning, and are designed to show how well learners can apply what they have learned to real-world situations. In this publication, the performance assessment tasks for the three modes of communication are

written at the beginning of the unit template, immediately following the essential question and unit goals. This placement models the philosophy of *Understanding by Design* (Wiggins & McTighe, 2005): beginning with the end in mind. Summative assessments capture the most important learning of the unit and provide a venue for learners to apply that learning to real-life situations. This model is patterned after the Integrated Performance Assessment (IPA) elaborated by Adair-Hauck, Glisan, and Troyan (2013). The summative performance assessment tasks are designed to be integrated throughout the unit of instruction. For example, because the texts in the Interpretive Mode inform the content for the Presentational and Interpersonal summative tasks, it is recommended that the learners complete Interpretive tasks after they have had sufficient practice reading, listening, or viewing authentic tasks. These assessments do not have to take place at the very end of the instructional unit.

Formative Assessments: Techniques for Monitoring Learner Progress. There are many ways to monitor learner progress during lessons. The teacher may choose to track performance during various activities. Learners may monitor their peers and provide feedback, or learners may self-assess or reflect at different points during the lesson. A learner-centered classroom requires that learners take increased responsibility for their own learning and evaluate their individual progress toward goals and objectives.

Learner Can-Do Statements: Since goals were shared with learners at the beginning of the unit, learners need to monitor their progress toward those goals throughout the unit. A portion of a learner self-assessment template appears in Table 29. NCSSFL-ACTFL Can-Do Statements may be used to guide the creation of topic-specific Can-Do Statements. Collaboration between teacher and learners in writing Can-Do Statements for a thematic unit encourages learners to take responsibility for monitoring their own progress towards achieving these goals.

Table 29. Learner Can-Do Chart for the Interpersonal Mode

I can:	Yes	With help	Not yet
discuss my lifestyle routine and find out about how others spend their time			
discuss health/lifestyle balance issues and needs with others			
respond to and offer suggestions on how to create a balanced lifestyle			

Have learners add a check or date to indicate where they are in terms of meeting a goal and then allow time for them to re-evaluate progress throughout the unit. They may reflect individually or may be asked to prove to a peer that they can meet a goal. Challenge learners to reflect on how they might provide evidence for these statements, and then have them post that evidence in electronic portfolios. In class, learners may simply work with a partner to "prove" that they can meet the individual goals. We suggest that younger learners be given images to color or receive stickers to place on a chart as they accomplish key goals.

Teacher Can-Do Statements: With large classes, multiple sections, and a variety of preps during a regular teaching day, teachers may find it helpful to document learner performance toward goals throughout the unit. Knowing more precisely where individual learners are in the learning process allows for more informed feedback. Teachers can create an adapted version of the Learner Can-Do Chart described earlier. Run the unit goals across the top of the chart and the learner names down the left column. Table 30 is an example of the Teacher Can-Do Chart. As learners work in class, place a check when you hear or see that a learner has demonstrated meeting a goal. The advantage of such a system is that it serves as a continual reminder throughout the unit of who may need additional help or of which goals may need to be reintroduced.

Table 30. Teacher Can-Do Chart

	discuss my lifestyle routine and find out about how others spend their time	discuss health/ lifestyle balance issues and needs with others	respond to and offer suggestions on how to create a balanced lifestyle
Student 1			
Student 2			
Student 3			

Vocabulary or Grammar Self-Checks. Quick checks allow learners to assess their understanding of a concept. The teacher may opt to give a short vocabulary or grammar quiz. Learners complete the quiz and then check their own work. As the teacher circulates, learners check their answers against the posted answers and are encouraged to ask questions of the teacher or classmates if they do not understand. The teacher has the learners track their own performance and encourages them to make notes about what they know and their personal areas for improvement. This allows learners to reflect on their own learning and on skills that they will need for the summative performance assessment tasks. The responsibility for learning is shifted to the learner.

Fluency Counts. Fluency counts are another way to allow learners to self-assess. Pick a topic and ask learners to write on that topic for a specific amount of time. Tell them not to worry too much about accuracy; the goal is to get their ideas on paper. When time is called, have learners count the number of words they wrote about the topic. Do this frequently so that learners can see that they are writing more in the same amount of time. If learners get stuck, encourage them to write the same word over and over until they think of something else to write. A similar fluency count can be used for speaking tasks. Pair learners. Have one learner do a monologue for a certain amount of time; have the other learner count the number of words or sentences that are said; when time is called, have the listener give the count, but also give suggestions on what else might have been said. Learners should see the quantity of speech increasing over time (Tuttle & Tuttle, 2012). To move from Presentational speaking to Interpersonal speaking, pair learners for spontaneous conversations. Create the context for a meaningful conversation, and challenge learners to engage in conversation for a specific amount of time. Tell them to start over if they run out of things to say, or to redo the conversation with a change in the order of their ideas. Doing this type of conversation practice frequently allows learners to see that it is getting easier to sustain a meaningful conversation for longer and longer periods of time. It may seem contrived to time the conversations of the learners, but language learning is a skill, and many skills are assessed with timers. The runner who runs a 100-meter race is delighted to take a second off his time. Language learners feel a similar success as they increase their performance within a specific time frame.

T.A.L.K. Scores. During pair or group work, circulate and monitor individual learners for staying in the target (T) language, for their accuracy (A) on specific structures, for their ability to listen (L) and respond appropriately, and for their ability to be kind (K) by being an equal conversational partner in an activity. T.A.L.K. scores allow teachers to track learner performance during various speaking activities. Create a chart (Table 31) that has a column for each domain across the top and the name of each learner on the vertical column. Use a system to indicate performance such as + Consistently, ✓ Few difficulties, – Many difficulties (Shrum & Glisan, 2016).

Table 31. T.A.L.K. Scores

	Target Language	Accuracy	Listen	Kind
Student A	+	−	✓	✓
Student B	+	✓	+	−
Student C				

Index Cards: Create an index card for each learner (Table 32). Allow learners to pair using a strategy such as think–pair–share. Then, call on three or four non-volunteering learners to give the answer. Learners who have practiced with their partner or group should be able to give a solid answer. A good answer scores a 10. A zero is given only when learners do not know what they are supposed to do and have obviously not used the practice time to develop answers. Use the index cards over the course of a marking period to increase individual accountability during pair and group work. Online tracking tools can also be used in similar ways.

Table 32. Index Card

Student Name						
Question #1	10	9	8	7	6	0
Question #2	10	9	8	7	6	0
Question #3	10	9	8	7	6	0

Exit Slips. The sample lesson in Chapter Three used an exit slip near the end of the class. Exit slips work well when the teacher would like to see in writing how well an individual learner is able to meet the lesson objective. In this case, the learners were asked to write words and phrases that explained an expression introduced in class. Direct the learners to write as much as they can for a specific amount of time. Collect the exit slips as learners leave. Exit slips are formative assessment (i.e., assessment for learning), and there is no need to grade this work. Instead, simply review the exit slips and pull out the ones for learners who did not make sufficient progress toward the lesson objective. Keep those slips as a reminder to provide additional support to those learners during the next lesson. Use overall impressions from the exit slips to plan subsequent lessons.

Summative Assessments: Rubrics and Scoring Guides. Evaluating performance on summative tasks requires careful thought.

As teachers design the performance assessment tasks for a unit, they should concurrently determine the characteristics of high-quality performance. Based on those characteristics, the teacher creates rubrics to provide the learner with clear criteria by which the performance will be evaluated. Those rubrics then provide feedback on the strengths of the performance and suggestions for continuous improvement. Tedick (2002) states that rubrics also:

1. help learners set goals and take responsibility for their learning by clarifying expectations for performance;
2. help learners develop their ability to self-assess their own work in terms of quality;
3. help others (parents, administrators, colleagues) understand the criteria for excellent performance;
4. increase an assessment's reliability through well-defined criteria that can be applied consistently across individual performances; and
5. align criteria to standards, curriculum, and performance descriptors.

At this point it may be helpful to review the distinctions between proficiency and performance. The ACTFL Proficiency Guidelines and NCSSFL-ACTFL Can-Do Statements provide the frameworks for assessing language learning. Figure 14 reintroduces the context for language use and illustrates the difference between performance and proficiency.

Figure 14. Contexts for Performance and Proficiency

Performance	Proficiency
Within an instructional setting	Beyond the classroom
Based on specific instructional goals	Independent of specific instruction or curriculum
Familiar content and contexts	Broad content and contexts
Practiced vocabulary and functions	Spontaneous, unrehearsed

As described in Chapter One, the image on the left shows a classroom, reminding us that performance describes what learners can demonstrate based on what they have learned and practiced in an instructional setting. Performance is based on familiar contexts and content areas (ACTFL, 2015). On the right is an image of the world, a reminder that proficiency describes what learners can do regardless of where, when, or how the language was acquired, and is not limited to the content or curriculum of a particular course.

The NCSSFL-ACTFL Can-Do Statements are helpful to classroom teachers as they determine the criteria for performance tasks for a unit of instruction. A teacher might think while planning the assessment: "This task is for my second year learners. I know that they are still functioning as Novices, but for this particular interview task, I am going to ask them to include a variety of questions for the interview that they create. This will be a good way to nudge them beyond asking the memorized questions we have practiced since the beginning of the year. Because we are working on questions in class, I know that they have the scaffolding needed to create a variety of questions for the interview. My students are still Novice learners, but they are starting to practice some of the skills (understanding, asking, and answering a variety of questions) they will need in order to be considered Intermediate learners. I referred to the NCSSFL-ACTFL Can-Do Statements to help me think about where my learners are now, and what the next step is to advance them towards greater proficiency." This teacher is able to design the rubric based on the background knowledge of what learners can do at the Novice, Intermediate, and Advanced levels, and the notes she had written about the Qualities of Performance (Language Control, Vocabulary, Communication Strategies, Cultural Awareness) as she was designing the unit's summative performance assessment tasks.

You will see in the examples that a three-tiered rubric is recommended, with headers of "Strong Performance," "Meets Expectations," and "Approaching Expectations." With a three-tiered rubric, all three levels describe varying degrees of success in completing the task. In a four-tiered rubric, the fourth column is labeled "Does Not Meet Expectations" and generally includes descriptors that indicate that the requirements for the product or performance were not met. This advocacy for the three-tiered rubric is based on the belief that when units are constructed according to the guidelines in this publication, teachers will provide the scaffolding that learners need in order to demonstrate the unit goals. Later in this section is a discussion about using a checklist of "non-negotiables" to help learners self-assess, making sure that they have met the requirements for the product or performance. Learners can achieve one of the described levels of performance in a three-tiered rubric if they pay attention to the criteria by which

they will be evaluated, actively participate in all the learning activities in and outside of class leading up to the summative assessment, and act on the feedback suggestions given on formative assessments. A performance that is below "Approaching Expectations" requires sending the learner "back to the drawing board" to work on improving the performance.

Notice that the headers describing levels of performance are not "Novice," "Intermediate," and "Advanced." The rubrics are designed to give feedback to the learners on a specific performance with specific criteria. Therefore, it is more appropriate to describe the product or performance as "Strong," "Meets Expectations," or "Approaching Expectations." While the rubric is informed by the characteristics of Novice, Intermediate, or Advanced levels, the rubric needs to be task-specific in order to provide focused feedback for improvement.

Interpersonal Rubric for the Performance Assessment Task in *A Balanced Lifestyle.* Table 33 on the following page is a rubric for the Interpersonal Mode used to evaluate performance in the sample unit about a balanced lifestyle. The final Interpersonal performance task states:

> In pairs or small groups, learners share what they have learned about their lifestyle and the lifestyle of peers in France in terms of a balanced lifestyle. They compare their daily routines and schedules and make and respond to suggestions to adjust their lifestyle.

Notice these features of this rubric:

- The criteria used to evaluate performance are presented in the form of questions. This allows the learners to self-assess their performance; the questions are free of jargon, making them easy to understand. The domains of the Qualities of Performance are listed after each question.
- There are five questions to evaluate performance, which is a manageable number for both the learner and the teacher to keep in mind during the performance.
- The question associated with the domain of cultural awareness asks: "What cultural knowledge and understandings do I share?" The descriptors of performance address both knowledge and behaviors.
- This rubric is a three-tiered rubric with the ratings of "Strong Performance," "Meets Expectations," and "Approaching Expectations." The "Strong Performance" appears first if you read left to right. This sets the stage for the learners, describing excellence in inter-

Table 33. Interpersonal Rubric for the Performance Assessment Task in A Balanced Lifestyle - Novice High through Advanced

	Strong Performance 10 9	Meets Expectations 8	Approaching Expectations 7
How well am I understood? (Domain: Language Control)	I am easily understood. Errors in speaking are minor and do not interfere with communication.	I am understood most of the time. I may need to repeat or reword occasionally. Errors in speaking do not interfere with communication.	I am difficult to understand at times. I may ask for help expressing ideas (e.g., "How do you say…?"). Some errors in speaking may interfere with communication.
How involved am I in the conversation? (Domains: Functions, Text Type)	I ask a variety of relevant questions to keep the conversation going. I can respond to questions and/or add follow-up comments/information. I encourage others to participate.	I ask relevant questions to keep the conversation going. I can respond to questions and/or make a follow-up comment.	I ask a few relevant questions. I respond to questions simply.
What communication strategies do I use? (Domain: Communication Strategies)	I ask for clarification as needed. If I don't know a word, I can explain it another way (circumlocution).	I ask for repetition as needed. If I don't know a word, I can use gestures and drawings to express what I mean.	I can say "I don't understand" as needed. If I don't know a word, I quit talking.
How do I demonstrate that I can correctly use the new vocabulary from the unit? (Domains: Vocabulary, Contexts/Content)	I successfully use many new words related to the unit to discuss the assigned topic.	I successfully use a few new words related to the unit to discuss the assigned topic.	I successfully use familiar words related to the unit to discuss the assigned topic.
What cultural knowledge and understandings do I share? (Domain: Cultural Awareness)	I add relevant information about the target culture. I use cultural gestures and/or expressions that imitate those that a native speaker would use.	I refer to relevant information about the target culture. I may imitate some cultural gestures and/or expressions that a native speaker would use.	I make limited or no references to the target culture. I may use a cultural gesture or expression that I have learned in class.

personal communication. This rubric does not include a fourth rating of "Not Meeting Expectations." Instead, the rubric describes performances that reflect acceptable degrees of competence, placing all learners on the pathway towards proficiency.

- The three tiers of the rubric have numbers for scoring the performance: 10 or 9 = strong performance; 8 = meets expectations; 7 = approaching expectations. The ratings for each category can be added together to arrive at a score that can be transferred to a grade book.
- The descriptors in this rubric can be applied to Novice High through Advanced level language learners. In Interpersonal communication, the characteristics of successful performance remain the same. However, the topics that learners discuss become more detailed and complex as they advance.
- The descriptors for "How well am I understood?" allow for minor errors that do not interfere with communication. It is important for learners to understand that the emphasis is on comprehensibility, not perfection.

A scoring guide is an effective assessment tool for both formative and summative assessments for the Interpersonal Mode.

The scoring guide in Table 34 presents a continuum of desired characteristics for someone participating in an Interpersonal exchange. On the left-hand side are characteristics that learners should avoid. On the right-hand side are desirable characteristics. In between the two extremes is a space to rate the learners on a scale of 1 to 5 about how closely they are demonstrating the characteristics on the right-hand side.

Table 34. Interpersonal Scoring Guide

Move from:	1 - 3 - 5	Move to:
Uses English frequently		Uses the target language all the time
Only responds when asked		Volunteers comments related to the discussion
Asks random questions		Asks follow-up questions related to what someone else said
Gives short responses		Gives responses with details, reasons, explanations
Dominates the discussion		Invites others to give their opinions, ideas
Repeats ideas that others already contributed		Adds ideas, insights, additional information to make the discussion more interesting
Does not pay attention during the discussion		Actively listens to what others are saying

**"Polished" Presentational Assessment Task and Rubric in
A Balanced Lifestyle.** Presentational tasks require detailed
explanations so that the time invested in preparing the task is
well spent, and the intent of the rubric is clear. The descriptor
for the Presentational assessment task for *A Balanced
Lifestyle* is:

> Learners will work in small groups to create a presenta-
> tion that can be shared via the Internet based on multiple
> sources of information highlighting ways to promote
> a balanced lifestyle for peers. The presentation will be
> shared with another French class.

This task allows learners to determine the types of media they
will use to create the product. The overview for the project
states that the information in the presentation must be based
on multiple sources, the topic must be about ways to promote
balanced lifestyles for peers, and the product must be able to
be shared via the Internet.

Presentational tasks require rough drafts or rehearsals, with
coaching and/or feedback to improve the final product, because the final product will be shared with an audience beyond
the classroom. It is advisable to provide guidelines for the final
product that are "non-negotiables" designed to outline the
minimum requirements of content for the product. Here is a
potential list of non-negotiables for the task about a balanced
lifestyle:

- Work collaboratively with one or two other people.
- Create a bibliography documenting the sources for the
  presentation.
  - Sources discussed in class should be included as
    appropriate.
  - Three authentic French sources not discussed in
    class must be included.
  - You may include up to three resources that are
    not in the target language. (Note that this option
    is included to encourage honest documentation of
    resources that learners consulted. These resources
    can be considered background knowledge to help
    learners use target language resources more suc-
    cessfully.)
- Incorporate written and spoken text in the final product.
- Include at least three ways to promote a balanced life-
  style.
- Include references to balanced lifestyles of French
  teenagers.
- Upload the final product to the class webpage.

The checklist of non-negotiables helps learners verify that
they have followed directions and included the components
needed for evaluation. A product that does not conform to
these guidelines should not be evaluated, because the product
is incomplete. The requirement to meet all the non-negotiables
before submitting the product for evaluation allows the evaluation to focus on the quality of the final product as described
in the rubric.

When preparing a Presentational task, learners benefit from
following the Five-Step Scripting Process in Table 35 below.
This process is applicable to any written, signed, or oral Presentational task. Notice that feedback is given throughout the
process by peers and the teacher so that the final product is
polished and ready for publication or performance.

Table 35. Five-Step Scripting Process

Five-Step Scripting Process	
Step 1: Brainstorming • Brainstorm ideas about the topic. • Look for information from among the reading, listening, and viewing tasks completed during the unit.	• Research further information online. • Create a bibliography listing all the sources you consulted.
Step 2: Drafting • Create categories related to the topic. • Organize the information into topics. • Look for similarities and differences in the information. • Determine a key message for your presentation.	• Create an outline of ideas you plan to use in your presentation. • Determine the type of media you will use to deliver your presentation • Write a script for your presentation. • Exchange your script with another group in order to give feedback to each other about the content.
Step 3: Revising • Discuss the feedback received from another group. • Make changes to your script as appropriate.	• Look up unknown words in a dictionary. • Read your script aloud to your group to see if it makes sense. • Submit your script to your teacher for comment.
Step 4: Final editing • Review the comments from your teacher. • Make corrections to the script; clarify any comments from the teacher that you do not understand.	• Have your peer review group read the corrected version and make comments. • For oral presentations, practice the script out loud; for written presentations, create the final product.
Step 5: Publishing/Broadcasting • Share the finished product.	

Table 36 is a rubric to evaluate the balanced lifestyle Presentational task. Notice that this rubric is designed to evaluate a product that has been produced by a group where all group members receive the same grade. It is a three-tiered rubric; the criteria to evaluate performance are presented as five questions, with the associated domains listed after each question. The descriptors reflect qualities of a multimedia presentation. Cultural understanding is evaluated based on the explanation of how a cultural product is connected to a cultural practice, and how they both work together to provide insights into the target culture (perspectives). Because of the five-step scripting process (Table 35) with feedback on the drafts of the script for the final presentation, the language in the final presentation should be accurate and is, therefore, not addressed as a separate item in the rubric. The intent is to create a product that is ready for publication. The descriptors in this rubric can be applied to Novice High through Advanced learners.

"On Demand" Presentational Assessment Task and Rubric for *A Balanced Lifestyle*. Performance or products generated in the Presentational Mode are meant to be polished, benefiting from multiple drafts and rehearsals, with ongoing feedback, because the final performances or products are shared with an audience beyond the classroom. Learners work to showcase their very best writing or speaking. However, there are times when a teacher may want to gather evidence of how well learners write or speak without the benefit of drafts and feedback. This is often referred to as "on-demand" writing or speaking. At beginning proficiency levels, learners may be able to write or say a few simple sentences; at more advanced levels, they may write or speak in one or more paragraphs on a topic. "On-demand" tasks are usually completed in class to allow the teacher to have a clear sense of what a learner can do without outside support. For the balanced lifestyle unit, learners might be asked to write or speak on demand to describe their lives in terms of balance. The instructions might be:

> Consider your lifestyle in terms of balance. Explain what you do and don't do. Compare your actions to French youth, drawing on information from the texts we have

Table 36. Presentational Multimedia Rubric for the Performance Assessment Task in A Balanced Lifestyle

	Strong Performance 10 9	Meets Expectations 8	Approaching Expectations 7
Are we understood? (Domain: Language Control)	Pronunciation imitates a French accent. Any errors in pronunciation do not interfere with understanding. Speech is smooth and natural with few hesitations.	Accent generally imitates a French accent. Errors in pronunciation rarely interfere with understanding. Speech sounds like a script is being read at times, and/or may be delivered too quickly.	Accent sounds more American than French. Errors in pronunciation may occasionally interfere with understanding. Speech sounds like a script is being read, and delivery lacks natural intonation.
How are tech tools used in the presentation? (Domain: Communication Strategies)	Visuals and sound and design are used effectively to emphasize the key ideas in the presentation, to help the audience follow the storyline of the presentation, and to maintain the audience's attention.	Visuals and/or sound and design in the presentation help the audience focus on the key ideas and follow the sequence of information.	Visuals and/or sound and design are used in the presentation. Key ideas are sometimes difficult to identify because at times there may be too many visuals or sound/design elements.
Is the presentation interesting and informative? (Domains: Functions, Contexts/Content)	The content of the presentation is thoughtfully selected with the audience and purpose in mind. The information is accurate, and the recommendations for balance provide useful tips and tools for teenagers.	The content of the presentation is selected with the audience and purpose in mind. The information is accurate, and the recommendations for balance are appropriate for teenagers.	The content of the presentation is selected according to instructions but needs more careful thought in terms of what information is interesting and informative for an audience of teenagers. The information is accurate.
How rich is the vocabulary? (Domain: Vocabulary)	Wide variety of familiar vocabulary is used correctly and appropriately, incorporating many new expressions from the current unit of study.	Variety of familiar vocabulary is used correctly and appropriately, incorporating several new expressions from the current unit of study.	Simple, familiar vocabulary is used correctly, incorporating a few new expressions from the current unit of study.
How are knowledge and understanding of the target culture represented? (Domain: Cultural Awareness)	Information about the target culture is accurately presented; the relationships among products, practices, and perspectives are included and justified within the presentation.	Information about the target culture is accurately presented; products, practices, and perspectives are identified, and some relationships are included within the presentation.	Information about the target culture is presented; products, practices, and perspectives are identified.

used in class. End by setting a personal goal, and explain why this goal is appropriate for you.

The rubric for on-demand writing would be similar in structure to the one used for the Presentational multimedia task, but the questions and domains would change slightly to reflect the fact that learners wrote or spoke on their own without additional support. Table 37 shows a rubric for on-demand writing.

Interpretive Rubric and Scoring Guides for the Performance Assessment Tasks in A Balanced Lifestyle.

For the unit *A Balanced Lifestyle*, the Interpretive assessment includes three authentic texts: (1) reading a blog written by a teenager; (2) watching a commercial; and (3) reading the daily schedule of a top athlete. The information gained from the Interpretive tasks contributes to the completion of the Presentational and Interpersonal tasks.

For that reason, the Interpretive tasks do not have to be completed at the end of the unit. The teacher can use one of the texts as a summative assessment at a point in time during the unit when the learners have sufficient vocabulary and strategies to interpret that text independently.

Adair-Hauck, Glisan and Troyan (2013) suggest that learners process texts for both literal and interpretive meanings. At the literal level, learners identify key words, main ideas, and important, supporting details found in the text. At the interpretive level, learners identify how a text is organized, guess the meaning of new words using context clues, infer overall meaning by understanding what is not literally stated in the text, identify the author's perspective, and identify cultural perspectives by connecting practices and products to perspectives. They suggest that the same rubric could be used across proficiency levels, since the qualities of successful understanding remain the same; it is the text that changes to match the proficiency level of the learner. More information on assessing the Interpretive Mode in an IPA is available in *Implementing Integrated Performance Assessment* by Adair-Hauck, Glisan, and Troyan (2013), an ACTFL publication.

For the Interpretive tasks in the Balanced Lifestyle unit, we are using scoring guides to evaluate performance. Since the focus is on comprehension of the texts, teachers may ask that learners use some English to demonstrate comprehension, especially for beginning language learners with limited vocabulary. Shrum and Glisan (2016) note that several research studies show that learners demonstrate greater comprehension of a text when they can use their native language to explain what they understood. Shrum and Glisan recommend that teachers

Table 37. Presentational "On-Demand" Writing Rubric for the Performance Assessment Task for A Balanced Lifestyle

	Strong Performance 10 9	Meets Expectations 8	Approaching Expectations 7
Am I understood? (Domain: Language Control)	My writing is clearly understood. Errors do not interfere with the message.	My writing is generally understood; reader may have to occasionally reread a phrase or sentence to understand. Errors do not interfere with message.	My writing is understood, but the reader may have to be willing to make a guess or reread to understand. Errors occur and do cause some confusion for the reader.
How rich is my vocabulary? (Domain: Vocabulary)	I use a variety of familiar vocabulary correctly and appropriately incorporate new expressions from the current unit of study. I may include personal vocabulary.	I use familiar vocabulary correctly and appropriately incorporate a few new expressions from the current unit of study.	I use simple, familiar vocabulary correctly, and I may use a few new expressions from the current unit of study.
How well do I complete the task? (Domain: Functions, Content and Context)	I complete all of the task, adding some details.	I complete each part of the task.	I complete most of the task.
How organized is my writing? (Domain: Text Type)	My ideas are presented in an organized manner. My sentences are varied and interesting.	My ideas are presented in a somewhat logical manner. I write some interesting sentences.	My ideas are shared in a random fashion. My sentences follow a repetitive pattern.
How are knowledge and understanding of the target culture represented? (Domain: Cultural Awareness)	Comparisons between French and American culture are accurately presented.	Information about the target culture is accurately presented.	Information about the target culture is presented, but may or may not be accurate.

consider the proficiency levels of the learners and the task they are asked to accomplish in determining the need for learners to use English in Interpretive tasks.

For the assessment based on a blog about what a French teenager does daily, learners demonstrate understanding by checking off the activities that the teenager does from a list of possible activities. The responses are either correct or incorrect. Next, the learner evaluates the balance in the French teenager's life based on the activities that the teenager does, and compares them to his/her own and what he/she has learned about lifestyles of French teenagers in general. The evaluation is a simple scoring guide with space for comments about the responses. Table 38 shows the scoring guide for this task.

Table 38. Scoring Guide for Interpretive Task in A Balanced Lifestyle: Blog

	Yes	Partially	No
1. Your evaluation of the degree to which the French teenager leads a balanced lifestyle is based on evidence from the blog and is logical.			
2. You compare your French peer's schedule to your own, indicating similarities and differences.			
3. You conclude with observations about the degree to which the French teenager's lifestyle reflects what you learned in this unit about lifestyles of French teenagers.			
Comments:			

The second Interpretive task states:

Learners watch a commercial for a product that promises to make life easier or less stressful, and demonstrate comprehension by analyzing the effectiveness of the message and product.

For this task, the learner demonstrates comprehension of the language through the analysis of the commercial. Based on two criteria that advertising agencies consider in designing effective commercials, learners respond to questions that check understanding of the language and also analyze the quality of the commercial. The final question asks learners to make cultural comparisons. Learners respond to these prompts:

1. The visual matches the product.
   a. What is the name of the product?
   b. What is the product used for?

c. Does the visual match the product? Why or why not?
2. The message is honest.
   a. What does the commercial say that the product will do?
   b. Is the claim an honest assessment of the product? Why or why not?
3. The product is made and sold in France.
   a. Do you think that this product is popular in France? Why or why not?
   b. Do you think this product would be popular in the United States? Why or why not?

The scoring guide evaluates the learner's responses. The teacher indicates if the response is accurate/logical and complete. Note that the teacher will need to explain and give examples of the qualities of "accurate," "logical," and "complete" responses before the learners complete the task. Table 39 shows the scoring guide for this task.

The third Interpretive task asks learners to read a schedule of a top athlete to determine how he spends the hours in his day, deciding what elements are part of a balanced lifestyle and what elements are missing. Learners check off the items on the athlete's schedule that contribute to a balanced lifestyle. Next the learners list the elements of balance that are missing. Finally, the learners explain why the checked items on the schedule contribute to a balanced lifestyle and how the missing items would improve the athlete's balance in life. Table 40 shows the scoring guide for this task.

Summary: Evaluating Summative Performance Assessment Tasks. Together, the rubrics and scoring guides for the three modes of communication give a complete picture of how well the learners can understand and use the target language on the topic of a balanced lifestyle. In terms of culture, notice that cultural awareness is a separate category in the rubrics for the Interpersonal and Presentational tasks. For the Interpretive Mode, in two of the three tasks, the learners need to make cultural comparisons as part of the comprehension questions for the texts.

Table 39. Scoring Guide for Interpretive Task in A Balanced Lifestyle: Commercial

	The response is accurate/logical .			The response is complete .		
	Yes	**Partially**	**No**	**Yes**	**Partially**	**No**
1a. What is the name of the product?						
1b. What is the product used for?						
1c. Does the visual match the product? Why or why not?						
2a. What does the commercial say that the product will do?						
2b. Is the claim an honest assessment of the product? Why or why not?						
3a. Do you think that this product is popular in France? Why or why not?						
3b. Do you think this product would be popular in the United States? Why or why not?						
Comments:						

Table 40. Scoring Guide for Interpretive Task in A Balanced Lifestyle: Athlete's Daily Schedule

	Yes	Partially	No
1. You accurately identified the portions of the athlete's schedule that contribute to a balanced lifestyle.			
2. You accurately identified the elements that are missing from a balanced lifestyle.			
3. The explanation you wrote about balance in the athlete's lifestyle is based on evidence from his schedule and what you have learned about a balanced lifestyle.			
Comments:			

Growth in Intercultural Communication

Documenting Growth. As learners increase their abilities to understand and communicate in a language other than English, they are also growing in their understanding of how the cultural context influences successful communication. The Council of Europe (2008) describes the connection between language learning and culture: "Language learning helps learners to avoid stereotyping individuals, to develop curiosity and openness to others, and to discover other cultures. Language learning helps learners to see that interaction with individuals having different social identities and cultures is an enriching experience" (p. 29).

The World-Readiness Standards for Learning Languages (The National Standards Collaborative Board, 2015) summarizes the purpose for learning languages as represented through the 5 Cs of Communication, Cultures, Connections, Comparisons, and Communities: "Knowing how, when, and why to say what to whom" (p. 12), making it clear that it takes both language and cultural understanding for successful communication.

Byram (1997) discusses the influence of culture on communication, which he calls Intercultural Communicative Competence. He identifies five *savoirs* that deepen a person's understanding and ability to communicate with people from other cultural backgrounds:

- *Savoirs:* Knowledge of social groups and their related products and practices within one's own country and within the country of the person with whom you are communicating; knowledge of historical and contemporary relationships among countries;
- *Savoir être:* Curiosity and openness, readiness to suspend disbelief about other cultures and belief about one's own;
- *Savoir comprendre:* Ability to interpret a document or event from another culture, explain it, and relate it to documents and events from one's own culture;
- *Savoir apprendre/faire:* Ability to acquire new knowledge of a culture and cultural practices, and ability to use this knowledge to interact with people from other cultures in real time; and

- *Savoir s'engager*: Ability to evaluate, critically and on the basis of explicit criteria, products, practices, and perspectives in one's own and in other cultures and countries.

Taken collectively the five *savoirs* represent the characteristics that grow and develop as a person interacts with people of different cultural backgrounds. Capturing growth in learners' intercultural communication is an ongoing challenge because, as stated earlier, it is growth in understanding of and attention to how the cultural context influences successful communication. Learners' extensive background knowledge and experience in one cultural setting is not a guarantee of the same level of understanding in a different cultural setting. Learners' ongoing curiosity, observation skills, and withholding of judgment as they try to understand how a new cultural context influences communication is a critical mindset in the development of Intercultural Communicative Competence.

As a way to provide evidence of growth in Intercultural Communicative Competence, Schulz (2007) suggests that learners keep a portfolio that documents their interactions with other cultures and their reflections on those interactions:

> Just as second language acquisition is not a uniform, instantaneous event but occurs in a spiral fashion over time, necessitating repeated language input and output opportunities, the development of cultural awareness and cross-cultural understanding also occurs over time in cyclical fashion, permitting learners to document their emerging awareness and understanding with new data and insights (p. 9).

Schulz identifies the following objectives for a cultural portfolio, and gives suggestions for ways to meet each objective:

1. Students develop and demonstrate an awareness that geographic, historical, economic, social/religious, and political factors can have an impact on cultural products, practices, and perspectives, including language use and styles of communication.
   - Suggested task: Compare the United States and target country in at least 10 ways. Use the information researched to discuss at least five similarities/differences and how they influence the culture.
   - Suggested task: Identify at least five culture products and explain why the products are popular in the target country.
2. Students develop and demonstrate an awareness that situational variables such as age, gender, religion, place of residence, and time shape interactions and behaviors among people in important ways.
   - Suggested task: Comment on a minimum of three examples of observed differences in native or first language (L1) usage by, for example, younger and older persons, male and female speakers, southern and northern speakers.
   - Suggested task: Examine authentic texts from the second or target language (L2) culture to find examples of how people address each other.
   - Suggested task: Describe and comment on a minimum of three behaviors that illustrate similarities and differences between the target culture and your own.
3. Students recognize stereotypes or generalizations about the home and target cultures and evaluate them in terms of supporting evidence.
   - Suggested task: Give three examples of stereotypes of people from the target culture and discuss how these might have developed.
   - Suggested task: Conduct a survey of friends, family, and community members to explore stereotypes they might hold about the people from the target culture.
4. Students develop and demonstrate an awareness that each language and culture has culture-conditioned images and culture-specific connotations of some words, phrases, proverbs, idiomatic expressions, gestures, and symbols.
   - Suggested task: List and explain culture-specific connotations in words or phrases you have encountered in L2.
5. Students develop and demonstrate an awareness of some types of causes of cultural misunderstanding between members of different cultures.
   - Suggested task: using newspaper articles, advertisements, or websites, compare how an event, product, or practice of the home culture is viewed in the target culture and attempt to explain the reasons for the views.

Schulz's recommendation that growth in Intercultural Communication be documented via portfolio honors the diversity of cultural experiences and recognizes that cultures adapt and change over time.

Intercultural communication begins with an awareness that each person has a story. For successful communication, learners need to know the stories of the people with whom they interact. To learn those stories, they need to draw on Byram's "*savoirs*," and then reflect on the interactions and what they learned about the person/people and themselves. Perhaps "growth" then is most appropriately measured in the reflections of learners about their interactions with people of diverse cultural backgrounds, their reactions to these interactions, and what they are learning about themselves and others through those interactions.

Summary. This chapter provided multiple examples of formative and summative tools for assessing growth in both linguistic skills and cultural understanding. The importance of developing learners' ability to self-assess their progress in both these areas was highlighted through the use of portfolios. In the concluding chapter, we describe the mindset for curriculum development.

Application

1. You are working with a group of colleagues to design a rubric for Interpersonal tasks. A colleague wants to use proficiency levels as the levels in the rubric. What would you say and how would you explain your rationale?

2. You are working with a colleague to design an Interpretive assessment at the Novice level. Your colleague wants to write all of the comprehension questions in the target language. You believe strongly that English should be used. What would you say to justify your point of view?

3. You are working with a new colleague who has very large classes. She is struggling to implement formative assessment as a part of her lessons. What would you suggest?

Reflection

1. How does my gradebook reflect performance in the three modes of communication? To what extent are the learners' grades reflective of what they can do with the language and their ability to use the language beyond the classroom?

2. What strategies do I have in place for learners to self-assess? How are these practices having an impact on learning and motivation?

3. How do I know that my students are developing intercultural communicative competence?

Chapter 5 | Curriculum Design

Learning to speak another's language means taking one's place in the human community. It means reaching out to others across cultural and linguistic boundaries. Language is far more than a system to be explained. It is our most important link to the world around us. Language is culture in motion. It is people interacting with people.

— Sandra Savignon

Figure 15. Curriculum Design for Learning Languages in the 21st Century

Identity/Belonging

Challenges

Creativity

Discovery

Exploring Time and Place

Well-being

What Does a Curriculum for Learning Languages Look Like in the 21st Century?

Mindset for Curriculum Design. Mickan (2013) states, "A curriculum is an inventory of what is to be taught and how it will be taught and assessed for the realization of particular goals…a selection of content, resources, and activities organized and sequenced for consistency and continuity of instruction" (pp. 24–25). Figure 15 serves as a visual reminder of the curriculum mindset that has been discussed in this publication. An effective curriculum must bring all required elements together to create an articulated scope and sequence that allows learners to advance to the highest possible levels of proficiency given the type of program. The documents need to be written in a format that is easily understood and accessible to educators. Enduring understandings offer a starting point for curriculum development.

Enduring Understandings. As educators we want to ensure that our learners retain the big ideas—the enduring understandings that are at the heart of our discipline. For that to happen, we must focus on ideas that have value beyond the classroom. Wiggins and McTighe (2005) state that an enduring understanding may provide a conceptual foundation for basic skills: "All skills derive their value from the strategic principles that help us know when and how to use the skill" (p. 115). As stated previously, the overarching enduring understanding for all language learning is based on the goal statement in the World-Readiness Standards for Learning Languages (2015): "To study another language and culture gives one the powerful key to successful communication: *knowing how, when, and why, to say what to whom*" (p. 12). Developing our discipline-specific enduring understandings challenges us to determine what it is that we want our learners to remember long after they have left our classrooms. Enduring understandings that are reflected through the World-Readiness Standards give direction to all programs, no matter what the structure of a particular program might be. The goal areas of the Standards—Communication, Cultures, Connections, Comparisons, and Communities—are implicit in the enduring understandings that follow:

- Knowledge of another language fosters a better understanding of one's own language and culture, fostering the development of Intercultural Communicative Competence.
- Communicating in another language is a vehicle to gain knowledge and understandings that can only be acquired through that language and its culture(s).
- Learning other languages enables an individual to actively participate in multilingual communities locally and globally.

Components of a 21st Century Curriculum for World Languages. In the previous chapters we have focused on the design of individual thematic units and lessons and have explained the concepts that are integral to the development of those units and lessons. Figure 16 shows the components that must be addressed when creating a curriculum document that is vertically aligned across all levels of instruction.

Figure 16. Components of a 21st Century Curriculum for World Languages

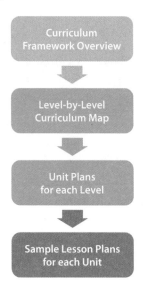

The role that each component plays in a 21st Century Curriculum for World Languages is explained next.

Curriculum Framework Overview

Although key to the development of individual units and lessons, the components listed below are also integral to the design of a curriculum framework overview for world languages:

- World-Readiness Standards for Learning Languages
- Themes
- Topics and Essential Questions
- Key Language Functions
- Text Type

World-Readiness Standards for Learning Languages. The graphic representation of curriculum design explained in Chapter One shows the 5 Cs of the World-Readiness Standards encircling the world. "The five goal areas of the Standards establish an inextricable link between **Communication** and **Cultures**, which is applied in making **Connections** and **Comparisons** and in using this competence to be part of local and global **Communities**. The *World-Readiness Standards for Learning Languages* create a roadmap to guide learners to develop competence to communicate effectively and interact with cultural competence to participate in multilingual communities at home and around the world" (The National Standards Collaborative Board, 2015). The 5 Cs serve as the foundation for curriculum design. Strong units of instruction incorporate all 5 Cs (Appendix A).

Themes. With the World-Readiness Standards as the foundation, themes serve as the pillars of the curriculum framework. Like the World-Readiness Standards, themes remain constant across all levels of instruction. They reflect the broad content areas that learners explore throughout their language learning journey in order to actively participate in global communities. We suggest that programs adopt the Advanced Placement (AP), the International Baccalaureate (IB), or the Global Themes in *Keys to Planning for Learning* to guide the development of instructional units for all levels of a language program. Table 40 shows the AP, IB, and Global Themes:

Table 40. Suggested Overarching Themes to Guide Curriculum Development

Advanced Placement (AP)	International Baccalaureate (IB)	Global Themes
• Personal and Public Identities • Families and Communities • Global Challenges • Beauty and Aesthetics • Science and Technology • Contemporary Life	• Communication and Media • Global Issues • Social Relationships • Cultural Diversity • Customs and Traditions • Leisure • Health • Science and Technology	• Identity/ Belonging • Challenges • Creativity • Discovery • Exploring Time and Place • Well-being

While we recommend these overarching themes to guide your curriculum, you may decide to create your own set of themes to reflect the goals of your program. Use the themes suggested in Table 40 as your inspiration and pay attention to the range of themes from personal identity to global issues. We also suggest that you limit the number of themes to a maximum of six, and that you commit to revisiting those themes throughout your program in order to build vocabulary, connect ideas, and deepen understanding of those themes across levels.

We want to clarify that the themes, while rich in their own right, do not need to be represented by individual units in the curriculum every year. For example, if we use the six Global Themes from *Keys to Planning for Learning*, we might elect to combine Identity/Belonging with Creativity at the Intermediate level to develop a thematic unit on self-expression through the fine arts. What is important is to make sure that all the themes are addressed every year in a language program in order to build a progression of language and content across all levels of instruction.

Topics and Essential Questions. With the program themes in place, select topics and essential questions with both the proficiency level and the developmental level of the learner in mind. Topics are more specific than themes and serve to narrow the focus of the theme. In selecting topics, think about the interests of the learners and the resources you have. Think also about the progression of topics across levels in your program. A well-articulated curriculum links topics throughout a year of instruction. It also links topics vertically from year to year.

With the theme and topic in place, begin to craft the essential question that further defines the theme and topic. As you

brainstorm questions, refer to the criteria for essential questions in Table 14 of Chapter 2. Consider the age, interests, and language level of the learners so that the question encourages the learners' curiosity. Table 41 shows an example of how essential questions for the theme of Discovery might change from the Novice to the Intermediate and Advanced proficiency levels. A chart showing sample essential questions for each of the 21st Century Global Themes is found in Appendix G.

Table 41. Theme and Essential Questions

Theme	Novice Range	Intermediate Range	Advanced Range
Discovery	Who are the inventors?	How are advances in science impacting my life today?	How do inventions impact the quality of life on earth?

Key Language Functions. The thematic unit plan introduced in Chapter 2 requires that language functions be identified as part of the Toolbox. These language functions are key to developing competency in another language. We suggest that the following six high-frequency functions be revisited by learners multiple times as they build their communication skills toward greater proficiency:

- Describing people, places, things, how, and how well something is done;
- Asking and answering questions;
- Expressing feelings and emotions;
- Expressing advice, opinions, preferences;
- Telling and retelling stories, sequencing;
- Expressing hopes, dreams, future plans.

The complete Chart of Key Language Functions is found in Appendix J. Table 42 shows the first section of the chart for the Key Function: Describing People, Places, Things, How, and How Well. In addition to the six key language functions, each key function includes "Related Language Functions." Notice in Table 42, that Related Language Functions for Describing include "categorize," "illustrate," etc. We have also suggested sample progressions for each of the six key language functions moving from Novice to Intermediate to Advanced proficiency levels. The progressions are meant to be examples of how the complexity of the six key language functions increases as learners become more skilled communicators.

Text Type. The ACTFL Proficiency Guidelines explain the progression that learners make as they move from words to

Table 42. Key Function: Describing People, Places, Things, How, and How Well

Describing People, Places, Things, How, and How Well				
Give a description using one or two short adjectives or adverbs.	Give a basic description and make simple comparisons using frequently used adjectives and adverbs.	Give more detailed descriptions including comparatives, contrasts, and superlatives.	Give detailed descriptions using a variety of precise adjectives and adverbs.	Give detailed descriptions using a wide variety of precise adjectives and adverbs.
Related Language Functions				

- *Analyze*
- *Categorize*
- *Classify*
- *Clarify*
- *Compare*
- *Contrast*
- *Count*
- *Define*

- *Describe physical characteristics*
- *Describe the weather*
- *Differentiate*
- *Edit*
- *Evaluate*
- *Explain*
- *Give biographical information*
- *Give examples*

- *Identify*
- *Illustrate*
- *Infer*
- *Interpret*
- *Label*
- *List*
- *Locate*
- *Name*

- *Paraphrase*
- *Present*
- *Rephrase*
- *Restate*
- *Rewrite*
- *Summarize*

Table 43. Sample Progression of Tasks

Novice → **Intermediate** → **Advanced**

Type of task by mode of communication	These tasks are examples of a progression from short, memorized language to longer, more complex language.			
Maintaining a conversation in person or virtually (Interpersonal)	Exchange greetings/ farewells, memorized biographical information.	Participate in a short conversation on a very familiar topic, asking and answering simple questions.	Initiate and carry on a conversation on a familiar topic, asking and answering a variety of questions and some follow-up questions.	Initiate and maintain a longer conversation with ease and confidence on a variety of topics.	Sustain a conversation on a wide variety of topics and appropriately handle an unexpected event or complication.
Interpreting authentic written texts (Interpretive)	Identify a few words/ phrases I have learned on a sign, advertisement, etc., accompanied by strong visual support.	Identify the main idea of a short message, advertisement, or article that includes visuals on a very familiar topic.	Identify the main ideas and some details of a short literary or informational text that includes visuals on a familiar topic.	Identify the main ideas and supporting details of a longer literary or informational text on a familiar topic.	Identify the main ideas and supporting details of a literary or informational text on familiar and some unfamiliar topics.
Summarizing authentic oral texts (Interpretive)	Identify a few words/ phrases accompanied by strong visual support on a very familiar topic.	Respond appropriately to simple, short announcements or directions, accompanied by visual support.	List the main ideas and some details of a short radio/television program, movie, or podcast on a familiar topic.	Identify the main idea and supporting details of a radio/television program, movie, or podcast on a familiar topic.	Identify the main idea and supporting details of a radio/television program, movie, or podcast on familiar and some unfamiliar topics.
Presenting information orally (Presentational)	Introduce myself, giving simple biographical information.	Give a short presentation on a very familiar topic.	Give an informational or demonstration speech on a topic of personal interest.	Give a persuasive speech on an issue of current importance.	Present a detailed, researched report on an academic topic, including evidence-based insights.
Presenting information in writing (Presentational)	Label an image about a very familiar topic.	Describe a person or place or event using simple sentences.	Write a story about a personal experience or other familiar topic.	Write a short essay about a topic of personal interest.	Write a detailed, researched report on an academic topic, including evidence-based insights.

sentences to paragraph-length narration. Text type is one way to explain in simple, concrete terms how learners use increasingly more complex language over time. To illustrate how text type might be represented in the three modes of Communication, we created a sample progression of tasks for the three modes, moving from short, memorized language to longer, more complex language (Table 43). Teachers might use the progression of tasks to create formative or summative assessments that are appropriate for the targeted level of performance.

Encouraging learners to say more and write more goes hand-in-hand with building learners' active vocabulary. Teachers need to monitor learners as they practice expressing their thoughts and ideas, noting gaps in what they trying to say or write. It is especially important to gradually introduce transition words that add sophistication to their text. Examples include "for example," "because," "especially," "but," "except," "however," and "meanwhile." Learners can also take ownership for their vocabulary by adding words that they need in order to express their ideas. This is the role of personal vocabulary. We suggest that they record these words in their journals with examples of how they are using them. Teachers can give feedback through the journals related to the appropriate use of the word that the learner selected.

Curriculum Overview. At this point it is time to create an overview of your curriculum framework (Table 44). The purpose of this overview is to present in chart-form all levels of instruction in a program on a single page highlighting how the themes and key functions are repeated each year but each year has new topics and essential questions. This overview is the first step in vertical and horizontal articulation. Check to see if connections can be made from topic to topic over the course of a year. Then check to see if connections can be made from one year to the next. Identifying potential connections both vertically and horizontally facilitates the spiraling of vocabulary and grammatical structures. This overview shows only the Key Function that will be emphasized during the unit. This is to ensure that each one of the Key Functions receives focused attention over the course of the year. Related Functions for each unit are included in the unit plan and in the detailed curriculum map for each level of instruction.

The Grade 7 overview is designed to introduce the (French-speaking) world while connecting learners to their own lives. The autobiography theme is a way for learners to meet their classmates and will include their names, ages, **describing** their

Table 44. Curriculum Framework Overview Grades 7 and 8 of a World Languages Program for Grades 7 – 12

GRADE 7 — NOVICE RANGE						
Themes	Identity/Belonging	Well-being	Exploring Time and Place	Discovery	Creativity	Challenges
Topics	Autobiography	Food	Geography	Explorers	Art & Photography	Environment
Essential Questions	Who am I?	What is a healthy meal?	Where in the world do people speak (French)?	Who are the explorers?	What do you see?	How green is your lifestyle?
Key Functions	Describing people, places, things, how, and how well	Expressing advice, preferences, opinions	Asking and answering questions	Telling or retelling stories	Expressing feelings and emotions	Expressing hopes, dreams, future plans

GRADE 8 — NOVICE RANGE						
Themes	Identity/Belonging	Well-being	Exploring Time and Place	Discovery	Creativity	Challenges
Topics	Friends	Free Time Activities	Famous people	City life	Celebrations	Making a difference
Essential Questions	Are all friends the same?	How much free time do you need?	How do you become famous?	What makes a city special?	What and how do people celebrate?	How do our actions here influence what is happening globally?
Key Functions	Describing people, places, things, how and how well	Asking and answering questions	Telling, retelling stories	Expressing advice, preferences, opinions	Expressing feelings and emotions	Expressing hopes, dreams, future plans

immediate family, and some activities they like to do. This unit connects to the second unit on food when learners state **preferences** for foods they like and learn about foods that people in the (French-speaking) world like comparing how healthy the foods are. Unit three connects the foods people eat in different parts of the world to a focus on all the places where (French) is spoken. This unit introduces young people living in the (French-speaking) world through short interviews where they **ask and answer questions**. Unit four introduces explorers who expanded the (French-speaking) world. Learners **retell a simple story** about the explorers' adventures. Unit five poses the question: What do you see?" Through artwork and photography, learners view places where (French) is spoken, with an emphasis on landscapes. Learners **express feelings and emotions** as they view these various landscapes. This leads to the final unit on the environment. Responding to the question: "How green

is your lifestyle?" learners talk about what they **can do now and in the future** to help maintain a green planet represented in the landscapes they viewed in the prior unit. This unit lends itself to activities in the outdoors and how those activities are influenced by where people live (swimming in the ocean, skiing in the mountains, etc.).

There are clear advantages to creating this overview of the curriculum framework. The themes reoccur throughout the language program, encouraging teachers to connect and re-cycle topics in more complex ways so that learners can build on what they have learned. The topics and essential questions for each grade level allow teachers to see how content changes across levels. The key function is identified for each unit. Condensing the curriculum overview to one page creates a "snapshot" of the language learning program that is easily referenced by teachers and learners throughout the year. An

Table 45. Level-by-Level Curriculum Map

	Level Two Performance Range Novice High - Intermediate Low				
	UNIT ONE	**UNIT TWO**	**UNIT THREE**	**UNIT FOUR**	**UNIT FIVE**
Theme	Identity/Belonging	Well-being/Creativity	Exploring Time and Place	Challenges	Discovery
Topic	Leisure Activities with Family and Friends	Healthy Foods	Cities	Daily Life	Famous People
Essential Question	How do my family, friends, and where I live influence my free time activities?	How can meals be healthy and creative?	What makes a city special?	How balanced is my lifestyle?	Who are the inventors?
Functions	• **Asking and answering questions** • Listing • Expressing likes and dislikes • Comparing	• **Describing** • **Asking and answering questions** • Expressing preferences • Agreeing/ Disagreeing	• **Expressing opinions** • Ask for and give directions • Describing places • Expressing interest/ boredom	• **Expressing feelings and emotions** • Expressing daily routines • Expressing frequency • Sequencing • Giving advice	• **Expressing hopes and dreams** • **Retelling an event** • Asking/giving biographical information
Structures/Patterns	This is… I like/don't like… Informational questions Tennis is more interesting than…	Adjective agreement Informational questions I prefer Negatives	Prepositions of location Expressing past events	Reflexive verbs Sequencing words You should….	Informational questions Past and future tenses
Priority Vocabulary	Family members Activities Sports Often Every day Sometimes Never	Meals Food pyramid Healthy, unhealthy Tastes (sweet, sour, spicy, bland)	Places in a city Street, intersection, Pedestrian zone, Sidewalk Traffic	Daily routine actions Adverbs of frequency: daily, weekly, often, sometimes, rarely, once in a while	Because of… Innovation Efficient Time-saving Life-saving Convenient

overview to Grade 8 is also included as an example to show how vertical articulation can be monitored across levels.

Level-by-Level Curriculum Map

Now that you have the overview to the curriculum for your language program, the next step is to create detailed curriculum maps for each level or course in your language program.

Table 45 shows what a curriculum map might look like, providing the basic building blocks for one level or course in a world language program. It is recommended that level-by-level curriculum maps identify performance targets for each level or course. The performance range serves as a reminder that learners are demonstrating what they know and can do based on topics they have practiced during classroom instruction.

Teachers can see at a glance the units for a particular course or level. The theme, topic, and essential question appear on the map. The language functions are listed next, with the **key language function** emphasized in each unit listed first in boldface type. This is to ensure that each one of the Key Functions receives focused attention over the course of the year. The structures and patterns that are needed to support those functions appear right after the functions. The priority vocabulary that learners need in order to meet the goals of the unit completes the map. The overview is formatted so that all of the units for a given level or course fit on a page, allowing teachers easy visual access to the curriculum for one level. To ensure that the curriculum is vertically articulated with repetition of key language and related functions from level to level, it may be helpful to track functions by unit across each level. Table 46 shows what this might look like for the level 2 course outlined above.

Teachers can now design their unit plans, which include the World-Readiness Standards, Summative Performance Assessment Tasks, Can-Do Statements, Key Learning Activities/Formative Assessments, Resources, and suggestions for Technology Integration. With unit plans in place, sample lesson plans can be designed to suggest how the unit might be taught. In order to show how learners progress over the course of the unit, we suggest designing sample lesson plans for the beginning, middle, and end of a unit.

Curriculum design as a dynamic process. Although we have guided you step-by-step through curriculum design, the process, in reality, is not linear. With each step, you look back to see if all the steps align. As you write the goals for the unit, you may realize that the unit goals are not appropriate for the the language level or developmental level of the learners. You may find that, as you design the summative performance assessments, the essential question needs to be reworded or changed. As you locate authentic text, you may realize that you have to adjust the Can-Do Statements or the priority vocabulary. As you teach the unit, you may make adjustments to better meet the needs of the learners. Let's consider three final questions.

How Many Units Should I Teach Each Year? The number of units really depends on the actual teaching situation, and arguments could easily be made for a certain number of units in any given situation. Academic-year calendars and grading cycles could affect the number of units. A typical high school system with four quarters and four grading periods might include five or six units per year, making certain that units never end during the last week of a grading period. An elementary class that meets twice a week for 25 minutes might opt for only two or three units a year given the limited number of contact minutes. Beyond the practical considerations of the calendar, think

Table 46. Articulation of Key and Related Functions: Level 2 Course

Key and Related Functions	Leisure Activities with Family and Friends	Healthy Foods	Cities	Daily Life	Famous People
Describing people, places, things, how, and how well	√	√	√		√
Asking and answering questions	√	√	√	√	√
Expressing feelings and emotions			√	√	
Expressing advice, opinions, preferences	√	√	√	√	
Telling and retelling stories; sequencing			√	√	√
Expressing hopes, dreams, possibilities					√

about the impact on student learning. How much time will teachers and learners need for meeting unit goals? If learners are to meet unit goals successfully, they will need time to develop their skills within each mode of communication. Learners need time to acquire new vocabulary and new structures that are used in meaningful contexts as they discuss, acquire, and present the ideas of the unit. They will need time to surface their own questions and time to explore those questions. They will need time to create their products in the Presentational Mode, to revise their work in collaboration with others, and to share those final products. Teachers need time to work with individual learners to create opportunities for feedback at critical points in the unit. The most frequently voiced concern in terms of curriculum is that there is never enough time. As thematic units are implemented, teachers are empowered to make more efficient use of time in ways that empower student learning.

What About Grammar? At this point, some readers are surely asking themselves about grammar. Remember that every language function requires key structures. The Toolbox for the thematic unit required that functions be listed first, followed by the structures associated with those functions. This places grammar in the appropriate context. It is presented and addressed when it is needed for specific communicative purposes. This intentional placement allows teachers and learners to focus on what is essential—the ability to communicate a message to an intended audience. The intentional spiral that occurs as certain key functions are revisited also allows the supporting structures to be re-integrated and allows for increased control of specific structures over time. With recognition that full control does not come early in the process, teachers and learners benefit by knowing that errors are a natural part of the language learning process. Crockett advocates a culture where error correction is replaced by encouragement and praise for communicating a message, and adds that the result is a classroom where the culture is warmer and more welcoming (in Zilmer, 2013). This does not mean that there is no need for error correction; rather, error correction occurs at appropriate moments.

What more needs to be considered when developing a highly effective curriculum? The curriculum documents described throughout this volume have focused primarily on the teachers and learner. Teachers bear primary responsibility for ensuring that learners meet the objectives conveyed by the written curriculum. However, all stakeholders—instructional leaders,

teachers, policymakers and parents contribute to the desired outcomes. Those who wish to consider curriculum development from the point of view of other stakeholders may wish to consult the guide *Starting with the End in Mind Planning and Evaluating Highly Successful Foreign Language Programs* (Couet, Duncan, Eddy, Met, Smith, Still, Tollefson, 2008).

Summary. This chapter presented details that must be considered in the development of a well-articulated scope and sequence for a world language program. While a publication is limited to what can be conveyed in print, we believe that the templates and overviews presented here will transfer easily to the numerous electronic curriculum tools that are in use today. Without a doubt, there is a great deal of energy, thoughtfulness, creativity, and time involved in developing a curriculum with units and lessons that allow learners to reach program goals and, more importantly, their personal goals. The creativity involved in curriculum development is most certainly the same process that creates a great work of art.

> *A great piece of art is composed not just of what is in the final piece, but equally important, what is not. It is the discipline to discard what does not fit—to cut out what might have already cost days or even years of effort—that distinguishes the truly exceptional artist and marks the ideal piece of work, be it a symphony, a novel, a painting, a company or, most important of all, a life.*
>
> (Collins, 2003)

Application

1. You are the designated mentor to a new colleague. You need to explain your program goals. What would you say? What documents would you share? How do you explain how well prepared the learners should be at the end of the course they are taking?

2. You and your department members are ready to make some changes. You want to teach fewer units and place more emphasis on student performance. What rationale would you share with administration to convince them to offer time and/or funding for curriculum development work?

Reflection

1. How do I address key functions throughout the curriculum?

2. Given that I have a limited amount of time, what is a logical next step for me in terms of curriculum, unit, and lesson design?

Final Thoughts
For Ongoing Reflection

We opened this publication on curriculum, unit, and lesson design by describing the 21st century learner and educator. We described the learner as "hyper-connected to the world" and ready to explore multiple sources of information almost simultaneously with the click of a button. We described the 21st century educator as a facilitator, providing space, time, and guidance to learners as they traveled the world from their laptop, tablet, or smartphone. In the 21st century, educators are tasked not with teaching learners *what* to think, but rather with teaching learners *how* to think. Technology is truly the bridge builder of the 21st century, connecting people around the world. The 21st Century Skills of Communication, Critical Thinking, Creativity, and, most importantly, Collaboration are essential skills for all learners. The language classroom is the ideal place to bring all those skills together for global collaboration.

Classrooms and schools in the United States are connecting with classrooms and schools around the world to discuss issues of importance that transcend boundaries. The 21st century learner is also connecting as an individual through social networks. "Learning is social"—that statement has never been truer than it is today. Learners who live in rural areas no longer have to feel isolated. The world is just a click away. Furthermore, language learners have the advantage of being able to click and connect in more than one language. Think of the possibilities!

Let's return to our original question: What does a curriculum for learning languages look like in the 21st century? First and foremost, it is flexible and encourages learners to be curious about the global community in which they live. With flexibility in mind, we have selected six global themes—Identity/Belonging, Challenges, Creativity, Discovery, Exploring Time and Place, and Well-being—designed as lenses through which learners can simultaneously learn about people, places, and cultures around the world as they learn about themselves. While there are no prescribed topics within the themes, the 5 Cs of the World-Readiness Standards for Learning Languages—Communication, Cultures, Connections, Comparisons, and Communities—give depth and breadth to the content. In fact, the beauty of the global themes is that they can be interpreted in a multitude of ways. You may recall that

in describing the unit on a balanced lifestyle, we showed how it could be connected to each of the Global Themes, depending on how learners wanted to explore the topic.

Second, the 21st century language learning curriculum encourages curiosity. With that goal in mind, we encouraged unit planning around a theme and topic, and an essential question related to that theme and topic. Because the themes are intentionally broad, we felt it important to encourage unit designers to focus on a topic related to the theme as an intermediary step to the more important step of designing an essential question to guide the learning in the unit of study. In the 21st century language classroom, learners should determine questions and, ultimately, the essential question they want to explore as a way to foster their natural curiosity about the world. We know that motivation is essential to the learning process. How better to motivate learners than by putting them in the driver's seat, letting them ask questions, and then having them connect with people around the world to find answers?

Third, the 21st century language learning curriculum requires global collaboration. There are not enough creative and innovative ideas in any one classroom to address all of the challenges facing today's global citizens. The challenges are complex and require people of diverse backgrounds to bring their perspectives and knowledge to a virtual roundtable. Language learners need highly developed skills in Intercultural Communicative Competence to make those virtual discussions successful collaborations. Again, language learners are uniquely poised to be leaders in these discussions, because they have grappled with the intricacies of communicating effectively with people from other cultures. Kramsch (1993) expressed the importance of teaching culture in language classes:

> Culture in language teaching is not an expendable fifth skill, tacked on, so to speak, to the teaching of speaking, listening, reading, and writing. It is always in the background, right from day one, ready to unsettle the good language learners when they expect it least, making evident the limitations of their hard-won communicative competence, challenging their ability to make sense of the world around them (p. 8).

We cannot prepare language learners for successful global collaboration unless we emphasize that learning a language is learning a culture. Fallows (2010) in the book, *Dreaming in Chinese,* eloquently expresses how language and culture are inextricably linked:

I often found a connection between some point of the language—a particular word or the use of a phrase, for example—and how that point could elucidate something very "Chinese" I would encounter in my everyday life in China. The language helped me understand what I saw on the streets or on our travels around the country—how people made their livings, their habits, their behavior toward each other, how they dealt with adversity, and how they celebrated. This book is the story of what I learned about the Chinese language, and what the language taught me about China (p. 15).

Finally, the 21st century language educator, just like educators of all disciplines, is teaching learners *how* to learn and not *what* to learn. The pathway to proficiency guides language learners to continuously expand their understanding and communication skills in an expanding number of contexts, beginning with words, phrases, memorized sentences, and questions, and branching out to express their own ideas by creating with language in longer sentences and questions, eventually moving to paragraph-length narration. Learners who reach that level of proficiency and who seek to continue to develop their linguistic and cultural skills will be well-prepared to take their place in a global society.

We would like to leave you with this vision for language study:

To prepare young people for meaningful interactions with people around the world, helping them understand the inextricable link between language and culture as they work to understand and communicate with respect in the language they are learning, and, at the same time, deepening their understanding of their own language and culture; to prepare young people to be explorers: being curious, asking questions, being open to sharing new experiences and new ideas, ultimately with the goal of creating networks of collaboration to address the challenges facing today's world.

Appendix A | World-Readiness Standards

GOAL AREAS	STANDARDS		
COMMUNICATION Communicate effectively in more than one language in order to function in a variety of situations and for multiple purposes	**Interpersonal Communication:** Learners interact and negotiate meaning in spoken, signed, or written conversations to share information, reactions, feelings, and opinions.	**Interpretive Communication:** Learners understand, interpret, and analyze what is heard, read, or viewed on a variety of topics.	**Presentational Communication:** Learners present information, concepts, and ideas to inform, explain, persuade, and narrate on a variety of topics using appropriate media and adapting to various audiences of listeners, readers, or viewers.
CULTURES Interact with cultural competence and understanding	**Relating Cultural Practices to Perspectives:** Learners use the language to investigate, explain, and reflect on the relationship between the practices and perspectives of the cultures studied.	**Relating Cultural Products to Perspectives:** Learners use the language to investigate, explain, and reflect on the relationship between the products and perspectives of the cultures studied.	
CONNECTIONS Connect with other disciplines and acquire information and diverse perspectives in order to use the language to function in academic and career-related situations	**Making Connections:** Learners build, reinforce, and expand their knowledge of other disciplines while using the language to develop critical thinking and to solve problems creatively.	**Acquiring Information and Diverse Perspectives:** Learners access and evaluate information and diverse perspectives that are available through the language and its cultures.	
COMPARISONS Develop insight into the nature of language and culture in order to interact with cultural competence	**Language Comparisons:** Learners use the language to investigate, explain, and reflect on the nature of language through comparisons of the language studied and their own.	**Cultural Comparisons:** Learners use the language to investigate, explain, and reflect on the concept of culture through comparisons of the cultures studied and their own.	
COMMUNITIES Communicate and interact with cultural competence in order to participate in multilingual communities at home and around the world	**School and Global Communities:** Learners use the language both within and beyond the classroom to interact and collaborate in their community and the globalized world.	**Lifelong Learning:** Learners set goals and reflect on their progress in using languages for enjoyment, enrichment, and advancement.	

Appendix B | ACTFL Proficiency Guidelines Summary

Reading	
Novice	Readers can understand key words and cognates, as well as formulaic phrases that are highly contextualized. They are able to get a limited amount of information from highly predictable texts in which the topic or context is very familiar, such as a weather map. They may rely heavily on their own background knowledge and extralinguistic support (such as the imagery on the weather map) to derive meaning. They are best able to understand a text when they are able to anticipate the information in the text. Recognition of key words, cognates, and formulaic phrases makes comprehension possible.
Intermediate	Readers can understand information conveyed in simple, predictable, loosely connected texts. They rely heavily on contextual clues. They can most easily understand information if the format of the text is familiar, such as in a weather report or a social announcement. They are able to understand texts that convey basic information such as that found in announcements, notices, and online bulletin boards and forums. These texts are non-complex and have a predictable pattern of presentation. The discourse is minimally connected and primarily organized in individual sentences and strings of sentences containing predominantly high-frequency vocabulary. They are most accurate when getting meaning from simple, straightforward texts. They are able to understand messages found in highly familiar, everyday contexts. They may not fully understand texts that are detailed or those texts in which knowledge of language structures is essential in order to understand sequencing, time frame, and chronology.
Advanced	Readers can understand the main idea and supporting details of authentic narrative and descriptive texts. They are able to compensate for limitations in their lexical and structural knowledge by using contextual clues. Comprehension is likewise supported by knowledge of the conventions of the language (e.g., noun/adjective agreement, verb placement, etc.). When familiar with the subject matter, readers are also able to derive some meaning from straightforward argumentative texts (e.g., recognizing the main argument). They are able to understand texts that have a clear and predictable structure. For the most part, the prose is uncomplicated and the subject matter pertains to real-world topics of general interest. They demonstrate an independence in their ability to read subject matter that is new to them. They have sufficient control of standard linguistic conventions to understand sequencing, time frames, and chronology. However, these readers are likely challenged by texts in which issues are treated abstractly.

Listening	
Novice	Listeners can understand key words, true aural cognates, and formulaic expressions that are highly contextualized and highly predictable, such as those found in introductions and basic courtesies. They understand words and phrases from simple questions, statements, and high-frequency commands. They typically require repetition, rephrasing, and/or a slowed rate of speech for comprehension. They rely heavily on extralinguistic support to derive meaning. They are most accurate when they are able to recognize speech that they can anticipate. In this way, these listeners tend to recognize rather than truly comprehend. Their listening is largely dependent on factors other than the message itself.
Intermediate	Listeners can understand information conveyed in simple, sentence-length speech on familiar or everyday topics. They are generally able to comprehend one utterance at a time while engaged in face-to-face conversations or in routine listening tasks such as understanding highly contextualized messages, straightforward announcements, or simple instructions and directions. They rely heavily on redundancy, restatement, paraphrasing, and contextual clues. They understand speech that conveys basic information. This speech is simple, minimally connected, and contains high-frequency vocabulary. They are most accurate in their comprehension when getting meaning from simple, straightforward speech. They are able to comprehend messages found in highly familiar everyday contexts. Intermediate listeners require a controlled listening environment where they hear what they may expect to hear.
Advanced	Listeners can understand the main ideas and most supporting details in connected discourse on a variety of general interest topics, such as news stories, explanations, instructions, anecdotes, or travelogue descriptions. They are able to compensate for limitations in their lexical and structural control of the language by using real-world knowledge and contextual clues. They may also derive some meaning from oral texts at higher levels if they possess significant familiarity with the topic or context. They understand speech that is authentic and connected. This speech is lexically and structurally uncomplicated. The discourse is straightforward and is generally organized in a clear and predictable way. They demonstrate the ability to comprehend language on a range of topics of general interest. They have sufficient knowledge of language structure to understand basic time-frame references. Nevertheless, their understanding is most often limited to concrete, conventional discourse.

Writing	
Novice	Writers at the Novice level are characterized by the ability to produce lists and notes, primarily by writing words and phrases. They can provide limited formulaic information on simple forms and documents. These writers can reproduce practiced material to convey the most simple messages. In addition, they can transcribe familiar words or phrases, copy letters of the alphabet or syllables of a syllabary, or reproduce basic characters with some accuracy.
Intermediate	Writers at the Intermediate level are characterized by the ability to meet practical writing needs, such as simple messages and letters, requests for information, and notes. In addition, they can ask and respond to simple questions in writing. These writers can create with the language and communicate simple facts and ideas in a series of loosely connected sentences on topics of personal interest and social needs. They write primarily in present time. At this level, writers use basic vocabulary and structures to express meaning that is comprehensible to those accustomed to the writing of non-natives.
Advanced	Writers at the Advanced level are characterized by the ability to write routine informal and some formal correspondence, as well as narratives, descriptions, and summaries of a factual nature. They can narrate and describe in the major time frames of past, present, and future, using paraphrasing and elaboration to provide clarity. Advanced-level writers produce connected discourse of paragraph length and structure. At this level, writers show good control of the most frequently used structures and generic vocabulary, allowing them to be understood by those unaccustomed to the writing of non-natives.
Speaking	
Novice	Novice-level speakers can communicate short messages on highly predictable, everyday topics that affect them directly. They do so primarily through the use of isolated words and phrases that have been encountered, memorized, and recalled. Novice-level speakers may be difficult to understand even by the most sympathetic interlocutors accustomed to non-native speech.
Intermediate	Speakers at the Intermediate level are distinguished primarily by their ability to create with the language when talking about familiar topics related to their daily life. They are able to recombine learned material in order to express personal meaning. Intermediate-level speakers can ask simple questions and can handle a straightforward survival situation. They produce sentence-level language, ranging from discrete sentences to strings of sentences, typically in present time. Intermediate-level speakers are understood by interlocutors who are accustomed to dealing with non-native learners of the language.
Advanced	Speakers at the Advanced level engage in conversation in a clearly participatory manner in order to communicate information on autobiographical topics, as well as topics of community, national, or international interest. The topics are handled concretely by means of narration and description in the major time frames of past, present, and future. These speakers can also deal with a social situation with an unexpected complication. The language of Advanced-level speakers is abundant, the oral paragraph being the measure of Advanced-level length and discourse. Advanced-level speakers have sufficient control of basic structures and generic vocabulary to be understood by native speakers of the language, including those unaccustomed to non-native speech.

Appendix C | Methods, Theories, and Approaches of Language Acquisition

Methods/Theories/ Approaches	Teacher	Student	Summary	Example: Teaching *Bonjour*/Hello
Grammar Translation	• uses authentic texts • explains grammar, vocabulary, and culture in native language • prepares grammar and vocabulary exercises	• reads silently • listens to explanations • memorizes words and rules • prepares written translations	Learners memorize the rules of the language in order to read and translate texts.	*"Bonjour" learned by vocabulary lists and by translating.* *Bonjour = Hello* *Hello = Bonjour*
Direct/Natural	• uses language actively in classroom • uses actions and demonstration to convey meaning • focuses on pronunciation • teaches grammar inductively	• repeats the language, correct pronunciation important • figures out grammar rules	Learners repeat and memorize oral dialogues. They ask and answer formulaic questions in class, work in language labs. Dictation is a common practice.	*"Bonjour" learned through numerous, frequent repetitions.* *T: Bonjour* *S: Bonjour*
Audio-Lingual Method (ALM)	• introduces dialogues that are typical of certain situations—post office, restaurant, etc.	• reads and repeats dialogues • memorizes dialogues	Learners memorize formal dialogues that do not capture authentic ways of speaking.	*"Bonjour" learned in numerous, frequent dialogues.* *- Bonjour, Pierre.* *- Bonjour, Anne.*
Functional– Notional	• selects topics relevant to learners' lives • determines function needed for topic • teaches grammar when it is needed	• interacts conversationally using functions and grammatical structure	Learners interact in realistic ways about topics of interest. Language is often constrained by requiring learners to use certain structures tied to functions.	*"Bonjour" becomes a way to meet and greet someone.*
Communicative Competency Proficiency-Based	• engages learners in conversation • creates scenarios to perform functions in a range of contexts • places focus on meaning and form	• participates in conversational role plays • attends to meaning and form	Learners use language in situations that approximate real-life, but are not always real to students.	*"Bonjour" becomes part of role-plays, games, and simulations.* Teacher gives the task: You are meeting a foreign exchange student for the first time. Greet him or her.

Methods/Theories	Teacher Approach	Student Activities	Summary	Example: Teaching *Bonjour*/Hello
Total Physical Response (TPR) **Total Proficiency Through Reading and Storytelling (TPRS)**	• develops comprehension before speech • gives commands in the target language • makes use of gestures, and physical action to convey meaning • creates and shares stories using previously learned vocabulary	• infers meaning from commands and stories • acts out commands • acts out stories • retells story; creates own versions of stories by recombining learned elements	Learners demonstrate comprehension by their actions and responses. They are able to recombine elements to create personal stories.	*"Bonjour" is acted out or becomes part of a story.* Student hears *Bonjour* and waves hand. Student creates a story that incorporates *Bonjour*.
Task-Based **Project-Based**	• develops tasks that require learner to use target language to meet a specific objective • designs task for use of selected grammar and vocabulary items	• negotiates meaning to understand others • uses language to complete tasks	Learners complete tasks, but may be able to do so without use of the target language or by avoiding intended linguistic structures and vocabulary.	*"Bonjour" is an element of a task.* Teacher assigns task: You will be welcoming visitors from various countries. Design a multimedia, print, and audio campaign that greets everyone appropriately.
Content-Based	• uses the target language 100% of the time • teaches grade-level content • integrates language skills as content is taught	• learns content in the target language • uses language skills to demonstrate comprehension of content	Learners use language to access and understand content while developing increased language skills.	*"Bonjour" is not necessarily part of the unit.* *Bonjour* may or may not be learned as students work with the life cycle of a butterfly in science class.
Sociocultural	• uses authentic text as cultural artifacts • focuses on culturally respectful communication • plans tasks that allow learners to perform beyond current ability but within the Zone of Proximal Development (Vygotsky)	• develops language skills by interacting with others • work extensively with authentic text • attends to cultural and communicative competence	Learners engage with language by working with concepts, language, and symbols in ways that language speakers do.	*"Bonjour" occurs in an authentic situation (e.g., learners may watch a movie).* Learners interact with authentic text to learn *Bonjour*.

Based on information from Horowitz (2008), Mickan (2013), and Shrum and Glisan (2010).

Appendix D | Challenges: Education

Language and Level/Grade	French – High School	Approximate Length of Unit	6 weeks
Performance Range	Novice High/Intermediate Low	Approximate Number of Minutes Weekly	250 minutes/weekly
Theme/Topic	Challenges: Education		
Essential Question	Why can't all young people go to school?		

Unit Goals

What should learners know and be able to do by the end of the unit?	Learners will be able to: • Describe the current status of education of young people locally, nationally, and globally. • Identify and categorize economic, political, and social reasons why young people around the world cannot go to/stay in school. • Give reasons why going to school is important to oneself and locally, nationally, globally. • Give examples of initiatives to support schooling for all young people around the world. • Connect with a school in (country) to learn more about the school; collaborate to develop a plan for continued communication.

Summative Performance Assessment Tasks

• *These tasks allow learners to demonstrate how well they have met the goals of the unit.* • *The tasks follow the format of the IPA, but are integrated throughout the unit.* • *The template encourages multiple Interpretive tasks.* • *The Interpretive tasks inform the content of the Presentational and Interpersonal tasks.* • *The tasks incorporate 21st Century Learning.*	**Interpretive Mode**

Watch a movie about a young girl in Sénégal who cannot go to school; identify reasons that prevent her from attending school.	Read an article about preparing for work and careers in the 21st century; identify reasons why it is important for all young people to go to school.	Listen to an appeal for support of an initiative to help young people stay in school; describe the main components of the initiative.

Presentational Mode	**Interpersonal Mode**
Polished: Work in groups to design a multimedia campaign to inform others of literacy rates around the world and ways that organizations are working to increase literacy rates globally. **On Demand:** Respond to these questions in writing: What are reasons that all children cannot go to school? What are some possible solutions to this global problem?	Share ideas about the role and importance of education for all, and barriers to school attendance for young people locally, nationally, internationally. In small groups, discuss ways that the class could collaborate with a school in (country) to support the school's education program.

Standards

Cultures (Sample Evidence) *Indicate the relationship between the product, practice, and perspective*	Relating Cultural Practices and Products to Perspectives
	Product: School **Practice:** Going to School **Perspective:** Importance of school for all young people in (country) **Product:** Daily class schedule **Practice**: Required vs elective courses **Perspective:** Purpose of school

Connections (Sample Evidence)	Making Connections to Other Disciplines	Acquiring Information and Diverse Viewpoints
	Social Studies: • Education as a right of the child (United Nations) • Global challenge of increasing literacy rates English Language Arts and Literacy: • Evaluation of the accuracy and validity of information from different Internet sources • Synthesis of information • Sharing information and ideas with others through discussions	• Reading articles and viewing video clips from a variety of authentic sources about education and literacy rates around the world • Interviewing native speakers of the target language about their attitudes towards school

Comparisons (Sample Evidence)	Language Comparisons		Cultural Comparisons
	• *Une année blanche* (a missed year of school) • *Passer le bac* (to take the French exam at the end of high school)		• Reasons to attend/not attend school • Final exams in high school
Communities (Sample Evidence)	School and Global Communities		Lifelong Learning
	Inform others about education around the world and opportunities for collaboration on a project related to education for all.		• Self-assess progress toward personal learning goals/Can-Do Statements. • Consider the role that education plays in your life and set goals related to how to continue your studies and/or explore new learning opportunities

Connections to Other Standards
• **21st Century Learning: Collaboration** Work together to determine how to best collaborate with another school • **21st Century Learning: Creativity** Create a mulit-media campaign on literacy • **21st Century Learning: Critical Thinking:** Evaluate the role that education plays in your life and set goals related to future learning opportunities • **Common Core: Reading 1:** Read closely to determine what the text says explicitly and to make logical inferences from it; cite specific textual evidence when writing or speaking to support conclusions drawn from the text. • **Common Core: Speaking and Listening 1:** Prepare for and participate effectively in a range of conversations and collaborations with diverse partners, building on others' ideas and expressing their own clearly and persuasively. • **Common Core: Writing 7:** Conduct short as well as more sustained research projects based on focused questions, demonstrating understanding of the subject under investigation.

Toolbox

Can-Do Statements

Interpretive	(Reading) I can understand infographics sharing statistics on school attendance around the world. (Reading + Listening) I can understand when others share their opinions about the importance of an educataion. (Listening) I can understand details from a video that presents information on literacy and the challenges associated with literacy around the world.
Presentational	(Speaking + Writing) I can share information about a specific school making suggestions for how to engage with that school. (Speaking + Writing) I can state my opinions about education and the role of education in my life and society. (Speaking + Writing) I can make others aware of similarities and differences in schools around the world.
Interpersonal	• I can exchange opinions about school and the role that education plays in society. • I can share information about a school in another culture. • I can discuss challenges associated with the right to an education for all children.

Supporting Functions	Supporting Structures / Patterns	Priority Vocabulary
Compare *various components of school systems/ schedules*	*plus de, moins de, autant de* (more of, less of, as much of)	• school subjects • school classrooms
Describe *attitudes toward attending school*	*Il est important que, Il est nécessaire que, il est dommage que, afin que, pour que* (It's important that, it's necessary that, it's too bad that, so that, in order that)	*Les droits de l'enfant* (rights of the child) *Manquer de formation* (lack training/schooling) *Aller à l'école* (to go to school) *Assister aux cours* (to attend classes)
Express opinions *on the importance of school*	*Il est important que, Il est nécessaire que, il est dommage que, afin que, pour que* (It's important that, it's necessary that, it's too bad that, so that, in order that)	*Réussir/échouer* (to pass/to fail) *Relier/Partager/Echanger* (to connect, to share, to exchange) *L'alphabétisation* (literacy)
Ask and answer questions *to learn more about schooling in other cultures*	Interrogatives	*Obligatoire/facultatif* (required/ optional)

Key Learning Activities/Formative Assessments		
This is a representative sample of activities/assessments across the 3 modes of communication.		
Learning Activity/Formative Assessment *(Sample activities are listed from the beginning to the end of the unit).*	How does this activity support the unit goals or performance tasks?	Mode of Communication
Small groups: brainstorm why we have schools	Introduce the role and importance of school	Interpersonal
Listen to song Sacre Charlemagne: identify who invented schools according to the song; determine attitude toward school in song	Provide background information on school	Interpretive
Read short biography of Charlemagne and his view on the importance of education	Provide historic context for schools	Interpretive
Read "l'histoire de l'école" and create a timeline of important dates related to schools http://www.copaindumonde.org/5136.0.HTML	Provide historic context for schools	Interpretive Presentational
Compare school systems in various countries around the world	Provide information on schools	Interpretive Presentational
Small groups: brainstorm reasons why all young people locally, nationally, internationally can't go to school	Assess background knowledge	Interpersonal
Read http://www.copaindumonde.org/5145.0.HTML and list the current situation related to children's rights to school.	Provide current information on schooling	Interpretive
View film explaining the importance of education for all children at http://www.YouTube.com/watch?v=OI3eK2r75T8= ; afterwards discuss in small groups the degree to which you agree with the film's perspective	Viewpoint on why education is important	Interpretve Interpersonal
View: http://prezi.com/_9icbrqc-uhg/education-counts/	Provide global context	Interpretive

Resources	Technology Integration
La Petite Vendeuse de Soleil – film about girl in Sénégal World Wise Schools website about education http://wws.peacecorps.gov/wws/educators/lessonplans/lesson.cfm?lpid=3578 Film explaining importance of education for all children http://www.youtube.com/watch?v=OI3eK2r75T8 Additional resources available at: http://clementi-terrill2012.wikispaces.com	www.epals.com allows you to connect with classrooms around the world www.skype.com allows you to connect with others via live video education.weebly.com allows you to create an interactive website

Appendix E | Common Core Anchor Standards

Reading

Key Ideas and Details

R1: Read closely to determine what the text says explicitly and to make logical inferences from it; cite specific textual evidence when writing or speaking to support conclusions drawn from the text.

R2: Determine central ideas or themes of a text and analyze their development; summarize the key supporting details and ideas.

R3: Analyze how and why individuals, events, and ideas develop and interact over the course of a text.

Craft and Structure

R4: Interpret words and phrases as they are used in a text, including determining technical, connotative, and figurative meanings, and analyze how specific word choices shape meaning or tone.

R5: Analyze the structure of texts, including how specific sentences, paragraphs, and larger portions of the text (e.g., a section, chapter, scene, or stanza) relate to each other and the whole.

R6: Assess how point of view or purpose shapes the content and style of a text.

Integration of Knowledge and Ideas

R7: Integrate and evaluate content presented in diverse formats and media, including visually and quantitatively, as well as in words.

R8: Delineate and evaluate the argument and specific claims in a text, including the validity of the reasoning as well as the relevance and sufficiency of the evidence.

R9: Analyze how two or more texts address similar themes or topics in order to build knowledge or to compare the approaches the authors take.

Range of Reading and Level of Text Complexity

R10: Read and comprehend complex literary and informational texts independently and proficiently.

Writing

Text Types and Purposes

W1: Write arguments to support claims in an analysis of substantive topics or texts, using valid reasoning and relevant and sufficient evidence.

W2: Write informative/explanatory texts to examine and convey complex ideas and information clearly and accurately through the effective selection, organization, and analysis of content.

W3: Write narratives to develop real or imagined experiences or events using effective technique, well-chosen details, and well-structured event sequences.

Production and Distribution of Writing

W4: Produce clear and coherent writing in which the development, organization, and style are appropriate to task, purpose, and audience.

W5: Develop and strengthen writing as needed by planning, revising, editing, rewriting, or trying a new approach.

W6: Use technology, including the Internet, to produce and publish writing and to interact and collaborate with others.

Research to Build and Present Knowledge

W7: Conduct short as well as more sustained research projects based on focused questions, demonstrating understanding of the subject under investigation.

W8: Gather relevant information from multiple print and digital sources, assess the credibility and accuracy of each source, and integrate the information while avoiding plagiarism.

W9: Draw evidence from literary or informational texts to support analysis, reflection, and research.

Range of Writing

W10: Write routinely over extended time frames (time for research, reflection, and revision) and shorter time frames (a single sitting or a day or two) for a range of tasks, purposes, and audiences.

Speaking and Listening

Comprehension and Collaboration

SL1: Prepare for and participate effectively in a range of conversations and collaborations with diverse partners, building on others' ideas, and expressing their own clearly and persuasively.

SL2: Integrate and evaluate information presented in diverse media and formats, including visually, quantitatively, and orally.

SL3: Evaluate a speaker's point of view, reasoning, and use of evidence and rhetoric.

Presentation of Knowledge and Ideas

SL4: Present information, findings, and supporting evidence such that listeners can follow the line of reasoning and the organization, development, and style are appropriate to task, purpose, and audience.

SL5: Make strategic use of digital media and visual displays of data to express information and enhance understanding of presentations.

SL6: Adapt speech to a variety of contexts and communicative tasks, demonstrating command of formal English when indicated or appropriate.

Language

Conventions of Standard English

L1: Demonstrate command of the conventions of standard English grammar and usage when writing or speaking.

L2: Demonstrate command of the conventions of standard English capitalization, punctuation, and spelling when writing.

Knowledge of Language

L3: Apply knowledge of language to understand how language functions in different contexts, to make effective choices for meaning or style, and to comprehend more fully when reading or listening.

Vocabulary Acquisition and Use

L4: Determine or clarify the meaning of unknown and multiple-meaning words and phrases by using context clues, analyzing meaningful word parts, and consulting general and specialized reference materials, as appropriate.

L5: Demonstrate understanding of figurative language, word relationships, and nuances in word meanings.

L6: Acquire and use accurately a range of general academic and domain-specific words and phrases sufficient for reading, writing, speaking, and listening at the college and career readiness level; demonstrate independence in gathering vocabulary knowledge when considering a word or phrase important to comprehension or expression.

Appendix F | NCSSFL-ACTFL Can-Do Proficiency Benchmarks

	NOVICE PROFICIENCY BENCHMARK	INTERMEDIATE PROFICIENCY BENCHMARK
COMMUNICATION		
INTERPRETIVE	*I can* identify the general topic and some basic information in both very familiar and everyday contexts by recognizing practiced or memorized words, phrases, and simple sentences in texts that are spoken, written, or signed.	*I can* understand the main idea and some pieces of information on familiar topics from sentences and series of connected sentences within texts that are spoken, written, or signed.
INTERPERSONAL	*I can* communicate in spontaneous spoken, written, or signed conversations on both very familiar and everyday topics, using a variety of practiced or memorized words, phrases, simple sentences, and questions.	*I can* participate in spontaneous spoken, written, or signed conversations on familiar topics, creating sentences and series of sentences to ask and answer a variety of questions.
PRESENTATIONAL	*I can* present information on both very familiar and everyday topics using a variety of practiced or memorized words, phrases, and simple sentences through spoken, written, or signed language.	*I can* communicate information, make presentations, and express my thoughts about familiar topics, using sentences and series of connected sentences through spoken, written, or signed language.

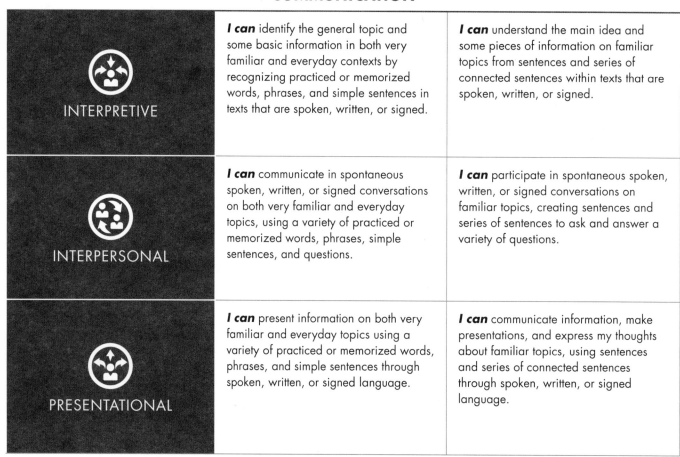

Find the complete NCSSFL-ACTFL Can-Do Statements at *www.actfl.org/resources/ncssfl-actfl-can-do-statements.*

ADVANCED PROFICIENCY BENCHMARK	SUPERIOR PROFICIENCY BENCHMARK	DISTINGUISHED PROFICIENCY BENCHMARK	
COMMUNICATION			
I can understand the main message and supporting details on a wide variety of familiar and general interest topics across various time frames from complex, organized texts that are spoken, written, or signed.	*I can* interpret and infer meaning from complex, academic and professional texts on a range of unfamiliar, abstract, and specialized issues that are spoken, written, or signed.	*I can* interpret and infer meaning from dense, structurally sophisticated texts on a wide range of global issues and highly abstract concepts, with deeply embedded cultural references and colloquialisms and dialects that are spoken, written, or signed.	INTERPRETIVE
I can maintain spontaneous spoken, written, or signed conversations and discussions across various time frames on familiar, as well as unfamiliar, concrete topics, using series of connected sentences and probing questions.	*I can* participate fully and effectively in spontaneous spoken, written, or signed discussions and debates on issues and ideas ranging from broad general interests to my areas of specialized expertise, including supporting arguments and exploring hypotheses.	*I can* interact, negotiate, and debate on a wide range of global issues and highly abstract concepts, fully adapting to the cultural context of the conversation, using spoken, written, or signed language.	INTERPERSONAL
I can deliver detailed and organized presentations on familiar as well as unfamiliar concrete topics, in paragraphs and using various time frames through spoken, written, or signed language.	*I can* deliver extended presentations on abstract or hypothetical issues and ideas ranging from broad general interests to my areas of specialized expertise, with precision of expression and to a wide variety of audiences, using spoken, written, or signed language.	*I can* deliver sophisticated and articulate presentations on a wide range of global issues and highly abstract concepts, fully adapting to the cultural context of the audience, using spoken, written, or signed language.	PRESENTATIONAL

Appendix G | Essential Questions

	Novice Range	→	Intermediate Range	→	Advanced Range
Identity/Belonging	Who am I?	→	How is family defined?	→	Why is global collaboration important?
	How do I contribute to my community?		How can I gain the skills that I need for my future?		How does learning another language and culture influence who I am and my view of the world?
Challenges	What are the rights of a child?	→	Why can't all young people go to school?	→	Why is lifelong learning a necessity in the 21st century?
	What is hunger?		What is the connection between clean water and quality of life?		How does overpopulation impact quality of life around the world?
Creativity	How do I contribute to society?	→	How do you use your imagination?	→	How can schools encourage creativity and innovation?
	What do artists do?		How do music and art reflect society?		What makes a piece of literature a classic?
Discovery	Who are the inventors?	→	How are advances in science impacting my life today?	→	How do inventions influence the quality of life on earth?
	Who are the explorers?		What parts of our world need to be explored?		Where are the next frontiers to explore?
Exploring Time and Place	What dates are important on my personal timeline?	→	What events from (France's) past continue to influence (France) today?	→	Why do people say that history repeats itself?
	What makes a city special?		How does where I live influence my lifestyle?		Why do people say: It's a great place to visit, but I wouldn't want to live there?
Well-being	How do people here and in (the French-speaking world) describe a balanced lifestyle?	→	What impact does technology have on our lifestyles?	→	What role does media play in shaping public opinion?
	Where does our food come from?		Eat to live or live to eat: What is the difference?		Why consider joining the "slow food" movement?

Appendix H | Well-being: A Balanced Lifestyle

Language and Level / Grade	French – High School	Approximate Length of Unit	6 weeks
Performance Range	Novice Mid/ Novice High	Approximate Number of Minutes Weekly	250 minutes/weekly
Theme/Topic	**Well-being:** A Balanced Lifestyle		
Essential Question	How do people here and in the (French)-speaking world describe a balanced lifestyle?		

Unit Goals

What should learners know and be able to do by the end of the unit?	Learners will be able to: • *Describe their daily/weekly routines and categorize their activities in terms of relaxation, social life, physical fitness, academics, work (jobs or volunteer).* • *Compare their daily/weekly routine to their classmates' routines.* • *Explore several health and wellness websites in order to identify elements of a balanced lifestyle here and in (the French-speaking world).* • *Link with a classroom in the (French-speaking world) in order to learn about their daily/weekly routines.* • *Compare daily/weekly routines of young people in the US to the routines of young people in the (French-speaking world).* • *Create a definition for a "balanced lifestyle" for teenagers based on information from websites, readings, and interviews with teenagers in the (French-speaking world).* • *Make recommendations for a daily/weekly routine that reflects the definition developed in this unit.* • *Create a presentation for (the community) highlighting ways to encourage a balanced lifestyle.*

Summative Performance Assessment Tasks

Interpretive Mode

• *These tasks allow learners to demonstrate how well they have met the goals of the unit.* • *The tasks follow the format of the IPA, but are integrated throughout the unit.* • *The template encourages multiple interpretive tasks.* • *The Interpretive tasks inform the content of the Presentational and Interpersonal tasks.* • *The tasks incorporate 21st Century Learning.*	Read a blog written by a teenager where he discusses his activities. Demonstrate comprehension by completing a graphic organizer based on information found in the text.	Watch a commercial for a product that promises to make life easier or less stressful and identify audience, purpose, and message.	Read a schedule of a top athlete to determine how he spends the hours in his day. Decide which elements are part of a balanced lifestyle and which elements, if any, are missing.

Presentational Mode	**Interpersonal Mode**
Polished: Create a presentation based on multiple sources of information highlighting ways to promote a balanced lifestyle for teenagers. Share the presentation with another French class. **On Demand:** Write a paragraph explaining how balanced your lifestyle is, making simple comparisons to balanced lifestyles in the target culture.	In pairs or small groups, share what they have learned about their lifestyle and the lifestyle of teenagers in (the French-speaking world) in terms of balance. Compare daily routines, making and responding to suggestions to adjust their lifestyle.

Standards

Cultures	**Relating Cultural Practices and Products to Perspectives**	
(Sample Evidence) *Indicate the relationship between the product, practice, and perspective*	**Product:** Café **Practice:** Stopping with friends for coffee **Perspective:** It's not the coffee, it's the conversation. **Product:** School year calendar **Practice**: Regular breaks, holidays **Perspective:** Balance	
Connections (Sample Evidence)	**Making Connections to Other Disciplines**	**Acquiring Information and Diverse Viewpoints**
	Health and wellness: Compare recommendations for healthy lifestyles. **Media studies:** Consider impact of media on lifestyle considerations like diet and exercise.	• Differences in school schedules • Importance of vacation and family time • Tradition of *"Fermature annuelle"* (annual closing) in France

Comparisons (Sample Evidence)	Language Comparisons	Cultural Comparisons
	• *la joie de vivre* (joy of living) • *métro, boulot, dodo* (subway, work, sleep) • Ne t'en fais pas! (Don't worry!) • *la détente* (relaxation)	• Work time/leisure time • Mealtime with/without family • Weekend activities

Communities (Sample Evidence)	School and Global Communities	Lifelong Learning
	Share information on wellness with community.	• Self-assess progress toward personal learning goals/Can-Do Statements. • Examine personal lifestyle and make adjustments as needed.

Connections to Other Standards	
	• **21st Century Learning: Collaboration** Work together to design materials to promote balance. • **21st Century Learning: Creativity** Create a persuasive piece that can be shared with others. • **21st Century Learning: Critical Thinking:** Evaluate your lifestyle in terms of balance from an American and a (French) perspective. • **Common Core: Reading 1:** Read closely to determine what the text says explicitly and to make logical inferences from it; cite specific textual evidence when writing or speaking to support conclusions drawn from the text. • **Common Core: Language 4:** Determine or clarify the meaning of unknown and multiple-meaning words and phrases by using context clues, analyzing meaningful word parts, and consulting general and specialized reference materials as appropriate. • **Common Core: Writing 6:** Use technology, including the Internet, to produce and publish writing and to interact and collaborate with others. • **Common Core: Writing 7:** Conduct short as well as more sustained research projects based on focused questions, demonstrating understanding of the subject under investigation. • **Common Core: Speaking and Listening 1:** Prepare for and participate effectively in a range of conversations and collaborations.

Toolbox

Can-Do Statements

Interpretive	(Reading + Listening) I can understand when someone talks about their daily routine. (Reading + Listening) I can understand simple illustrated instructions for exercises to do to stay in shape. (Reading) I can understand a short interview where an athlete shares his daily routine to stay in shape. (Listening) I can understand people as they describe their daily routines.
Presentational	(Speaking + Writing) I can present information about the elements of a balanced lifestyle. (Speaking + Writing) I can present information comparing lifestyles in France and the U.S. (Writing) I can keep a diet and exercise journal to track what I do to stay healthy.
Interpersonal	• I can ask and answer questions about what I do each day to be healthy. • I can share how often I do certain activities each week. • I can exchange information about what people in (country) do to be healthy.

Supporting Functions	Supporting Structures / Patterns	Priority Vocabulary
Compare *lifestyle routines*	*plus que, moins que, aussi que* (more than, less than, as…as)	• expressions of time • adverbs of frequency • days, months • time • feelings *Une bonne hygiène de vie* (a healthy lifestyle) *Un régime équilibré* (a balanced diet) *La détente* (relaxation) *S'entraîner* (to exercise) *Se détendre/se dépêcher* (to relax/to hurry) *Être détendu/être stressé* (to be relaxed/to be stressed)
Describe *your daily schedule*	*(le) lundi…* (on Mondays)	
Ask and answer questions *about daily routines*	*oui/non* (yes/no), *ou* (either/or), *quand* (when), *à quelle heure* (at what time)	
Express frequency *saying when and how often you do certain things*	*tous les jours* (everyday) *une fois par semaine* (once a week), *rarement* (rarely)	
Express needs *saying what you need to do to be healthy*	*Il faut / Il me faut* (It's necessary/I need)	
Express opinions *about daily activities, schedules*	*Il est important de, Il est bon de* (It's important to/it's good to)	
Make suggestions *about ways to be healthy*	*Tu devrais / Vous devriez* (You should) *Il te/vous faut* (You need to)	

Key Learning Activities/Formative Assessments		
This is a representative sample of activities/assessments across the 3 modes of communication.		
Learning Activity/Formative Assessment *(Sample activities are listed from the beginning to the end of the unit).*	How does this activity support the unit goals or performance tasks?	Mode of Communication
Watch video clip of Song – *Ma Vie au Soleil* (My Life in the Sun), list activities that relate to *métro, boulot, dodo* (subway, work, sleep) and activities that relate to a more relaxed lifestyle.	Explore elements of a balanced lifestyle	Interpretive
Use *Libération* magazine headline and article on stress at school. Have learners complete graphic organizer with statistics from article and then compare to their own situations.	Impact of school on lifestyles	Interpretive Interpersonal
Read article on how French teenagers spend free time. Design survey questions to use with learners studying French. Create graphic organizer to compare school results to those in article. Discuss results in groups.	How French teens spend free-time and make comparisons	Interpretive Interpersonal Presentational
Work in groups to create a multi-media presentation that explains métro, boulot, dodo (subway, work, sleep) in the context of a teenager's life in the US.	Product that explains the lifestyle of a US teenager to French teens	Interpersonal Presentation
Watch silent movie – UNICEF clip on right of child to play. Discuss and compare to metro, boulot, dodo (subway, work, sleep).	Concept of balanced lifestyle from different perspective	Interpretive Interpersonal
Read French Girl in Seattle: *Une Visite au café* (A visit to the café). Select an image from the article or a personal image. Explain the role of the café from the perspective of the article and from your perspective. Post your image and comments.	Introduce learners to cafés; allows learners to process concept of café	Interpretive Presentational
Read article Les lycéens se retrouvent au café (*High school students meet in the café*); discuss what you like and don't like about the activities; consider what the equivalent might be in your community.	Consider role of café for teens and make comparisons	Interpretive Interpersonal
Compare two *Maisons des Jeunes* (*Youth recreation centers*) for hours and activities. Compare to local recreational facility.	Importance of teen centers and comparison to US	Interpretive
Create a proposal for a local teen café or an advertisement for one that already exists.	Determine needs of local community and address those needs	Presentational
Read article on importance of sleep; discuss typical sleep habits.	Summarize healthy behaviors; give advice; served as model of how they might present	Interpretive Interpersonal
View video La moitié des ados manquent de sommeil (*Half of teenager lack sleep*).	Listen for specific issues/advice	Interpretive
Select an article from the website *mangerbouger.fr* that deals with health and wellness. Read individually first. Then, identify key points with group. Decide how to best share information with other groups.	Initial preparation for possible wellness fair presentations	Interpretive Interpersonal Presentational
Resources	**Technology Integration**	
Ma Vie au Soleil -https://www.youtube.com/watch?v=NqyOJ7oUnbl http://www3.sympatico.ca/serge.richard2/ http://www3.sympatico.ca/serge.richard2/page5.html Additional resources available at: http://clementi-terrill2012.wikispaces.com	Teachers can create a safe, free space for learner blogs and more: http://kidblog.org	

Appendix I | Unit Template

Language and Level / Grade		Approximate Length of Unit	
Performance Range		Approximate Number of Minutes Weekly	
Theme/Topic			
Essential Question			

	Unit Goals
What should learners know and be able to do by the end of the unit?	Learners will be able to:

	Summative Performance Assessment Tasks

	Interpretive Mode
• These tasks allow learners to demonstrate how well they have met the goals of the unit. • The tasks follow the format of the IPA, but are integrated throughout the unit. • The template encourages multiple interpretive tasks. • The Interpretive tasks inform the content of the Presentational and Interpersonal tasks. • The tasks incorporate 21st Century Learning.	

Presentational Mode	Interpersonal Mode

	Standards

	Relating Cultural Practices and Products to Perspectives
Cultures (Sample Evidence) *Indicate the relationship between the product, practice, and perspective*	**Product:** **Practice:** **Perspective:** **Product:** **Practice:** **Perspective:**

Connections (Sample Evidence)	Making Connections to Other Disciplines	Acquiring Information and Diverse Viewpoints

Comparisons (Sample Evidence)	Language Comparisons	Cultural Comparisons

Communities (Sample Evidence)	School and Global Communities	Lifelong Learning

Connections to Other Standards	

Toolbox		
Can-Do Statements		
Interpretive		
Presentational		
Interpersonal		
Supporting Functions	**Supporting Structures / Patterns**	**Priority Vocabulary**

Key Learning Activities/Formative Assessments		
This is a representative sample of activities/assessments across the 3 modes of communication.		
Learning Activity/Formative Assessment (*Sample activities are listed from the beginning to the end of the unit*).	**How does this activity support the unit goals or performance tasks?**	**Mode of Communication**

Resources	Technology Integration

Appendix J | Key Language Functions and Sample Progressions

Novice	Intermediate	Advanced

Describing People, Places, Things, How and How Well

Give a description using one or two short adjectives or adverbs	Give a basic description & make simple comparisons using frequently used adjectives and adverbs	Give more detailed descriptions including comparatives, contrasts, and superlatives	Give detailed descriptions using a variety of precise adjectives and adverbs	Give detailed descriptions using a wide variety of precise adjectives and adverbs

Related Language Functions

- *Analyze*
- *Categorize*
- *Classify*
- *Clarify*
- *Compare*
- *Contrast*
- *Count*
- *Define*

- *Describe*
- *Describe physical characteristics*
- *Describe the weather*
- *Differentiate*
- *Edit*
- *Evaluate*
- *Explain*
- *Give biographical information*

- *Give examples*
- *Identify*
- *Illustrate*
- *Infer*
- *Interpret*
- *Label*
- *List*
- *Locate*

- *Name*
- *Paraphrase*
- *Present*
- *Rephrase*
- *Restate*
- *Rewrite*
- *Summarize*

Asking and Answering Questions

Respond to a simple question	Ask and respond to simple, memorized questions	Ask and respond with some details to a variety of informational questions and follow-up questions	Ask and respond with details to a wide variety of questions including follow-up questions that request details	Ask and respond with elaboration to a wide variety of questions, including follow-up questions that request detailed explanations

Related Language Functions

- *Ask for/give biographical Information*
- *Ask for/give clarification*
- *Ask for/give directions*

- *Ask for/give/refuse permission*
- *Ask for/give time, day, date*

- *Ask/respond to informational questions: who, what, when, where, how, why, how much, how many*

- *Ask and respond to what the weather is like*
- *Extend/accept/refuse invitations*
- *Request/respond*

Expressing Feelings and Emotions

Say that I am happy or sad	Express basic emotions and feelings	Express a variety of emotions and feelings	Express a wide variety of emotions and feelings, beginning to distinguish shades of meaning (ex: happy, thrilled, ecstatic)	Express a wide variety of emotions and feelings, choosing precise expressions appropriately to reflect shades of meaning

Related Language Functions

- *Apologize/forgive*
- *Attract attention*
- *Blame*
- *Complain*
- *Compliment*
- *Congratulate*

- *Express certainty/uncertainty*
- *Express doubt/indecision*
- *Express emotions/feelings*
- *Express interest/lack of interest/indifference/boredom*

- *Express regret*
- *Express surprise*
- *Express sympathy*
- *Mediate/conciliate*

- *Praise/criticize*
- *Thank*
- *Warn*

Novice		Intermediate		Advanced

Expressing Advice, Opinions, Preferences

Say I like or don't like something	Express preferences/ opinions in simple sentences	Express opinions/advice with reasons	Express opinions/advice with evidence-based justifications	Express opinions/advice with detailed rationales or arguments based on evidence

Related Language Functions

- *Accept/refuse invitations*
- *Agree/disagree*
- *Analyze/interpret*
- *Approve/disapprove*
- *Argue*
- *Confirm/admit/deny*
- *Contradict*

- *Criticize*
- *Critique*
- *Encourage*
- *Evaluate*
- *Explain*
- *Express likes/dislikes/preferences*
- *Express obligation*

- *Express opinions*
- *Express possibility/impossibility*
- *Express probability/improbability*
- *Give advice*
- *Give possible solutions*
- *Give reasons and explain causality*
- *Judge*

- *Justify*
- *Negotiate*
- *Offer alternatives/solutions*
- *Persuade/dissuade*
- *Recommend*
- *Suggest*

Telling and Retelling Stories; Sequencing

Recount what I am doing in short, memorized sentences	Tell someone about my day, activities, an event in a simple sequence of sentences	Tell a story or recount an event in a logical sequence of sentences	Tell a detailed story about something that happened, logically sequencing the events	Recount a story or event using paragraph-length narration

Related Language Functions

- *Compile*
- *Compose*
- *Construct*
- *Create*
- *Depict*
- *Describe*
- *Document*

- *Explain*
- *Express cause & effect*
- *Express daily routines*
- *Give commands*
- *Give directions*
- *Give supporting details*
- *Illustrate*

- *Instruct*
- *Narrate*
- *Outline*
- *Organize*
- *Present information*
- *Recount experiences/events*
- *Report*

- *Retell*
- *Sequence*
- *Summarize*
- *Tell*

Expressing Hopes, Dreams, Possibilities

Express my plans simply for later in the day, the next day, weekend	Express hopes, plans for the future simply (ex: I hope to…; I will…)	Express hopes, dreams, plans for the future with some details (ex: I would like to…; in order to become X, I will need to…)	Express hopes, dreams, plans, possibilities with explanations (ex: If I could live anywhere in the world, I would live in X because….)	Express hopes, dreams, plans, possibilities with detailed explanations

Related Language Functions

- *Express hopes*
- *Express intentions*
- *Express needs/want*
- *Express wishess*

- *Formulate*
- *Hypothesize*
- *Make appointments, arrangements, reservations*

- *Make recommendations*
- *Plan*
- *Predict*
- *Promise*

- *Speculate on the future*
- *Talk about the future*

Appendix K | Lesson Plan Template

Performance Range		Grade		Date		Day in Unit		Minutes	
Theme/Topic									
Essential Question									
Daily Topic									

STANDARDS		LESSON OBJECTIVES		
What are the communicative and cultural objectives for the lesson?	**Communication and Cultures**	*Which modes of communication will be addressed?* ☐ Interpersonal ☐ Interpretive ☐ Presentational	**Learners can:**	
If applicable, indicate how this lesson connects to other standards.	**Connections**			
	Comparisons			
	Communities			
	Other Standards			

Lesson Sequence	Activity/Activities What will learners do? What does the teacher do?	Time* How many minutes will this segment take?	Materials/Resources/Technology Be specific. What materials will you develop? What materials will you bring in from other sources?
Gain Attention/ Activate Prior Knowledge			
Provide Input			
Elicit Performance/ Provide Feedback			

Provide Input	*If applicable*		
Elicit Performance/ Provide Feedback	*If applicable*		
Closure			
Enhance Retention & Transfer			
Reflection/ Notes to Self	• What worked well? Why? • What didn't work? Why? • What changes would you make if you taught this lesson again?		

* Remember that the maximum attention span of the learner is approximately the age of the learner up to 20 minutes. The initial lesson cycle (gain attention/activate prior knowledge, provide input and elicit performance/provide feedback) should not take more than 20 minutes. The second cycle (provide input and elicit performance/provide feedback) should be repeated as needed and will vary depending on the length of the class period.

Appendix L | Chinese Lesson Plan for Third Grade

Language Level	Novice	Grade	3	Date	xxx	Day in Unit	xxx	Minutes	30

Theme/Topic	**Families and Communities:** Agriculture in China's 5 regions

Essential Question	How does where I live influence what I eat?

STANDARDS			LESSON OBJECTIVES	
What are the communicative and cultural objectives for the lesson?	**Communication and Cultures**	*Which modes of communication will be addressed?* ✔ Interpersonal ☐ Interpretive ☐ Presentational	**Learners can:** • Identify agricultural products of the five regions of China.	
If applicable, indicate how this lesson connects to other standards.	**Connections**	Associate geography with agricultural products		
	Comparisons			
	Communities			
	Other Standards	**Speaking and Listening 1.** Prepare for and participate effectively in a range of conversations and collaborations with diverse partners, building on others' ideas and expressing their own clearly and persuasively.		

Lesson Sequence	Activity/Activities What will learners do? What does the teacher do?	Time* How many minutes will this segment take?	Materials/Resources/Technology Be specific. What materials will you develop? What materials will you bring in from other sources?
Gain Attention/ Activate Prior Knowledge	• Teachers share geography visuals. • Learners will work in small groups to place geography visuals on the map of China. • After completing this activity, learners will take turns placing large velcro visuals on a shower curtain map of China so that everyone can check their group maps for accuracy.	5	• Shower curtain map of China • Velcro images of geography of different regions of China • Blank maps of China for Learner groups • Envelopes of geography images to accompany blank maps of China
Provide Input	• Learners will repeat the names of agricultural products as the teacher shows them to the class.	3	
Elicit Performance/ Provide Feedback	• Learners will move to five different stations around the room, identify the region and the geographic features of the region (review) and learn the agricultural products associated with the region. • After learners move to a new station, the learners identify the region and geographic feature, learn the agricultural products associated with the new region. • The teacher makes simple comparisons between regions: Does the (north) have (chicken)? What region has (chicken)?	15	

Provide Input	*if applicable*		
Elicit Performance/ Provide Feedback	*if applicable*		
Closure	• Learners return to their groups and maps of China. They place agricultural products on the maps. • After completing this activity, learners take turns placing large velcro visuals on a shower curtain map of China so that everyone can check their group maps for accuracy. The teacher asks: What region has (chicken)?	7	• Shower curtain map of China • Velcro images of agricultural products • Blank maps of China for groups • Envelopes of agricultural products for groups
Enhance Retention & Transfer			
Reflection/ Notes to Self	• What worked well? Why? • What didn't work? Why? • What changes would you make if you taught this lesson again?		

Glossary

Authentic Tasks: An authentic task is one which requires the student to use knowledge or skills to produce a product or complete a performance that is useful beyond the classroom.

Authentic Texts: Those written and oral communications produced by members of a language and culture group for members of the same language and culture group (Shrum & Glisan, 2016, p. 84).

Backward Design: The teacher starts with desired outcomes and acceptable evidence and then plans appropriate learning activities to reach those outcomes (Wiggins & McTighe, 2005).

Bloom's Taxonomy of Thinking: Classification of learning objectives created by Benjamin S. Bloom and colleagues in 1956. It was updated in 2000 by Loren Anderson, a former student of Bloom. The updated taxonomy moves from lower order to higher order thinking skills: Remember, Understand, Apply, Analyze, Evaluate, Create.

Brain-Based Learning: Those practices that are compatible with what we know about how the brain learns.

Can-Do Statements: Based on the ACTFL Proficiency Guidelines, Can-Do Statements tell what language learners can understand and communicate in the language(s) they are learning.

Circumlocution: The use of language that one does know in order to explain a specific word that one does not know (ACTFL 2012 Proficiency Guidelines Glossary).

Code-Switching: Switching from one language to another to complete an idea, thought, or sentence, sometimes when one lacks the word or phrase in the language one started off in (ACTFL 2012 Proficiency Guidelines Glossary).

Cognates: Words between languages that have a common origin and are therefore readily understood. For example, the French word "leçon" and the English word "lesson" (ACTFL 2012 Proficiency Guidelines Glossary).

Cohesive Devices: Language components that link ideas for smooth flow within and among sentences and paragraphs, such as conjunctions, relative pronouns, pronoun substitutions (subject, verb), adverbs of time, and subordinate clauses (ACTFL 2012 Proficiency Guidelines Glossary).

Common Core State Standards: The Common Core State Standards Initiative is a state-led effort that established a single set of clear educational standards for kindergarten through 12th grade in English language arts and mathematics that states voluntarily adopt. The standards are designed to ensure that students graduating from high school are prepared to enter credit bearing entry courses in two or four year college programs or enter the workforce (www.corestandards.org).

Communication Strategies: How the language learner makes himself understood (repeating, paraphrasing, etc.) and what he does to understand others (e.g., asks for repetition, slowing of speech).

Comprehensible Input: The amount of language a learner can fully understand plus a little more, $i + 1$ (Krashen, 1982).

Content: Topics that the learner can understand and discuss.

Context: Situation within which the language learner understands and communicates.

Cultural Awareness: How the language learner uses knowledge of the target culture to understand and communicate in the target language.

Culture Triangle: The relationship of cultural products and practices to the underlying perspectives of a people.

Curriculum: Curriculum includes the knowledge and skills that successful students are expected to learn, organized to plan learning. In the case of world language instruction, the curriculum is based on the Proficiency Guidelines that describe the pathway to increased understanding and communication in the target language.

Differentiation: The process of providing students with different ways of presenting concepts and ideas so that all students can learn regardless of their abilities.

Discourse: Communication of ideas or information through speech or writing.

Domains of Performance: Describe the language learners' performance in terms of functions, contexts, text type, language control, vocabulary, communication strategies, and cultural awareness.

Enduring Understanding: Statements summarizing important ideas that are central to a discipline and have lasting value beyond the classroom.

Essential Questions: "Questions that are not answerable with finality in a brief sentence . . . Their aim is to stimulate thought, to provoke inquiry, and to spark more questions—including thoughtful student questions—not just pat answers" (Wiggins & McTighe, 2005, p. 106).

European Language Portfolio: The ELP is a document in which those who are learning or have learned a language—whether at school or outside school—can record and reflect on their language learning and cultural experiences. It is a project of the Council of Europe.

Feedback: Information communicated to the student about performance in order to improve learning.

Fluency: The flow in spoken or written language as perceived by the listener or reader. Flow is made possible by clarity of expression, the acceptable ordering of ideas, and use of vocabulary and syntax appropriate to the context (ACTFL 2012 Proficiency Guidelines Glossary).

Formative Assessment: Monitoring student learning during instruction and providing ongoing feedback to improve learning.

Formulaic: Constituting or containing a verbal formula or set form of words such as "How are you?/Fine, thank you." "Thanks very much./You're welcome." (ACTFL 2012 Proficiency Guidelines Glossary).

Functions: Communicative tasks that a learner can complete in the target language.

Genre: Any category of art, music, film, literature, etc., based on a set of stylistic criteria (ACTFL 2012 Proficiency Guidelines Glossary).

Interculturality: The interaction of people from different cultural backgrounds using authentic language appropriately in a way that demonstrates knowledge and understanding of the cultures. It is the ability to experience the culture of another person and to be open-minded, interested, and curious about that person and culture (www.learnnc.org/lp/editions/linguafolio/6122).

Interpersonal Communication: Two-way exchange of information, ideas, and opinions, both oral and written, that is unrehearsed and requires negotiation of meaning.

Interpretive Communication: Listening, reading, or viewing a message. It is one-way communication without the opportunity for clarification or rephrasing.

Instructional Repertoire: The learning strategies and theories that facilitate instruction in the world language classroom.

Learner-Centered Instruction (or student-centered learning, or student-centered instruction or learner-centered teaching): Student-centered learning (SCL), or learner-centeredness, is a learning model that places the student (learner) in the center of the learning process. In student-centered learning, students are active participants in their learning; they learn at their own pace and use their own strategies; they are more intrinsically than extrinsically motivated; learning is more individualized than standardized. Student-centered learning develops learning-how-to-learn skills such as problem solving, critical thinking, and reflective thinking. Student-centered learning accounts for and adapts to different learning styles of students (National Center for Research on Teacher Learning, 1999) (www.intime.uni.edu/model/center_of_learning_files/definition.html).

Lexical: Of or relating to the words or the vocabulary of a language as distinguished from its grammar and structure (ACTFL 2012 Proficiency Guidelines Glossary).

LinguaFolio®: LinguaFolio® is a formative assessment tool to help language learners self-assess their progress in learning languages. LinguaFolio® was developed by members of the National Council of State Supervisors for Languages and is the result of a transatlantic dialogue (sponsored by the Goethe-Institut) among members of the Council of Europe, delegates from the European Ministries of Education, and representatives from state departments of education in the United States.

Literacy: The National Council of Teachers of English (2013) has expanded the traditional definition of literacy (ability to read and write), stating that active, successful participants in this 21st century global society must be able to develop proficiency and fluency with the tools of technology; build intentional cross-cultural connections and relationships with others so to pose and solve problems collaboratively and strengthen independent thought; design and share information for global communities to meet a variety of purposes; manage, analyze, and synthesize multiple streams of simultaneous information; create, critique, analyze, and evaluate multimedia texts; and attend to the ethical responsibilities required by these complex environments.

Mode: A manner of communicating; the National Standards specify three modes of communication: Interpersonal, Interpretive, and Presentational.

Multiple Intelligences: An intelligence is a capacity to process information in certain ways. Each intelligence can be activated in an appropriate cultural setting (Shrum & Glisan, 2016, p. 325).

Narrative: The relating of a story or account of events, experiences, etc., whether true or fictitious, told in a logical and chronological order (ACTFL 2012 Proficiency Guidelines Glossary).

Non-Negotiables: Criteria for a project or assignment that must be met before the project or assignment can be submitted for evaluation.

On-Demand Writing: Writing that is completed during a set period of time without feedback or other outside assistance.

Pacing: The amount of time within a lesson spent on each part of the lesson.

Paragraph: A self-contained, cohesive unit of spoken or written discourse that generally consists of multiple sentences linked by internal organization and connectors (ACTFL 2012 Proficiency Guidelines Glossary).

Paraphrase: Restating the meaning of something spoken or written in one's own words.

Presentational Communication: Polished speaking or writing for an audience. The writer or speaker benefits from rehearsals, feedback, and editing in preparation of the message.

Proficiency: What individuals can do with language in terms of speaking, writing, listening, and reading in real-world situations in a spontaneous, non-rehearsed context (ACTFL 2012 Proficiency Guidelines).

Range of Performance: Descriptors of what the language learner can do at the Novice, Intermediate, and Advanced levels.

Rubric: A document that describes criteria for a project or assignment with levels of quality from "excellent" to "needs more work."

Scaffolding: Providing assistance to the learner to accomplish a task, making it easier for the learner to succeed.

Scoring Guide: A document that lists the expectations for a project or assignment along with indicators showing that the expectation was fully met, partially met, not met.

Specialized Vocabulary: Words, expressions, technical terms, etc., that are meaningful to members of a specific group or field of study or endeavor (ACTFL 2012 Proficiency Guidelines Glossary).

Strings of Sentences: A series of isolated or discrete sentences typically referring to a given topic but not grammatically or syntactically connected (ACTFL 2012 Proficiency Guidelines Glossary).

Summative Assessment: Used to evaluate student learning at the end of a unit or semester or course.

Target Language: The language other than one's native language that is being learned.

Text Type: Words, phrases, sentences, strings of sentences, or paragraphs.

Theme: A unifying subject or idea of an instructional unit.

Toolbox: Part of the Standards-Based Thematic Unit Template, the Toolbox includes the Language Functions and Related Structures and Patterns, Vocabulary, and Resources needed to achieve the instructional goals of the unit.

Twenty-First Century Skills: Identified by business and education leaders, 21st Century Skills are the skills that students need to succeed in work, school, and life (www.p21.org).

Bibliography

American Council on the Teaching of Foreign Languages (ACTFL). (2012a). *ACTFL proficiency guidelines–speaking, writing, listening and reading*, (3rd ed.). Alexandria, VA: Author. Retrieved from http://actflproficiencyguidelines2012.org/

American Council on the Teaching of Foreign Languages (ACTFL). (2015). *ACTFL performance descriptors for language learners.* Alexandria, VA: Author. Retrieved from http://www.acfl.org/publications/guidelines-and-manuals/actfl-performance-descriptors-language-learners

American Council on the Teaching of Foreign Languages (ACTFL). (2012c). *Alignment of the national standards for learning languages with the common core state standards.* Alexandria, VA: Author. Retrieved from http://www.actfl.org/sites/default/files/pdfs/Aligning_CCSS_Language_Standards_v6.pdf

American Council on the Teaching of Foreign Languages (ACTFL). (2012, July 30). *Use of the target language in the classroom* [Press release]. Retrieved October 03, 2013, from http://www.actfl.org/news/position-statements/use-the-target-language-the-classroom

American Council on the Teaching of Foreign Languages (ACTFL). https://www.actfl.org/about-the-american-council-the-teaching-foreign-languages/actfl-global-engagement-initiative/recognized-global-engagement-initiative-programs). Retrieved April 10, 2017.

American Council on the Teaching of Foreign Languages (ACTFL). https://www.actfl.org/assessment-professional-development/career-resources/careers-using-language-skills. Retrieved May 7, 2017.

American Council on the Teaching of Foreign Languages (ACTFL). (https://www.actfl.org/news/position-statements/global-competence-position-statement. Retrieved April 10, 2017.

Ames, C. A. (1990). Motivation: What teachers need to know. Teachers *College Record, 91*(3), 409–421. Retrieved June 30, 2013, from http://web.uncg.edu/soe/bf_course669/docs_session_6/motivtion-whatteachersneedtoknow.pdf

Anderson, L. W., Krathwohl, D. R., & Bloom, B. S. (2001). *A taxonomy for learning, teaching, and assessing: A revision of Bloom's taxonomy of educational objectives.* New York: Longman.

Babson Survey Research Group. (2016). Online Report Card - Tracking Online Education in the United States, 2015. Retrieved October 20, 2017, from https://onlinelearningconsortium.org/read/online-report-card-tracking-online-education-united-states-2015/

Barcroft, J. (2004). Second language vocabulary acquisition: A lexical input processing approach. *Foreign Language Annals, 37*(2), 200–208.

Beck, I. L., McKeown, M. G., & Kucan, L. (2002). *Bringing words to life: Robust vocabulary instruction.* New York, NY: Guilford.

Beck, I. L., McKeown, M. G., & Kucan, L. (2008). *Creating robust vocabulary: Frequently asked questions and extended examples.* New York, NY: Guilford.

Bergmann, J., Overmyer, J., & Wilie, B. (2012, April 14). The flipped class: Myths vs. reality. *The Daily Riff.* Retrieved June 24, 2013, from http://www.thedailyriff.com/articles/the-flipped-class-conversation-689.php

Bisson, C., & Luckner, J. (1996). Fun in learning: The pedagogical role of fun in adventure learning. *Journal of Experimental Education, 9*(2).

Blachowicz, C. and Cobb, C. (2007). *Teaching Vocabulary Across the Content Areas: An ASCD Action Tool.* Alexandria, VA: ASCD.

Bloom, B. S. (1956). *Taxonomy of educational objectives: The classification of educational goals.* New York: Longman. Bloom's Digital Taxonomy. (n.d.). *Educational-origami.* Retrieved from http://edorigami.wikispaces.com/

Brandl, K. (2008). *Communicative language teaching in action: Putting principles to work.* Upper Saddle River, NJ: Pearson Prentice Hall.

Brookhart, S. M. (2012). Preventing feedback fizzle. *Educational Leadership, 70*(1), 25–29. Brookhart, S. M. (2013). Assessing creativity. *Educational Leadership, 70*(5), 28–34.

Brookhart, S. M. (2013). *How to create and use rubrics for formative assessment and grading.* Alexandria, VA: ASCD. Byram, M. (1997). *Teaching and assessing intercultural communicative competence.* Clevedon: Multilingual Matters.

Cai, L. (2010). The Mouse Marriage. *Learning Languages*, 15 (2).

Caine, R. N., & Caine, G. (1990). Understanding a brain-based approach to teaching and learning. *Educational Leadership, 48*(2), 66–70.

Carr, A. (2010, May 18). *The most important leadership quality for CEOs? Creativity.* Retrieved from http://www.fastcompany.com/1648943/most-important-leadership-quality-ceos-creativity.

Center for Excellence in Learning and Teaching. (n.d.). *CELT.* Retrieved from http://www.celt.iastate.edu/

Center for Media Literacy. (2011). *Media literacy: A definition and more.* Retrieved September 22, 2013, from http://www.medialit.org/media-literacy-definition-and-more

Center for Media Literacy. (n.d.). *About CML.* Retrieved October 23, 2017, from http://www.medialit.org/about-cml

Center for Open Educational Resources & Language Learning, The University of Texas at Austin. (n.d.). *Foreign Language Teaching Methods: Motivation Predicts Success.* Retrieved October 23, 2017, from http://coerll.utexas.edu/methods/modules/learners/02/

Center for Open Educational Resources & Language Learning, The University of Texas at Austin. (n.d.). *Foreign Language Teaching Methods: Readability and the Holistic Approach.* Retrieved October 23, 2017, from http://coerll.utexas.edu/methods/modules/reading/01/readability.php

COERLL: https://coerll.utexas.edu/methods/modules/reading/01/readability.php). Retrieved April 15, 2017.

Collins, J. (2003, December 30). *Best new year's resolution? A 'stop doing' list.* Retrieved November 10, 2013, from http://www.jimcollins.com/article_topics/articles/best-new-years.html

Common Sense Media. (2015). *Common Sense Census: Media use by tweens and teens.* Retrieved from https://www.commonsensemedia.org/sites/default/files/uploads/research/census_executivesummary.pdf . May 5, 2017.

Common Sense Media. (2015). *The Common Sense Census: Media use by teens and tweens.* Retrieved October 20, 2017, from https://www.commonsensemedia.org/sites/default/files/uploads/research/census_executivesummary.pdf

Costa, Arthur L. and Kallick, Bena.(2005). *Learning and Leading with Habits of Mind.*

Couet, R., Duncan, G., Eddy, J., Met, M., Smith, M., Still, M., Tollefson, A. (2008). *Starting with the End in Mind: Planning and Evaluating Highly Successful Foreign Language Programs.* Boston, MA: Pearson Education, Inc. Retrieved from http://www.pearsonschool.com/index.cfm?locator=PS1c74&acornRdt=1&DCSext.w_psvaniturl=http%3A%2F%2Fwww%2Epearsonschool%2Ecom%2FEndinMind

Council of Europe. (2008). *White paper on intercultural dialogue: "Living together as equals in dignity."* Strasbourg, France: Council of Europe.

Crockett, L., Jukes, I., & Churches, A. (2011). *Literacy is not enough: 21st-century fluencies for the digital age.* Kelowna, B.C., Canada: 21st Century Fluency Project.

Crouse, D. (2012). Going for 90% plus: How to stay in the target language. *The Language Educator, 7*(5), 22–27.

Curtain, H. A., & Dahlberg, C. A. (2016). *Languages and learners, making the match: World language instruction in K–8 classrooms and beyond* (5th edition) Boston: Cengage Learning.

Cushman, K. (1994). Less is more: The secret of being essential. *Coalition of Essential Schools.* Retrieved July 07, 2013, from http://www.essentialschools.org/resources/34

Danesi, M. (2003). *Second language teaching: A view from the right side of the brain.* Dordrecht, The Netherlands: Kluwer Academic Publishers.

Danielson, L. M. (2009). Fostering reflection. *Education Leadership, 66*(5). Retrieved June 25, 2013, from http://www.ascd.org/publications/educational-leadership/feb09/vol66/num05/Fostering-Reflection.aspx

DeVoss, D. N., Eidman-Aadahl, E., & Hicks, T. (2010). *Because digital writing matters: Improving student writing in online and multimedia environments.* San Francisco: Jossey-Bass.

Dörnyei, Z. (2001). *Teaching and researching motivation.* Harlow, England: Longman.

Dörnyei, Z. (2005). *The psychology of the language learner: Individual differences in second language acquisition.* Mahwah, NJ: L. Erlbaum.

Dörnyei, Z., & Csizér, K. (1998). Ten commandments for motivating language learners: Results of an empirical study. *Language Teaching Research, 2*(3), 203–229.

Dougherty, E. (2012). *Assignments matter: Making the connections that help students meet standards.* Alexandria, VA: ASCD.

Dweck, C.S. (2010). Even Geniuses Work Hard. *68(1),* 16-20.

Duncan, G., & Met, M. (2010). *STARTALK: From paper to practice* (Publication). Retrieved June 10, 2013, from https://startalk.umd.edu/lesson-planning

Eastburn, M. (2007). Adventures Through Time and Space. *Learning Languages*, 12(2).

Eddy, J. (2007). Children and Art: Uncovering Cultural Practices and Perspectives through works of art in world language performance assessment. *Learning Languages*, 12(2).

Egan, K. (1986). *Individual development and the curriculum*. London: Hutchinson.

European Language Portfolio Intercultural Experiences and Awareness, August 2003/February 2011. Retrieved January 2012 https://rm.coe.int/16804932c1.

Fallows, D. (2010). *Dreaming in Chinese: Mandarin lessons in life, love, and language*. New York: Walker & Company.

Foreign Language Teaching Methods: The Language Learner. (n.d.). *Motivation predicts success*. Retrieved from http://coerll.utexas.edu/methods/modules/learners/02/

Fortune, T. (2012). Learning content through the target language. *Maintaining target language in the classroom: Comprehensible input and output* (Webinar Series). Alexandria, VA: ACTFL.

Frey, Nancy, and Douglas Fischer. *The Formative Assessment Action Plan: Practical Steps to More Successful Teaching and Learning*. Alexandria, VA: ASCD, 2011.

Gardner, H. (1983). *Frames of mind: The theory of multiple intelligences*. New York: Basic Books.

Gardner, H. (1999). *Intelligence reframed: Multiple intelligences for the 21st century*. New York: Basic Books.

Gardner, R. C. (1985). *Social psychology and second language learning: The role of attitudes and motivation*. London: E. Arnold.

Gardner, R. C., & Lambert, W. E. (1972). *Attitudes and motivation in second-language learning*. Rowley, MA: Newbury House.

Gewertz, C. (2013, April 8). Busting up misconceptions about formative 'assessment.' *Education Week*. Retrieved August 03, 2013, from http://blogs.edweek.org/edweek/curriculum/2013/04/httpwwwwestedorgonline_pubsres.html

Glaser, E. M. (1972). *An experiment in the development of critical thinking,*. New York: AMS Press.

Glisan, E., & Donato, R. (2017). *Enacting the work of language instruction: High-leverage teaching practices*. Alexandria, VA: ACTFL.

Graham, C. R. (1985). Beyond integrative motivation: The development and influence of assimilative motivation. In *On TESOL '84: A brave new world for TESOL*. Washington, D.C.: TESOL.

Hale, S. L., & Cunningham, M. K. (2011). *Evidence based practice using a thematic based unit for language development*.

Larmer, J., Mergandoller, J., & Boss, S. (2015). Gold Standard PBL: Essential Project Design Elements. Retrieved October 23, 2017, from http://www.bie.org/blog/gold_standard_pbl_essential_project_design_elements

Lecture. Retrieved July 26, 2013, from www.txsha.org

Lenhart, A. (2015, April 08). Teens, Social Media & Technology Overview 2015. Retrieved October 20, 2017, from http://www.pewinternet.org/2015/04/09/teens-social-media-technology-2015/

Hamilton, H. E., Crane, C., & Bartoshesky, A. (2005). *Doing foreign language: Bringing Concordia Language Villages into language classrooms*. Upper Saddle River, NJ: Pearson/Merrill/Prentice Hall.

Hattie, J. (2012). Know thy impact. *Educational Leadership, 70*(1), 18–23.

Himmele, P., & Himmele, W. (2011). *Total participation techniques: Making every student an active learner*. Alexandria, VA: ASCD.

Hirsch, E. D. (2003). Reading comprehension requires knowledge—of words and the world. *American Educator, 27*(1), 10-13.

Horrigan, J. B. (2015, April 20). The numbers behind the broadband 'homework gap'. Retrieved October 20, 2017, from http://www.pewresearch.org/fact-tank/2015/04/20/the-numbers-behind-the-broadband-homework-gap/

Horwitz, E. K. (2008). *Becoming a language teacher: A practical guide to second language learning and teaching*. Boston: Pearson/Allyn and Bacon.

Hudelson, S. (1994). Literacy development of second language children. In F. Genesee (Ed.), *Educating second language children: The whole child, the whole curriculum, the whole community* (pp. 129–152). Cambridge: University Press.

Hunter, R. C., & Hunter, M. C. (2004). *Madeline Hunter's mastery teaching: Increasing instructional effectiveness in elementary and secondary schools*. Thousand Oaks, CA: Corwin Press.

Jackson, S. (2013). Helping students ask good questions. Retrieved February 15, 2017, from http://www.scholastic.ca/education/teaching_tip/april2013.html.

Jacobson, W., Sleicher, D., & Burke, M. (1999). Portfolio assessment of intercultural competence. *International Journal of Intercultural Relations, 23*(3), 467–492.

Johnson, D. W., & Johnson, R. T. (1999). Making cooperative learning work. *Theory into Practice, 38*(2), 67–73.

Kramsch, C. J. (1993). *Context and culture in language teaching.* Oxford: Oxford University Press.

Krashen, S. D. (1982). *Principles and practice in second language acquisition.* Oxford: Pergamon.

Larmer, J., Mergendoller, J., & Boss, S. (2015). *Setting the standard for project based learning.* ASCD.

Leger, H. (2007). Insects: An Interdisciplinary Unit. *Learning Languages,* 12(2).

LeLoup, J. W., Ponterio, R., & Warford, M. K. (2013). Overcoming resistance to 90% target language use: Rationale, challenges, and suggestions. *NECTFL Review, 72,* 45–60.

Lent, R.C. (2012). *Overcoming textbook fatigue: 21st century tools to revitalize teaching and learning.* Alexandria, VA: ASCD.

LinguaFolio®–National Council of State Supervisors for Languages. (n.d.). *LinguaFolio®–National Council of State Supervisors for Languages.* Retrieved from http://www.ncssfl.org/links/index.php?linguafolio

LinguaFolio® online. Retrieved October 31, 2013, from https://linguafolio.uoregon.edu/

Little D. & Perclová, R. (2001). *The European language portfolio: A guide for teachers and teacher trainers.* Strasbourg, France: Council of Europe, Language Policy Division.

Little, D. & Simpson, B. (2003). *European language portfolio: The intercultural component and learning how to learn.* Strasbourg, France: Council of Europe.

Macintyre, P. D. (2007). Willingness to communicate in the second language: Understanding the decision to speak as a volitional process. *The Modern Language Journal, 91*(4), 564–576.

Marzano, R. J. (2006). *Classroom assessment & grading that work.* Alexandria, VA: ASCD.

Marzano, R. J. (2007). *The art and science of teaching: A comprehensive framework for effective instruction.* Alexandria, VA: ASCD.

McTighe, J., & Wiggins, G. P. (2013). *Essential questions: Opening doors to student understanding.* Alexandria: ASCD.

Media habits of teens and twenty-somethings 2012. (2012, July). Retrieved from http://www.google.com/think/research-studies/media-habits-of-teens-and-twenty-somethings-2012.html

Mickan, P. (2013). *Language curriculum design and socialisation.* Bristol: Multilingual Matters.

Minerva Programme. (n.d.). Project of study of the electronic European Language Portfolio. Retrieved from http://eelp.gap.it/default.asp.

Moeller, A. J., & Ketsman, O. (2010). Can we learn a language without rules? *In 2020 Vision for 2010: Developing Global Competence* (pp. 91–108). Richmond, VA: Robert Terry.

Moss, C. M., & Brookhart, S. M. (2012). *Learning targets: Helping students aim for understanding in today's lesson.* Alexandria, VA: ASCD.

National Capital Language Resource Center (NCLRC). 2003. Method: Learner-centered instruction. In *The essentials of language teaching: Teaching goals and methods.* Retrieved from http://www.nclrc.org/essentials/goalsmethods/method.htm

National Governors Association Center for Best Practices, Council of Chief State School Officers (CCSSO). (2010). *Common core state standards for English language arts and literacy in history/social studies, science, and technical subjects.* Washington, DC: Author.

National Standards in Foreign Language Education Project (NSFLEP). (1996). *Standards for foreign language learning: Preparing for the 21st century.* Yonkers, NY: Author.

National Standards in Foreign Language Education Project (NSFLEP). (1999). *Standards for foreign language learning in the 21st century* (2nd ed.). Lawrence, KS: Allen Press.

National Standards in Foreign Language Education Project (NSFLEP). (2006). *Standards for foreign language learning in the 21st century* (3rd ed.). Lawrence, KS: Allen Press.

NCTE position statements on literacy. (2013, February). *NCTE Comprehensive News.* Retrieved from http://www.ncte.org/positions/literacy

Online Learning Community. (2016). Babson Study: Distance Education Enrollment Growth Continues. Retrieved May 11, 2017, from: https://onlinelearningconsortium.org/news_item/babson-study-distance-education-enrollment-growth-continues-2/)

Ostroff, W. L. (2016). *Cultivating Curiosity in K–12 Classrooms: How to Promote and Sustain Deep Learning.* ASCD.

Oxford, R. L. (1990). *Language learning strategies: What every teacher should know.* New York: Newbury House Publisher.

Partnership for 21st Century Learning. (n.d.). *Collaboration*. Retrieved October 23, 2017, from http://www.p21.org/our-work/4cs-research-series/collaboration

Partnership for 21st Century Learning. (n.d.). *Communication*. Retrieved October 20, 2017, from http://www.p21.org/our-work/4cs-research-series/communication

Partnership for 21st Century Learning. (2016, January). *Framework for 21st Century Learning*. Retrieved October 20, 2017, from http://www.p21.org/storage/documents/docs/P21_framework_0816.pdf

Partnership for 21st Century Skills. (2011, March). *21st Century Skills Map*. Retrieved October 20, 2017, from http://www.p21.org/storage/documents/Skills%20Map/p21_worldlanguagesmap.pdf

The Partnership for 21st Century Skills. (n.d.). *Framework for 21st century learning*. Retrieved from http://www.p21.org/overview/skills-framework

Pew Research Center. (2016). Teens, Social Media & Technology Overview 2015. Retrieved May 10, 2017, from http://www.pewinternet.org/2015/04/09/teens-social-media-technology-2015/

Pew Research Center. (2016). The numbers behind the broadband 'homework gap.' Retrieved May 10, 2017, from http://www.pewresearch.org/fact-tank/2015/04/20/the-numbers-behind-the-broadband-homework-gap/)

Pew Research Center Analysis of U.S. Census Bureau's American Community Survey Demographic Research Data Sources http://www.pewresearch.org/methodology/demographic-research/data-sources/

Pink, D. H. (2009). *Drive: The surprising truth about what motivates us*. New York, NY: Riverhead Books.

Prensky, M. (2002). The motivation of gameplay: The real twenty-first century learning revolution. *On the Horizon, 10*(1), 5–11.

Prensky, M. (2012, May/June). *Teaching the right stuff*. Retrieved October 31, 2013 from http://marcprensky.com/writing/Prensky-TheRightStuff-EdTech-May-Jun2012.pdf

Ramirez, L. (2006). ¡Viva Columbia, Columbia Viva! A Fantasy Trip for the Five Senses. *Learning Languages*, 11 (2).

Reflective Thinking: RT. Retrieved April 11, 2017, from http://www.hawaii.edu/intlrel/pols382/Reflective%20Thinking%20-%20UH/reflection.html

Ritchhart, R., Church, M., & Morrison, K. (2011). *Making thinking visible: How to promote engagement, understanding, and independence for all learners*. John Wiley & Sons.

Robinson, K. (2011). *Out of our minds: Learning to be creative*. Oxford: Capstone.

Schmoker, M. J. (2011). *Focus: Elevating the essentials to radically improve student learning*. Alexandria, VA: ASCD.

Schulz, R. (2007). The challenge of assessing cultural understanding in the context of foreign language instruction. *Foreign Language Annals, 40*(1), 9–20.

Selivan, L. (2010, September). Revising lexis: Quality or quantity? *Teaching English | British Council | BBC*. Retrieved July 28, 2013, from http://www.teachingenglish.org.uk/

Shrum, J. L., & Glisan, E. W. (2010). *Teacher's handbook: Contextualized language instruction* (4th ed.). Boston, MA: Heinle. Shrum, J.L., & Glisan, E.W. (2016). *Teacher's handbook: Contextualized language instruction* (5th ed.). Boston, MA.

Sousa, D. A. (2006). *How the brain learns*. Thousand Oaks, CA: Corwin Press.

Stahl, S. (2003). How words are learned incrementally over multiple exposures. American Educator, 27(1), 18-19. Retrieved March 16, 2017, from http://www.aft.org/pdfs/americaneducator/spring2003/AE_SPRNG.pdf#page=6

Tedick, D. J. (2002). *The Minnesota articulation project's proficiency-oriented language instruction and assessment: A curriculum handbook for teachers*. Minneapolis, MN: Center for Advanced Research on Language Acquisition, University of Minnesota.

The 10 Skills you need to thrive in the fourth industrial revolution. (2016). Retrieved April 10, 2017, from https://www.weforum.org/agenda/2016/01/the-10-skills-you-need-to-thrive-in-the-fourth-industrial-revolution/

Tomlinson, C. A. (1999). *The differentiated classroom: Responding to the needs of all learners*. Alexandria, VA: ASCD. Tprstories.com. (n.d.). Retrieved from http://www.tprsstories.com/

TPRStories.com (2017). Teaching Proficiency Through Reading and Storytelling.

Trilling, B., & Fadel, C. (2009). *21st century skills: Learning for life in our times*. San Francisco: Jossey-Bass.

Tuttle, H. G., & Tuttle, A. R. (2012). *Improving foreign language speaking through formative assessment*. Larchmont, NY: Eye on education.

University of Hawaii. (n.d.). Reflective Thinking: RT. Retrieved October 23, 2017, from http://www.hawaii.edu/intlrel/pols382/Reflective%20Thinking%20-%20UH/reflection.html

Vatterott, C. (2009). *Rethinking homework: Best practices that support diverse needs.* Alexandria, VA: ASCD. Welcome to LEARN NC! (n.d.). *LEARN NC.* Retrieved from http://www.learnnc.org/lp/editions/linguafolio/6122

Wiggins, G. (2012). 7 keys to effective feedback. *Educational Leadership, 70*(1), 11–16.

Wagner, M., & Byram, M. (2015). Gaining intercultural communicative competence. *The Language Educator., 10*(3), 28-30.

Wiggins, G. P., & McTighe, J. (1998). *Understanding by design.* Alexandria, VA: ASCD.

Wiggins, G. P., & McTighe, J. (2005). *Understanding by design* (2nd ed.). Alexandria, VA: ASCD.

Wilkins, D. (1972). Do reading and interactive vocabulary instruction make a difference? An empirical study. *TESOL quarterly, 31*(1), 121-140.

Willis, J. (2005). Attention to have and to hold. *Journal of the National Council of Teachers of English, 8–9.* Retrieved May 29, 2013, from http://www.radteach.com/page1/page8/page9/page9.html

Willis, J. (2006). *Research-based strategies to ignite student learning: Insights from a neurologist and classroom teacher.* Alexandria, VA: ASCD.

World languages 21st century skills map. (n.d.). Retrieved from http://www.p21.org/storage/documents/Skills%20Map/p21_worldlanguagesmap.pdf

World-Readiness Standards for Learning Languages (2015). National Standards in Foreign Language Education Project NSFLEP.

Ziegler, N. A., & Moeller, A. J. (2012). Increasing self-regulated learning through the LinguaFolio®. *Foreign Language Annals, 45*(3), 330–348.

Zilmer, C. (2013). 90%+ target language, authentic texts, no isolated grammar? How? *The Language Educator, 8*(3), 26–29.

Zyzik, Eve C., and Charlene Polio. *Authentic Materials Myths: Applying Second Language Research to Classroom Teaching.* Ann Arbor: U of Michigan, 2017.